Dos Passos

Dos Passos

Artist as American

By Linda W. Wagner

University of Texas Press   Austin and London

Permission to quote from selected material in the John
Dos Passos Collection, the University of Virginia Library,
is gratefully acknowledged.

Library of Congress Cataloging in Publication Data

Wagner, Linda Welshimer.
  Dos Passos.
  Bibliography: p.
  Includes index.
  1. Dos Passos, John, 1896–1970—Criticism and
interpretation. 2. National characteristics, American,
in literature.
PS3507.0743Z925   813'.5'2   78-9922

ISBN 0-292-74011-5

For Howard O. Brogan

*. . . there is such a thing as writing for writing's sake.
A cabinetmaker enjoys whittling a dovetail because
he's a cabinetmaker; every type of work has its own
delight inherent in it.*
—John Dos Passos

Contents

Acknowledgments

This manuscript has been prepared with the support of the John Simon Guggenheim Foundation. Thanks go as well to Joseph J. Waldmeir, Russel B. Nye, Victor Howard, Townsend Ludington, Blanche Gelfant, David Sanders, Alan Hollingsworth, Clyde Grimm, and Jan McInroy.

Introduction:
The Americanization of
John Dos Passos

When John Dos Passos criticized the *New Masses* in 1926 because its editors were too little interested in "exploring America,"[1] he was in effect charting much of his own future. In most of his half century of writing, Dos Passos consistently tried to image—and thereby define—the character of the United States and its people. Unchastened by the enormity of his task, he wrote book after book in search of the national identity and its embodiment in a convincing American hero, beginning with *Manhattan Transfer*, the 1925 portrait of New York, and ending with the posthumously published *Century's Ebb* in 1975. For him, this literary exploration of America became "a prospecting trip, drilling in unexpected places, following unsuspected veins, bringing home specimens as yet unclassified."[2]

Enthusiastic as Dos Passos was about being the "chronicler" of American life, his early writing revealed little of that eventual interest. Nearly all his stories published in *The Harvard Monthly* had foreign settings, as did his poems and his first two published novels, *One Man's Initiation: 1917* and *Three Soldiers* (the novels, ostensibly, because they were about World War I). During his college and war years, travel was both Dos Passos' avocation and his love, and the writing he did from 1912 through the next decade reflects his fascination with foreign cultures. As early as 1918, however, he wrote of America with real affection and humor; and in 1920, for the first time since his Harvard days, he spent most of the summer in New York, a city that both "amused and appalled him."[3] In subsequent years of traveling, through both Europe and Asia Minor, Dos Passos' travel writing reflected his quandary: America, even with its scarcity of literary and cultural traditions, was exciting in its very naivete. While in some respects it could not compare with older cultures, in others it surpassed them. Dos Passos said in 1919,

"I admit that America is more dear to me than Europe—probably its colossal hideousness, its febrile insanity are evolving towards a better life for man";[4] and in 1920, writing from London, he echoed the sentiment: "America has an unhallowed attraction for me."[5] Then in 1922 came the first of his antitravel comments:

> At present I am bound for the U.S.A. having, bi Jasus, destroyed the illusion of geography—No more retchings after Cook's tours, or pinings to join the agile Mr. Neuman—in his Travel Talks—All of it is bunk. . . . There's as bad wine to be drunk in Tiflis as on Eleventh Street, the phonographs squawk as loud in Baghdad as they do in Sioux City, and politics are no more comic in Teheran than in Washington D.C.[6]

Dos Passos may have been gravitating toward an allegiance to "home," even in the midst of the expatriate culture many young American liberals had created abroad, but his writing had yet to illustrate that interest. His impressionistic war novels and 1923 *Streets of Night* were too obviously romantic to signal the innovation in approach and in theme that he felt a truly American literature demanded. He had written in his 1916 essay "Against American Literature" that too little American writing was native, that most of it was "foreign-inspired." American writers had yet to write about their primary themes and interests; neither had they yet presented any concept of what he called the American "national soul" (*âme nationale*). So unlike the passionless formality of the English, the American soul to Dos Passos was instead a "genial, ineffectual, blindly energetic affair." (He says this with the mild humor that came to mark most of his comments about the American character: even in his later somewhat more critical writing his anger was usually directed toward institutions and their abuses, seldom toward the American people per se.)

He complained that the American novel lacked "color and passion"; "Our books are like our cities; they are all the same." And he described that sameness as being "sincere, careful, and full of shrewd observation of contemporary life," using the novels of Edith Wharton and Robert Herrick as illustrations. Instead of these novels of manners, Dos Passos asked for novels of passion, filled with what he then called "earth-feeling." In short, he said, "The tone of the higher sort of writing in this country is undoubtedly that of a well brought up and intelligent woman, tolerant, versed in the things of this world, quietly humorous, but bound, tightly, in the fetters of 'niceness,' of the middle-class outlook." He objected as well to the methods of these novelists, criticizing them for relying on abstractions instead of using concrete images and representations of "human qualities." Little matter, said Dos Passos, that America had few folk traditions and a scant mystic and primitive heritage; by using what did exist, writers could infuse their work with power, as had Walt Whitman, the man Dos Passos considered America's only great poet.

The essay ends with the statement of the attitude that would pervade Dos Passos' writing for the next fifty years (an attitude remarkable for its consistency, if not for its perspicacity), that America and its literature had the potential for great fruition yet that, because of continual misdirection, its promise might remain only promise. Instead of becoming the home of great literature, America might rather become "the Sicily of the modern world," producing only "steel and oil and grain."[7]

Hardly definitive so far as the subject of American literature is concerned, this first (commercially) published essay[8] does indicate Dos Passos' major personal interests as writer—a deep involvement with American culture and the literature it might be expected to produce (here as yet undefined, except for his emphasis on Whitmanic subjects); a consistent interest in the artistic methods that would make such literature possible, especially in characterization; and a fascination with what he saw as the American character ("genial, ineffectual, blindly energetic"). The latter sometimes came surprisingly close to being his own character. The blurring between the observable persona of imaginative fiction and a revealing self-portrait was one of the most interesting of the changes in Dos Passos' half century of fiction. An autobiographical persona dominated both his early and his very late fiction: in the early, Martin Howe and John Andrews, impassioned if iconoclastic, and in the late, Ro Lancaster and Jay Pignatelli, authoritative yet bewildered.[9] As this study will show, the Dos Passos persona appears in each novel but often as only a minor character and seldom as an authorial voice. Not until *The Great Days*, *Midcentury*, and *Century's Ebb* did Dos Passos use a clearly recognizable self as protagonist. Though not unique, this pattern does show the comparative restraint that marked Dos Passos' writing. Convinced that objectivity was desirable, he tried to create distance between persona and self by turning from the single protagonist of *One Man's Initiation: 1917* to the multiple protagonists of *Three Soldiers* and then to the antiprotagonists of *Manhattan Transfer* and *U.S.A.* The effectiveness of his presentation, which was sometimes satiric, depended in part on the reader's concept of hero and in part on some knowledge of American "success" myths, because Dos Passos often played his characters against those expectations. His truly successful protagonists seldom conform to society's ideas of achievement.

Dos Passos' methods of presenting character were not those of the intensive psychological study; instead he used the panoramic or at least multiple, and often external, view. Because his method was so different from the more familiar modernist approach of, say, Conrad or Faulkner, for example, some readers thought him relatively disinterested in character, and it was a commonplace that Dos Passos was more sociological than psychological in his emphasis. Dos Passos himself contributed to this evaluation, especially during the 1930s, when he emphasized that his apprehension of America as country was his first purpose in writing, feeling as he did that the novelist's job was "to capture the snarl of the human currents of his time, so that there results an accurate permanent record of a phase of history."[10] Avidly interested in social and economic developments, Dos Passos thought that understanding such developments was crucial to the modern writer: "The writer has got to put his mind on the world around him. He has got to understand–I do not mean complain about, I mean understand–the industrial set-up that is so ruthlessly changing the basis of society. . . . His business is to justify the ways of machinery to man."[11]

Countless notes and notebooks among Dos Passos' papers attest that he worked hard to understand the vicissitudes of the financial/ industrial complex that America had become. Such an interest led to the subject matter of his later fiction–the taxicab war and labor union power structure in *Century's Ebb* and *Midcentury*; Washington bureaucracy in the *District of Columbia* trilogy; the dynamics of the film industry in *Most Likely To Succeed*. But his concern with economics was always subordinate to his larger purpose of describing the interaction among people: Dos Passos considered his primary role to be an observer of American morality. He felt constrained to protest, both in writing and in person, when justice was abused; thus he played active roles in the Sacco-Vanzetti protests, the Harlan County, Kentucky, mine activities, the Spanish Civil War, World Wars I and II, etc. As Alfred Kazin described Dos Passos' commitment, he had a genuine "passion for history, for retracing history's creative moments": "Alone among his literary cronies, Dos

Passos managed to add this idea of history as the great operative force to their enthusiasm for radical technique, the language of Joyce, and 'the religion of the word.'"[12] Harry T. Moore described him, similarly, as "the only major American novelist of the twentieth century who has had the desire and the power to surround the lives of his characters with what Lionel Trilling once called 'the buzz of history.' . . . He has given us an image of a major aspect of our experience that has hardly been touched by any other novelist of our time."[13] And Joseph Epstein concluded in a 1976 essay, "This joining of the artistic to the political is one of the things that made the early Dos Passos so appealing a figure. Along with being the most educated of the writers of the 1920's, he was also the most *engagé*."[14]

To the charge, often heard, that Dos Passos' political attitudes were inconsistent, one might answer that various shifts in the economic world made certain continuing stances impractical. In the 1920s and 1930s, for example, labor unions seemed to offer help to undervalued American workers. By the 1950s, however, corruption within most union leadership was depriving the workers of what little power they had won. Labor unions, for Dos Passos, changed from promising to threatening—less because of his personal politics than because of the composition of those bodies. As he explained in *The Best Times*, "When the meaning of political slogans turns topsy-turvy every few years, anyone who tries to keep a questioning mind . . . has to put up with having old friends turn into unfriends and even into enemies."[15] He had summarized as early as 1939, "My sympathies, for some reason, lie with the private in the front line against the brass hat; with the hodcarrier against the strawboss . . . ; with the laboratory worker against the stuffed shirt in a mortarboard; with the criminal against the cop."[16] For Dos Passos, the continuing struggle was that between the individual and an organized social, political, or financial structure. "The theme is freedom," he repeated often, coupled with his definition, "Individuality is freedom lived."[17]

It could also be said that differences in the critical estimation of Dos Passos' work were due not to his choice of subject or method so much as to the highly volatile intellectual temper of the 1920s and 1930s. Contrary to the generalizations of some critics, the only striking "change" in Dos Passos' writing occurred early and separated his first three novels, travel writing, and poems (work dominated by the themes of the lost son, the effete young man so far removed from life that he cannot find any place within it, reverence for and distance from women, and cultural and familial rootlessness) from the 1925 *Manhattan Transfer*, his first obvious use of the "exploration-of-America" theme. In one sense, after Dos Passos left off using clearly autobiographical subjects—at least so obviously—he seemed to begin thinking of himself as an American instead of some advantaged young wanderer. Part of his interest in the working-class character lay in that person's distance from his own situation; part stemmed from his war experiences, when he had learned to know a range of people and had developed a sense of "kinship with individual men and women."[18] Influenced further by the social unrest of the late 1920s, much of which surrounded the Sacco-Vanzetti protests, Dos Passos' fascination with labor and seemingly leftist characters coincided with the proletarian movement of the 1930s; therefore, and partly by accident, he became known as a "proletarian" novelist.

As Dos Passos said reluctantly, "There was a short period during which I actually believed that if you put underdog in Topdog's place he'd behave better. This was a very serious fallacy that made useless most of the thinking that stemmed from it."[19] When his romance with the working-class character ended, Marxist critics insisted that Dos Passos had changed political positions. A reading of his fiction, however, shows very little shift in attitude. While at one point he had looked to communism with hope, he remained skeptical, even during his Russian visit, and later, with the formation of *New Masses*, controversy between Dos Passos and the other contributors was evident from the beginning, as in his essay "The New Masses I'd Like." As Granville Hicks summarized in 1950,

> Nothing is deeper in the man than his fear of power. To begin with, he feared the power of the military, as he had experienced it in the first World War, and the power of men of wealth. The hatred of war and exploitation grew so acute that he accepted for a time the tempting radical doctrine that only power can destroy power. But what he saw of communism in Russia, in Spain, and at home convinced him that the destroying power could be more dangerous than the power it overcame. The New Deal, whatever its accomplishments, represented a great concentration of power, and he must always have been uneasy about it. As for war, Dos Passos hated it in and for itself and because it inevitably resulted in the piling of power upon power.[20]

By the time *Adventures of a Young Man*, a vehement exposé of communist sympathizers, was published in 1939, there was no way to pretend that Dos Passos was anything other than anti-Communist. The subsequent *District of Columbia* and the other late novels only reinforced his anti-Red and antipower position.

The undeniable sense of history in most of Dos Passos' writing is the bridge between his best-known work and the later history and fiction. Materials used in *1919*, the second book of the *U.S.A.* trilogy, which deals directly with World War I and its aftermath, and in *Mr. Wilson's War*, the historical treatment of the same period, are frequently similar and might also have appeared in *One Man's Initiation* and *Three Soldiers*. In addition to factual information, the books contain scenes, characters, and incidents that shape the larger attitudes of the reader. Dos Passos' imagistic method gives specific scenes a vividness that makes them memorable: the soldier whose girl surprises him with a large box of candy; the shelled waste of a cathedral; the distraught soldier who kills his hated lieutenant – for Dos Passos, material evoked method. The visual, direct presentation caught the real events – or the apparently real events – that sparked his primary interest. As he recalled in 1968, "I was thoroughly embarked on an effort to keep up a contemporary commentary on history's changes."[21]

Artist that he was, however, Dos Passos knew that his observations would be believed only if his techniques succeeded. The difference between his successful novels and those that seemed weak diatribes was often a difference of method. Characteristically, whether his writing was in fiction or history, the concrete scene, the specific detail, serves to suggest a philosophical attitude or situation. Whether one calls this attention to the concrete "imagism" (as the poets did), "expressionism" (the term in drama), "impressionism" (the fictional term, more appropriate to Dos Passos' first novels than to the mature work), or the "Camera Eye" (as he himself had labeled part of his method in *U.S.A*), method dominates his writing throughout his career. Given as he was to imaging his characters, his reliance on devices like those used in early films – juxtaposition resembling collage with its shifting content and point of view; emphasis on speed; noninterference by an authorial conscience – seems reasonable. Dos Passos' aim was, newsreellike, to present, to bombard, the viewer-reader with a spectrum of scenes and images, from which some sense of the real "history" being lived – whether personal or social – could accumulate. He recalled that his aim was "simultaneity":

> Direct snapshots of life. Reportage was a great slogan. The
> artist must record the fleeting world the way the motion pic-
> ture film recorded it. By contrast, juxtaposition, montage he
> could build drama into his narrative. Somewhere along the way
> I had been impressed by Eisenstein's motion pictures, by his
> version of old D. W. Griffith's techniques. Montage was
> his key word.[22]

An important corollary to this method was the idea of "reportage"
(later, *rapportage* in Dos Passos' vocabulary), the assumed objectivity of the viewer-author. Part of the difficulty with reading *Manhattan Transfer* and *U.S.A.* is that there is no announced authorial
perspective. Characters and events are literally presented without
directional language or situation: we are not sure, until we know
something of Dos Passos' narrative contexts, whether to criticize
or to applaud Daughter's love for Richard Savage or J. Ward Moorehouse's ambition. Dos Passos considered his fiction during these
years to be neither completely impartial nor charged in the sense of
the nineteenth-century novel. As he recalled later, "Artistic works
to be of lasting value must be both engaged and disengaged. They
must have a certain life, a certain aloofness that separates them
from the obsessions of the hour. At the same time they must en-
compass . . . the whole range of the human spirit."[23]

Dos Passos' concept of novels as history, history presented more
accurately and more deeply than conventional history–which he
came to describe as "contemporary chronicles"–has its inception in
his observation that a few great novels were really "chronicle novels" and drew much of their force from their mixture of history with
fictional narrative and character. Speaking of *Vanity Fair*, *War and
Peace*, and *La Chartreuse de Parme*, he explained that "the story is
the skeleton on which some slice of history is brought back to life.
Personal adventures illustrate the development of a society. Historical forces take the place of the Olympians of ancient Greek theater."[24] Plot exists to reveal the actual machinations of history (not
life, as the more common literary term "slice-of-life" would suggest); characters and their adventures exist not because they are of
interest in themselves but because they illustrate the ways in which
society has developed. And at the root of all of a person's troubles
lies neither Fate nor gods but "historical forces." Dos Passos' concept of the "chronicle novel" or his own "contemporary chronicles"
differed greatly from the standard literary translation of man-uni-
verse-power-plot and should be an essential consideration in any attempt to evaluate the success of his own work.

The application of these ideas to his aims in the *U.S.A.* trilogy is evident. "The narrative must carry a very large load," he explains, because American life during the present century is versatile, teeming. "Everything must go in. Songs and slogans, political aspirations and prejudices, ideals, hopes, delusions, frauds, crackpot notions out of the daily newspaper." The business of the modern novelist was to present enough valid historical images that the reader could accurately re-create the scene, the time, being presented. The centrality of his approach and method is clear from Dos Passos' observation that "the *U.S.A.* narratives were never supposed to end. They were followed by other chronicles from other points of view. Intermittently, and always trying to look out from the vantage point of style, to let the matter mould the style,"[25] the other chronicles kept coming.

His coining the term "contemporary chronicles" to describe his fiction suggests that Dos Passos realized the uniqueness of his work, this vividly imaged picture of America that was meant to be neither judgmental nor moralistic. Whenever he discussed his writing, however, whether midway through his career or toward its end, he seemed apologetic. His lack of any real financial success may have dampened his understanding of the value of his work, but the critic can view the continuum of his writing without the considerations of popular success and financial profit. The question today, critically, should be why Dos Passos' very important role in the development of modern American fiction need be considered with any tinge of apology. One has only to read the more contemporary fiction of writers like Günter Grass, E. L. Doctorow, or Norman Mailer to realize that Dos Passos' influence may be as great as Hemingway's. Jean Paul Sartre called Dos Passos "the greatest writer of our time";[26] D. H. Lawrence praised *Manhattan Transfer* as "the best modern book about New York that I have read."[27] Joseph Epstein, in retrospect, calls *U.S.A.* "the most ambitious single literary work ever undertaken in this country."[28] Thirty years ago, in 1947, Joseph Warren Beach saw the danger that Dos Passos' critical reputation might be eclipsed by the popularity of other writers and identified his interest in sociology, instead of psychology, as the quality of his fiction that would prompt that eclipse. In the age of the psychological novel, Dos Passos' emphasis on panorama instead of individual development was a handicap. As Beach pointed out, "The individual interests him, but mainly as a member of the social body."[29]

Consistent with this approach is the fact that Dos Passos tried to locate evil in social patterns rather than in individuals or their acts (World War I was, finally, *not* "Mr. Wilson's War," although Dos Passos' fictional treatment of it might have been more interesting had he felt that it were). We are still trained to be character-oriented readers, and Dos Passos' one consistent difference from other writers contemporary with him was his avoidance of the single psychological study in depth. He recognized the greatness in Faulkner's characterizations,[30] but his own aim—his personal intention in his fiction—was at times directed toward something else, toward "illustrating the development of a society." Again, the breadth of his aim forced him to choose different methods, but the heart of his own work—regardless of his comments about slogans, songs, and headlines—did remain America and its people.

By the time of the 1944 *State of the Nation*, Dos Passos had fully realized how central people were to his presentation of the *âme nationale*. As he arranged vignette after vignette, character sketch after character sketch, his implication was clear: the U.S.A. *is* its people. Farmers, factory workers, schoolteachers, piano players, barbers—identities exist through physical appearance, attitudes, and especially speech—language is usually Dos Passos' most important means of identifying character. People exist, however, as themselves, as individuals; they do not become so changed in Dos Passos' hands that they become "characters." Dos Passos accepts their external reality and shapes his panorama from it; he does not hypothesize or imagine things about these people that as an external observer he could not know.

The late fiction also shows this authorial caution to interpret the people of his imagination. The only characters Dos Passos draws with any psychological depth are those based on people he has known (Katy in Lulie or Hemingway in George Elbert Warner) or those that increasingly come to represent himself—Ro Lancaster and Jay Pignatelli. Most of the changes in method in the late novels come at least partly from his choice of characters who are more than external presentations.

The fact that Dos Passos chose somewhat different goals for his fiction gave him a distinction that time will prove valuable. Perhaps his panoramic vision will provide more insights to future readers than would a concentration on single characters, because through it the reader receives a great sense of the variety, richness, and complexity possible in any national identity, but particularly in the American modern. Dos Passos also consistently captured the motion of America—its energy, its life, the reality of its dealings and its work—as few other writers have ever done.

The only accurate critical view of Dos Passos in retrospect is that which recognizes his aims as writer and historian and considers those aims with the evident seriousness that shaped his life as writer. Even though he felt a responsibility to portray the realities of his culture, partly so that readers could better understand themselves, Dos Passos was adamant about the writer's necessity to be, first, an artist. Like so many of his contemporaries, Hemingway and Faulkner among them, Dos Passos believed in the religion of literature, the concept of writer as prophet, as seer. As he recalled, "There was, among many of the young people of my generation, a readiness to attempt great things. . . . It was up to us to try to describe in colors that would not fade, our America that we loved and hated. . . ."[31] As in so many of his remarks about art, America as subject shares his attention equally with his interest in craft.

One of the most accurate descriptions of the way Dos Passos saw his role as writer—as person concerned with this national soul, the craft of writing, and the morality of characters and life—occurs in his 1932 essay "The Workman and His Tools." Here Dos Passos grants that modern American writers write "to convince people of something," but he goes on to stress the joy writers find in the execution of their art: "There is such a thing as writing for writing's sake. A cabinetmaker enjoys whittling a dovetail because he's a cabinetmaker. . . ." For Dos Passos, the writer's delight in craft, in words, is more than "self-expression," although it is that also, precisely because the writer's keenest senses are focused outward, to the visible spectrum of life. The most interesting subject, finally, becomes history and the people who—in living—compose it; and his comments here suggest the relation of formal history to the writer's words, the living language with which any writer—but especially the American writer—should be working:

> The mind of a generation is its speech. A writer makes aspects of that speech permanent by putting them in print. He whittles at the words and phrases of today and makes forms for the minds of later generations. That's history. A writer who writes straight is an architect of history.[32]

In 1932 Dos Passos' aims ended with the preservation of what he considered history; by 1970, the history of the external world had merged with his own. For Dos Passos—no matter what his subject, no matter what his search—his writing became the means to picture, define, and eventually comprehend both the world around him and himself. As American, he was particularly conscious of his need for traditions, and his emphasis on history was a means of informing himself about the country that he both admired and satirized. But, in the process of searching for *âme nationale*, for hero, and for his own definition as writer, Dos Passos came to realize that every strong writer builds his own world, a creation ultimately subjective and personal.

Part I
The Development
of the Artist

1. Reaching Past Poetry

*Good writing was good writing under Moses and the Pharaohs
and will be good writing under a Soviet republic or a money
oligarchy. . . .*
–John Dos Passos, 1932

Although Dos Passos' writing eventually focused on American
themes, his earliest poetry and fiction were more self-conscious
than country-conscious. His favorite protagonist was a young, well-
educated naif–usually a Brahmin–hungering for all experience
simultaneously. There was much fascination with women, with sex
(although never explicit), and with travel, all described through a
romantic haze of impressionist color. There was also a strong sense
of rootlessness, and the most carefully drawn figures are those of
the boy's commanding, successful father and his genteel, passive
mother.

Dos Passos' early writing is also self-conscious in another sense,
in that it illustrates the artistic principles already important to the
fledgling author. These were the years of absorption in technique,
and most modern writers believed that, in order for any writer to
"write straight," he must have some kind of prolegomenon, some
set of artistic principles. Dos Passos' beginning aesthetic grew from
the contemporary emphasis on the concrete image, the scene–
whether in fiction, drama, or poetry–and on the arrangement of
those images and scenes into patterns resembling montage or collage. The pose of the objective author became one of his ideals, as
did the use of commonplace subjects.

The young author's first commitment to an aesthetic position
seems to have occurred early, during and just after his college years.
His letters to Rumsey Marvin, a younger friend who also wanted to
write, give a clear account of his own developing ideas about craft
and form, usually expressed in terms of the poetry he was then writing. His work of the first decade, both poetry and fiction, shows

not only the practice of his ideas about craft but also (perhaps more interestingly) the pervasive themes and character types that were to recur throughout his fifty years of work. For better or worse, the dominant characteristics of his writing are recognizable from the first, and one of the purposes of this study is to locate and trace those characteristic patterns.

Dos Passos' literary biography begins with his years at Harvard, 1913–16, where–with Robert Hillyer, E. E. Cummings, and others– he helped edit the relatively avant-garde *Harvard Monthly*, in which his essays, stories, and poems reveal his knowledge of contemporary artistic trends.[1] As a member of the Poetry Club, he heard such poetic innovators as Amy Lowell, Robert Frost, Vachel Lindsay, John Gould Fletcher, Conrad Aiken, and others and could disdainfully comment that too many Harvard students "chose to live in the 1890's."[2] For Dos Passos and his friends, he reminisced, "Currents of energy seemed breaking out everywhere. . . . [Americans were] groggy with new things in theatre and painting and music."[3] He described this "creative tidal wave" more specifically in his 1931 introduction to the translation of Blaise Cendrars' poem *Panama*:

> Under various tags: futurism, cubism, vorticism, modernism, most of the best work in the arts in our time has been the direct product of this explosion, that had an influence in its sphere comparable with that of the October revolution in social organization and politics and the Einstein formula in physics. Cendrars and Apollinaire, poets, were on the first cubist barricades with the group that influenced Picasso, Modigliani, Marinetti, Chagall; that profoundly influenced Maiakovsky, Meyerhold, Eisenstein; whose ideas carom through Joyce, Gertrude Stein, T. S. Eliot (first published in Wyndam's [sic] Lewis's "Blast").[4]

One central premise in the modernist aesthetic revolution was the importance of the image, and Dos Passos frequently refers to the imagist poets, particularly Ezra Pound and Richard Aldington, just as he often cites ideas that were first stated by Pound and F. S. Flint as early as 1913. The concentration on the concrete and the use of free or organic form and of rhythms determined by the spoken phrase rather than the rigidity of the metronome–these principles of imagism were to lay the foundation for most modern poetry and much prose as well.[5] The new aesthetic might be destructive of traditional forms and attitudes but, as Dos Passos explained in 1923,

"Explosions of fresh vitality in any art necessarily destroy the old forms."[6]

Dos Passos' poems, finally collected in the 1922 *A Pushcart at the Curb* (the manuscript of which in the University of Virginia collection suggests that the book was originally almost twice its published size),[7] do seem to have been influenced in some respects by the imagist doctrines. Short poems like "XV" from "Winter in Castile" are image-centered, highly descriptive, and succinct:

> *The weazened old woman without teeth*
> *who shivers on the windy street corner*
> *displays her roasted chestnuts invitingly*
> *like marriageable daughters.*[8]

Most of the longer poems also emphasize the image, although it may be only one element of a structure determined partly by the musicality of the total poem. Dos Passos' interest in the image is clear from his letters to Rumsey Marvin, where in 1915, for example, he stressed that "an idea or emotion has usually to be tied up in a picture, a figure of speech or something like that, before it is really available for poetry—in the highest sense. . . ."[9] In 1916 he wrote that "the game is to get musical-picture words and pack them with the desired emotion."[10] Later he referred to the importance of "concrete images," claiming to be interested in "originality" in their use before all else.[11]

Further comments to Marvin from 1915 to 1918 suggest his knowledge of other imagist principles. A "modern" writer, according to both Dos Passos and the imagists, was to use natural-sounding language rather than poetic diction. In 1918 he took Marvin to task for using archaisms. "In what language, except that of certain dead gentlemen, appears the word 'smooth'st'? For heaven's sake man—write live language not dead Keats and Shelley."[12] Several years earlier, he had criticized Marvin's language as being "a little high falutin', even for poetry" and advised him, "Try to run down the simple (not the hackneyed) and colorful words."[13] Dos Passos' own self-mocking poem "IV," from "Nights at Bassano," illustrates the controversy surrounding both "poetic" language and "poetic" subject matter:

> *O I would take my pen and write*
> *In might of words*
> *A pounding dytheramb* [sic]

Alight with teasing fires of hate,
Or drone to numbness in the spell
Of old loves long lived away
A drowsy vilanelle [sic].
O I would build an Ark of words,
A safe ciborium where to lay
The secret soul of loveliness. . . .

But my pen does otherwise.

All I can write is the orange tint with crimson
of the beaks of the goose
and of the wet webbed feet of the geese. . . . (PAC, pp. 99–100)

By shifting from subjects suitable for post-Victorian poetry to geese, Dos Passos also supports his 1915 contention to Marvin that "prize-fights are every bit as good a subject for poetry as fine ladies and illicit love affairs . . . every subject under the sun which has any thing to do with human beings–man, woman or child–is susceptible of poetic treatment. . . . And, moreover, one of the prime reasons why American literature isn't is that we as a nation have not that feeling of the infinite beauty and infinite poetry underlying things–love, war, sunsets, tin pans, lawnmowers, etc etc–."[14]

Comparing Dos Passos' poems with those of imagist poets like William Carlos Williams or H.D., however, shows some clear differences. Dos Passos seems to have been closer to the thinking of William Faulkner and Conrad Aiken in his feeling that, whatever its other properties, the modern poem should be "intensely musical."[15] The spare colloquial idiom of the modern American streetwalker or butcher theoretically may be the stuff of art, but Dos Passos had great admiration for the poems of Stevenson, Tennyson, and Swinburne, as well as for the work of Richard Aldington and Ezra Pound. As he wrote to Marvin,

> Do write more–and read Keats' Eve of St. Agnes, Shelley's Adonais–there you will learn something about words. . . . The main thing is to write what you see as simply as possible [sic] No, not exactly, the main thing is to keep the proper average between the music of the thing, the meter and the words–and don't be afraid of any word if it seems to fit– sincerely.[16]

Frequently, as in the following lines from "XIV," Dos Passos' poems are marked by heavy assonance, one means of creating musicality in language:

nights of clouds
terror of their flight across the moon.
Over the long still plains
blows a wind out of the north;
a laden wind out of the north. (PAC, p. 41)

From this device, it is only a short step to one of his most pervasive techniques, the repetition of phrase or line, a type of refrain, whether or not conventionally placed at the ends of stanzas. At its simplest, Dos Passos' repetition occurs to create mood, often through color imagery, as in "V" from "Winter in Castile," a poem that opens "Rain slants on an empty square" and closes with the mournful "in the grey rain, / in the grey city." In more ambitious poems, Dos Passos uses repetition to vary mood rather than to maintain it, as in "I" of "Nights at Bassano" (a poem titled in draft "Rondel to Our Lady of Abyssinia") and in "XIII," reminiscent of Vachel Lindsay's work:

There's a sound of drums and trumpets
above the rumble of the street.
(Run run run to see the soldiers.)
All alike all abreast keeping time
to the regimented swirl
of the glittering brass band. . . .

Dos Passos believed in the use of regular poetic forms so long as they achieved desired effects. Here, although the "run run run" line recurs as refrain, its context differs each time, and the author seems intent on achieving at least some effects that are unpredictable. The ending of this poem, for example, echoes key words from the opening stanza but places them in a very differently toned image:

old men in cloaks
try to regiment their feet
to the glittering brass beat.
Run run run to see the soldiers. (PAC, pp. 38–39)

This same density of verbal play, in both assonance and repetition, characterizes Dos Passos' later prose-poem writing in the Camera Eye and Biography segments of *U.S.A.* and the prefatory sections of the later novels.

Another element of Dos Passos' concept of musicality stemmed from his notion that free verse was never literally free but was "*meant* to have rhythm—it's not the same rhythm as so-called metrical verse; but it's a perfectly definite and sometimes quite

The next two stanzas give early and later events in the boy's life, with the metaphor at the close of the third charging the role of romance with greater importance than that of art.

> When I was small I sat and drew
> endless pictures in all colors on the walls;
> tomorrow the pictures should take life
> I would stalk down their long heroic colonnades.

> When I was fifteen a red-haired girl
> went by the window; a red sunset
> threw her shadow on the stiff grey wall
> to burn the colors of my pictures dead.

Rather than similes, to which he so often resorted, in this poem Dos Passos chose striking metaphors, occurring in both single figures and in the dominant patterns of room and windowpane, moon and shadow. The result is an exacting tautness, an accuracy of emotion that none of his other poems—either published or unpublished—matches. In the concluding stanzas the earlier imagery assumes even greater personal and immediate significance:

> Through all these years the walls have writhed
> with shadow overlaid upon shadow.
> I have bruised my fingers on the windowbars
> so many lives cemented and made strong.

> While the bars stand strong, outside
> the great processions of men's lives go past.
> Their shadows squirm distorted on my wall.

> Tonight the new moon is in the sky. (PAC, pp. 200–1)

Part of Dos Passos' fascination with World War I was that he had opportunity to watch these "great processions of men's lives"—to be, in fact, a part of them. "The fellows in my section are frightfully decent—all young men are frightfully decent. If we only governed the world instead of the swagbellied old foggies that do."[20] Much of the "plot" of both One Man's Initiation: 1917 and Three Soldiers concerns the dichotomy between Dos Passos' optimistic acceptance of his fellow soldiers and his later awareness of their sometimes disappointing actions under stress.

A greater part of his excitement about the war, however, seems to have been the accessibility of real experience as subject matter for his writing. As he recalled in The Best Times about his first year in the ambulance corps, he was still "absorbed in the problem of how to write clearly," but his primary interest lay in the war as subject: "War was the theme of the time. I was in a passion to put down everything, immediately as it happened, exactly as I saw it." It is interesting too that, as he continues to explain his heightened perceptions, he relies on the by-now-familiar use of concrete images juxtaposed one with another: "The chance of death sharpened the senses. The sweetness of the white roses, the shape and striping of a snail shell, the taste of an omelet, the most casual sight or sound appeared desperately intense against the background of the great massacres."[21]

It comes as no surprise that Dos Passos' first two published novels are war novels, written "imagistically" and centered on the searching young protagonists, Martin Howe and John Andrews. What makes the books better than some of his self-conscious technical pronouncements of these years might have indicated is that his emotional energy permeates them and commits him to writing powerfully about experiences and newly developed feelings. Even though he still felt somewhat trapped by what he viewed as the "bell-glass" atmosphere of Harvard and Boston society, his novels convince the reader that war is more than a rhetorical problem or a social one, that the lives of men are valuable, and that Dos Passos' purpose as writer is to present enough of the bones of the experience so that we ourselves can add on the flesh. In One Man's Initiation, for example, there is little attention to political events preceding and surrounding the war. Dos Passos' interest, and focus, falls on a few soldiers faced with their first encounter with death—of both physical bodies and cultural ones. The experience of the novel is accordingly immediate and concrete, rather than abstract and philosophical.

What makes the two novels a logical part of the artistic progression Dos Passos' writing career evinces is that the methods he uses in them are very similar to the methods he was then employing in his poetry. Instead of choosing a dramatic structure of rising action-climax-falling action, Dos Passos sets one scene against another; events separated in time become related thematically as they are presented in a nonchronological montage. His reaction against a time-sequential, plot-oriented novel is clear in his statement that "happenings meant nothing in themselves anyway—and . . . I tried to give that impression—by the recurrence of words and phrases"; this in answer to a criticism of his fiction as being "jerky, not elaborated enough."[22]

Like his poetry, the prose of *One Man's Initiation* is marked by factual detail presented concretely and by a painter's reliance on color. Yellow crates and white handkerchiefs are shaded with the brown light of the wharf as the novel opens, and soon "the rosy yellow and drab purple" buildings of the New York skyline pass the ship. Into the swatch of colors Dos Passos interjects the relatively stark dialogue of the young soldiers:

> "This your first time across?"
> "Yes. . . . Yours?"
> "Yes. . . . I never used to think that at nineteen I'd be crossing the Atlantic to go to war in France." The boy caught himself up suddenly and blushed. Then swallowing a lump in his throat he said, "It ought to be time to eat."
> > God help Kaiser Bill!
> > O-o-o old Uncle Sam.
> > He's got the cavalry,
> > He's got the infantry,
> > He's got the artillery;
> > And then by God we'll all go to Germany!
> > God help Kaiser Bill!
> The iron covers are clamped on the smoking room windows, for no lights must show. So the air is dense with tobacco smoke and the reek of beer and champagne. In one corner they are playing poker with their coats off. . . .[23]

The contrasting glimpses of bravado and nervousness take the story quickly from the early tone of comfortable pastiche to the stolid irony of the body of the novel. Throughout *One Man's Initiation*, or *First Encounter* as it was later and intermittently titled, Dos Passos sets the unrelieved horror of physical war against the propagandist version of that war, with snatches of popular songs serving as punctuation. These opposing views of war form the bases for the novel: scenes set in graphic montage to duplicate the effect the sights of war have on Martin Howe's awareness.

Even as the would-be soldiers drink and gamble to allay their fears, these fears surface in their conversation. Dos Passos shows fear in both the abstract and the specific, and in the latter, in a scene in which a soldier reports that death from the German's "new gas" means "five to seven days of slow choking," the fear results from home-front propagandists. Juxtaposed with this scene is the cloying dialogue between Howe and the patriotic girl (her unreality attested to by the image of her teeth, "white and regular as those in a dentist's show-case") who so vehemently hates all Germans and spreads atrocity stories to justify her hatred. Dos Passos' description of her prim delight at the evil points to the implicit contradictions between her enthusiasm and her outrage: "She raised a small gloved hand to her pink cheek in a gesture of horror, and settled herself comfortably in her deck chair" (p. 48).

In the much shorter second chapter, Dos Passos continues this direction by setting the flowers blooming in the French countryside against the soldiers' complaints about aggressive Frenchwomen and Howe's first glimpse of the reality of war, a sight that recurs as leitmotif elsewhere in the novel: "Between the pale-brown frightened eyes, where the nose should have been, was a triangular black patch that ended in some mechanical contrivance with shiny little black metal rods that took the place of the jaw" (p. 54). Shocking as this sight is for Howe, Dos Passos hammers home the irony of the image by next introducing an old woman selling flowers—roses (for good luck) and daisies (for love). This coupling of physical death with the harbinger of it leaves little to the reader's imagination. And, although he takes the flowers, Howe can see nothing of luck and love, only the mutilated face of the young soldier.

As the novel continues, each chapter adds another episode to Martin Howe's awakening horror, whether it be the destruction of the picturesque abbey, the slow deaths of the ambulance patients, or the depravity of the soldiers. Each scene is presented graphically, so that separate images stand clear at first and then gradually coalesce into more intense significance. This incremental pattern is illustrated by Dos Passos' use of the physical imagery of mutilation, which begins with the triangular patch, changes to "a depression, a hollow pool of blood lying where the middle of a man had been," and culminates in the recollection of a German prisoner's being blown to bits by an unexpected grenade. This last image recurs as the cause of psychological torment to a supposedly hardened soldier and, in subsequent descriptions, Dos Passos adds more graphic physical details.

What is most noticeable about this carefully modulated intensification of horror is that Martin Howe's understanding of the true nature of wounding and death parallels his realizations about other romantic ideals. His concept of the woman he might love differs wildly from the French prostitutes who surround him. His beliefs about the realities of war are also quickly shattered, and the tone of physical outrage and hostility becomes correspondingly dulled and resigned. The image Dos Passos used to represent all the glory of an enlightened culture—that of the abbey—is eventually shelled; its destruction, however, is described with quasi-dreamlike resignation: "So had the abbey in the forest gleamed tall in the misty moonlight; like mist, only drab and dense, the dust had risen above the tall apse as the shells tore it to pieces" (p. 100). Similarly described is a macabre crucifixion scene, in which Christ's crown of thorns is replaced with a crown of barbed wire and the physical imagery culminates in the shapeless, sacked bodies of the dead. Instead of pathos or sensationalism, the sight of those unnamed, uncounted dead provokes the narrator to that same ultracontrolled description, focusing on the procession of the "little carts" rather than on the bodies that are their contents.

The progression in the novel to its unrelievedly bitter end—with many of Howe's friends dead or dying and his observing the aftermath of another futile battle—follows effectively from the image clusters placed early in the book. *One Man's Initiation* also has its share of polemic—chance conversations, ironic interchanges, outright diatribe—but even this rhetoric is frequently saved by Dos Passos' graphic use of the language. The propaganda first described as "living, growing flypaper to catch and gum the wings of every human soul" becomes personified in the ideology of the berserk soldier who believes that "to stop the war you must kill everybody, kill everybody."

Such vignettes as this of the mad soldier loosely connected by Howe's presence and central consciousness and by the repetition of images and language create the structure of the book. Relatively free from personal antagonists, Howe moves through the war, often less aware than one might wish of the unending ironies surrounding him. His "initiation" appears to accrue from the gradual accumulation of vivid physical images—colors, flowers, sounds, wounds, fires. Only toward the end of the novel does Dos Passos show Howe trying clumsily to sort through the prevailing attitudes and philosophies about the war. In a chapter that seems overlong, Howe and Tom Randolph discuss such matters with a group of French soldiers; they part in agreement, and the two Americans give their ironic summaries:

> "With people like that we needn't despair of civilization," said Howe.
> "With people who are young and aren't scared you can do lots."

"We must come over and see those fellows again. It's such
a relief to be able to talk."

"And they give you the idea that something's really going
on in the world, don't they?"

"Oh, it's wonderful! Think that the awakening may come
soon." (p. 169)

Scarcely three pages later, the novel ends, with all the admirable
French soldiers dead. Events have proved even the most pessimistic of views too affirmative, and the brisk episodic structure of the
book brings the denouement home effectively.

Dos Passos' second war novel, *Three Soldiers*, is also a collage of
color and image, even though the book includes three protagonists
and their interrelationships. Nearly five times as long as *One Man's
Initiation*, this novel introduces the dichotomy that so much of Dos
Possos' earliest fiction explored: that of the well-educated protagonist who fears life and surrounds himself—and thereby contrasts
himself—with less sensitive men who can, and often do, act. John
Andrews is the typical early protagonist, foiled by the more active
characters Chris Chrisfield and Dan Fuselli. *Three Soldiers* consequently becomes not only a "war" novel but also a psychological
study of three men, men brought to some kind of essential portrait
through the extremities of war.

Three Soldiers also shows Dos Passos' inventive approach to
style. Whereas *One Man's Initiation* is written in largely under-
stated description, with vivid imagery held to a minimum and
thereby made all the more striking when it does occur, *Three Soldiers* is dotted with rich, highly colored description. Scenes are
marked with imagery that relates the loosely connected episodes,
particularly imagery of fire (battle, grenades, guns, and conflict) and
death (loss of consciousness, pain, wood and decay). As Stendhal in
The Red and the Black, Dos Passos here relies on a red and black
pattern, dominated by visual imagery and incantatory repetitions:

> The lieutenant stood out suddenly black against a sheet
> of flame. . . . crashing detonations and yellow tongues of
> flame. . . . white and red glows rose and fell as if the horizon
> were on fire. As they started down the slope, the trees sudden-
> ly broke away and they saw the valley between them full of
> the glare of guns and the white light of star shells. It was like
> looking into a stove full of glowing embers.[24]

The horror of gunfire at night, blackness laced and cut with red,
so permeates the book that any neutral color creates a tone of peace-

fulness. The reader hopes for grays, because red signals either injury or death and black usually connotes either fear or death.

Dos Passos also uses much description of the sense of touch or smell—more than elsewhere in his early writing—and these details work with the visual imagery to depict psychological states accurately. He also effectively plays with dream images, as in the scene when Chrisfield's fear of death becomes so intense (a fear we recognize from earlier smell and sight imagery) that he sees himself being court-martialed, victimized by his own men, but unable to hear any of the charges.

> They were reading things out of papers aloud, but, although he strained his ears, he couldn't make out what they were saying. All he could hear was a faint moaning. Something had a curious unfamiliar smell that troubled him. He could not stand still at attention, although the angry eyes of officers stared at him from all round. "Anderson, Sergeant Anderson, what's that smell?" he kept asking in a small whining voice. "Please tell a feller what that smell is." But the three officers at the table kept reading from their papers, and the moaning grew louder and louder in his ears until he shrieked aloud. (p. 182)

In desperation, Chrisfield throws a grenade at the officers, later imaged as "wasps" silhouetted against the "sheet of flame." A few pages later, as if prefigured by the dream, Chrisfield kills a young German, coolly, "very coolly," in just the same way, and several pages beyond that, he similarly murders his own commanding officer, Anderson. In this passage, which climaxes Chrisfield's brutalization by the war, Dos Passos uses not color imagery but touch. Chrisfield reaches for the grenade with cold hands but, once he sees Anderson die, a "warm joy" goes through him and he feels, Dos Passos emphasizes, "full of warmth and strength."[25]

Dos Passos also uses image to express theme, here in connection with the central protagonist, John Andrews. Andrews' admiration for John Brown, idealistic abolitionist, and his use of that figure in his most mature musical composition unify the last sections of the novel and lead us to see how ineffectual, finally, Andrews' desertion from the army has been. "No; he has not lived up to the name of John Brown," he decides at one point near the end of the book, but then he finds resolve and decides he can escape to Bordeaux. With typical wartime irony, however, MP's arrive, their voices interrupting strains from the song "John Brown's Body." Like Brown's, John

Andrews' life is sacrificed to a military ideal that Dos Passos has already shown, repeatedly, to be worthless. What is ambiguous about Andrews' situation—and therefore in keeping with the pervasively despairing tone of *Three Soldiers*—is whether his death will serve any purpose at all.

2. History as Autobiography: Dos Passos' Early Protagonists

Except for books his life had been a great bare room—he told himself—a room equipped with globes and mathematical tables, and all things he hated.
—John Dos Passos, "The Shepherd"

"You see, it has taken me so long to find out how the world is. There was no one to show me the way."[1] John Andrews' complaint near the end of *Three Soldiers* is a clear statement of one theme that dominated much of Dos Passos' writing, both early and late. Dos Passos' characters are usually searching for answers. Unlike the already initiated Hemingway protagonist, whose chief frustration lies in convincing others that they should agree with his philosophy, Dos Passos' protagonist is often trapped by personal indecision, more acted upon than acting (as are Martin Howe and the characters of his early short stories).

Dos Passos' characterization of John Andrews becomes important, then, partly because Andrews is the first well-developed, plausible character in his fiction and also the first spokesman for what becomes a continuing theme in Dos Passos' later fiction—that individuals seldom win against organized, inhuman social units, whether they be armies, governments, or labor unions. And Andrews is also the prototype of the characteristic Dos Passos persona, the naive, impassioned Bostonian who enjoys his culture and its accompanying sophistication and superiority while simultaneously resenting it. The very superiority that he enjoys cuts him off from what he sees as "reality." Connoisseur of wines, food, music, and art—and would-be connoisseur of women—Andrews longs to live a more physical life, as he tells the rough Chrisfield:

> "I'd rather be this than . . . than that," said Andrews bitterly. He tossed his head in the direction of a staff car full of

officers that was stalled at the side of the road. They were drinking something out of a thermos bottle that they passed round with the air of Sunday excursionists. They waved, with the conscious relaxation of discipline, at the men as they passed. (pp. 177–78)

Criticism of the educated, "tame" generation colors much of Dos Passos' characterization in the years between the wars.[2] Repeatedly, his protagonists go through an "initiation" process like that of Martin Howe in the first novel, following a continuum much like Andrews' realizations in *Three Soldiers*. The first stage is self-dissatisfaction and rejection of the education obtained from formal schooling. Meeting people who have less training (Chrisfield, for example, who left school at twelve) and finding them interesting, sane, even admirable is a corollary stage. Once the identification between sophisticated hero and primitive friend has been made, the protagonist begins to see that organized social forces are evil, that it was not other human beings, after all, that caused life's miseries but rather the impersonal agencies of abstract philosophies. The hero's subsequent battles are with these agencies. John Andrews ends his military career in prison because of the brutalization of the men who carry out the commands of the hated military machine (the turning point in his attitude really coming when the lieutenant, in the midst of an orderly conversation, unexpectedly beats him).

Convincing as Dos Passos' portrait of John Andrews is—and he was usually at his best with protagonists who faced the problems of resenting their education and tried to act against it, who at least thought they wanted to replace education with experience—*Three Soldiers* is filled with inconsistencies that keep Dos Passos' pattern from working out successfully. To begin with, the earthy common soldiers, Dan Fuselli and Chrisfield, are not only weak but also appear infrequently in the book. Instead of impressing us with their energy, warmth, sanity, like a Sancho Panza or a Lyaeus, they are fumbling, materialistic, unappealing. Rather than lighthearted and Bacchic, Fuselli is motivated by the most dehumanizing desire of all, to change status, to become a corporal. Rising within the ranks of the army machine demands that he relinquish much of his human sensibility, though that quality is hardly made clear when he first appears in the novel. (Dos Passos gives us only the scene of his girlfriend's exchanging a box of candy for Fuselli's American flag, a scene more anecdotal than memorable.)[3] Fuselli's frustrated attempts to reach the rank of corporal are what we remember about him, and even though Dos Passos tries to make his progress integral to the novel (usually by having Andrews meet mutual friends who envy Fuselli's resourcefulness and vigor), it is a lost cause. The Fuselli Dos Passos creates here would have been of no help—and of even less interest—to the more complex Andrews.

Chris Chrisfield is similarly unappealing, partly because of Dos Passos' inept handling of midwestern dialect, which here is a strange mixture of southern and midwestern speech. With even thinner motivation, Chris becomes a murderer, incensed by Sergeant Anderson's early treatment of him and the sergeant's subsequent promotion to lieutenant. Dos Passos does not show how Chris's anger becomes the obsession that leads him to kill Anderson. If he did, perhaps Chrisfield's character as an innocent-gone-astray or an Indiana Ahab mindful only of revenge would be interesting. As it is developed in *Three Soldiers*, however, Chrisfield's primitivism only mocks the idea of noble savage and leaves the reader skeptical at best. In his letters, Dos Passos speaks of the intensity of his own emotion about the novel and its characters:

> I want to express somehow my utter . . . Its [*sic*] not exactly that though. The feeling of revolt against army affairs has long crystalized itself into the stories of three people, a clerk in an optician's in San Francisco, a farmer's son from Indiana and a musical person who appers in S.T.R.W.J.—so much so that I cant get a word down on paper.[4]

If Fuselli and Chrisfield are to represent the reality of physical life, as Dos Passos' comments in letters and throughout the novel suggest, then John Andrews has clear enough reason to remain a meditative observer. When he too turns to a life of involvement—even if acting as he wants means breaking both military and social law—we are somewhat confused. But so Dos Passos presents Andrews' moment of resolution: "An enormous exhilaration took hold of him. It seemed the first time in his life he had ever determined to act. All the rest had been aimless drifting. The blood sang in his ears" (p. 226). The justification for Andrews' rebellion (and, by implication, for Fuselli's and Chrisfield's derelictions also) is the inhumanity of any war machine. Dos Passos works hard to establish this structure by titling the six sections of the novel as if the military process were industrialization. "Making the Mould" shows the soldiers' erratic, senseless early training. "The Metal Cools" follows the company to France and its acclimatization there. An early scene here of Fuselli in despair ("He was so far from anyone who cared about him, so lost in the vast machine") suggests that his dehumanization occurs because of the military, but Dos Passos includes the almost unnoticed death of the young Stockton to show how little even the young initiates like Fuselli were capable of caring.

With the third part, "Machines," Dos Passos gives us Chrisfield's murder of Anderson, complete with what justification is allowable, that Chrisfield has now become a machine: "Chrisfield looked straight ahead of him. He did not feel lonely any more now that he was marching in ranks again. His feet beat the ground in time with the other feet. He would not have to think whether to go to the right or to the left. He would do as the others did" (p. 190).

With "Rust," the fourth section, Dos Passos suggests that some people, Andrews at least, can escape brutalization. First wounded, then transferred to the school battalion, he studies music at the Sorbonne, hoping to escape the effects of his time in the military machine. His hysteria at finding himself "alone, free, with days and days ahead of him to work and think, gradually to rid his limbs of the stiff attitudes of the automaton" (p. 299), sets the tone for much of his dangerous behavior in the fifth part, "The World Outside." Seductive as the Parisian world of music, art, and women is, Andrews is not completely at ease. An early strain of Dos Passos' belief in America rather than France as the land of fulfillment surfaces in a conversation between Andrews and the beguiling Frenchwoman Géneviève Rod:

> "France is stifling," said Andrews all of a sudden. "It stifles you slowly, with beautiful silk bands. . . . America beats your brains out with a policeman's billy."
> "What do you mean?" she said, letting pique chill her voice.
> "You know so much in France. You have made the world so neat. . . ."
> "But you seem to want to stay here," she said with a laugh.
> "It's that there's nowhere else." (p. 366)

Dos Passos' resentment against the Brahmin quality of life obtains here with Andrews' against the rigid French attitudes, cultured yet stultifying. Yet, inexplicably, it is for Géneviève Rod, symbol and product of these attitudes, that Andrews risks his final chance at freedom. In "Under the Wheels," Dos Passos presents the last conflict, as Andrews—now legally and morally wrong in his military desertion–is betrayed by his French landlady and also by Géneviève and acts irrationally, in ways destined to fail. Instead of using his intellect and talent to work past bureaucratic obstacles, Andrews runs headlong into all of them. In a conversation with Géneviève, Dos Passos has Andrews admit his irrationality, but the admission does not excuse him from the responsibility for his acts: "'I must be, as you say, a little mad, Géneviève,' said Andres. 'But now that I, by pure accident, have made a gesture, feeble as it is, towards human freedom . . . ,'" (p. 460).

In this respect, *Three Soldiers* is an unfinished novel: it leaves the reader with that gesture, that Quixotic grasp at freedom reminiscent of a long tradition of romantic heroes. What Dos Passos adds, with the bleakness of view typical of a modernist, is the futility of that gesture, the ultimate destruction of Andrews under the wheels of a relentlessly moving society. The novel ends as it does to justify Andrews' own earlier pronouncement, "Human society has been always that, and perhaps will be always that: organizations growing and stifling individuals, and individuals revolting hopelessly against them, and at last forming new societies to crush the old societies and becoming slaves again in their turn . . ."(p. 458).

John Andrews' complaint near the end of *Three Soldiers* ("There was no one to show me the way") would surface repeatedly in Dos Passos' writing during the next ten years. Not only did he make countless physical journeys (to Spain, to the Orient, to Mexico, to Russia), the subjects of which gave him material for his travel books and poems, but he also spent much of the decade exploring new artistic and political attitudes. Moving a step beyond Andrews' stopping point in *Three Soldiers*, the blind rebellion against oppressive force, Dos Passos explored what seemed to be reflective alternatives, leading his life so as to open himself to new experience and new conviction. Blanche Gelfant, John Wrenn, Martin Kallich, and others have written convincingly of Dos Passos' search for identity and the importance of the father figure in his life, and his writing of the 1920s most definitely shows that quest. By the time of *The 42nd Parallel* in 1930, Dos Passos appears to have recognized many of his obsessive search patterns: the autobiographical reminiscence of the Camera Eye sections is accurate; the "heroes" of the biography sections stand up well; the story is set in what was to be Dos Passos' setting for the rest of his work, the United States. But his work at the beginning of the decade was much less confident about itself and its personae: John Andrews' confusion pervaded.

Streets of Night, although not published until 1923, was begun during Dos Passos' Harvard years and parallels *Three Soldiers* in many of its themes and attitudes.[5] J. Fanshaw MacDougan is much like Andrews, although lacking his final act of rebellion. Cambridge and its rigid social structure is in many respects as restrictive as the military and, although life there aims toward humanization through culture, in some ways as debilitating. The theme is also familiar. Fanshaw longs to free himself from convention, to travel, to love, to "live"; but he continues to make meaningless rounds of concerts, teas, and dinners, poisoning his friendships with his frustration and considering his work only another social convention:

> A trio we are, Nan and Wenny and I, a few friends my only comfort in this great snarling waste of a country. We don't fit here. We are like people floating down a stream in a barge out of a Canaletto carnival, gilt and dull vermilion, beautiful lean-faced people of the Renaissance lost in a marsh, in a stagnant canal overhung by black walls and towering steel girders. One could make a poem or an essay out of that idea, some people could; Wenny, if he weren't such a lazy little brute. Why couldn't I?[6]

Like Hawthorne's Fanshaw, Dos Passos' protagonist lives by constructing idylls. Throughout the novel, the imagery of Renaissance painting connects his musings—faces, colors, scenes, any image can prompt Fanshaw's return to the beautiful and safe past. As Dos Passos presents him, he uses this dodge whenever he feels physically threatened—by the sight of lovers on the bridge, the heavy smells of cheap restaurants, thoughts of sex. Fanshaw's revulsion to the sex that he considers emblematic of a gross world (always the non-Renaissance world) gives Dos Passos a reason for the envelope structure of the book. *Streets of Night* opens with a long scene describing two Harvard classmates, Fanshaw and the more rowdy Cham Mason, picnicking with two chorines, who are wearing identical pink and blue ruffled dresses. Fanshaw blames his distaste for his blue-clad damsel on her Mary Garden perfume and her use of the word *ain't* (because both are "common"), but his rejection of sex per se is apparent from the start. Cham's more relaxed approach to the sexual encounter provides the same kind of contrast in characterization that Wenny's appreciation for the sensual does throughout the central part of the book. Structurally, even the seemingly contrived Walpurgisnacht relates to the opening because it occurs at Cham's wedding. The episode is important as a means not only of exploring all the recurring themes of commitment and self-awareness but also of showing Fanshaw's fear of both those processes.

The frame tale closes the novel with a postwar episode in Italy, in which Fanshaw visits a pink-gowned prostitute, modern vestige of his romantic idyll. The experience is not altogether unpleasant, and Fanshaw almost breaks through his self-imposed restraint to stay abroad (reminiscent of James' Lambert Strether). But cultural and personal conventions are too strong for him, and he drifts back to his pseudo-artistic life in America. As Dos Passos recalled many years later, *Streets of Night* had been "an effort to recapture that strange stagnation of the intellectual class I'd felt so strangling during college. . . . I certainly didn't manage to get much of it on paper, due to youthful ignorance of men and their motives."[7]

Whether the novel fails because of Dos Passos' "youthful ignorance" or because of other more important artistic considerations, it is in some ways a more interesting book than the relatively successful *Three Soldiers*. It does share many conventions of the *fin de siècle* "art novel," and Dos Passos' enthusiasm for Joyce's *Portrait of the Artist* and for the novels of James and Hawthorn is clear. But it also includes apt characterization of Nancibel Taylor, his first strong female character; stream-of-consciousness sections that are more successful than many much later attempts (Hemingway's in *To Have and Have Not*, for example); and a reliance on imagery and juxtaposition of scenes that gives it—for its ostensible structure and theme—a rapid pace.

Although the foil character of Fanshaw in the novel would appear to be David Wendell, Wenny, the younger student who does—through suicide—attempt to break through the various stagnations depicted in the book, Dos Passos structures the novel so that the real opposing force to Fanshaw's apathy is Nan. By opening the novel with the extensive scene of the Harvard man and the chorus girls, Dos Passos suggests that Fanshaw's obsession is with finding an ideal woman. The short interior monologue at the close of the first chapter, in which Fanshaw dreams of "Annabel Lee" ("Marriage was for ordinary people, but for him, love, two souls pressed each to each, consumed with a single fire"), lead directly to the scene of Nan's tea, with Fanshaw, Wenny, and her linked as compatriots.

The imagery in this scene recurs throughout much of the novel; it is nearly all connected with Wenny, just as it is all sensual—the smell of lemon; the sight of the chrysanthemumlike star, "bristling with green horns of light"; the smell of Wenny's wet wool suit. Physically attracted by Wenny's masculinity, Nan yet turns to Fanshaw ("Fanshaw's voice was always so soothing. . . . She always felt sane where Fanshaw was"). The imagery of this opening scene establishes these ambivalent poles of attraction: Nan can hardly restrain herself from caressing Wenny, yet she thinks of his hard, hot hands as "ditchdigger's hands." Fascinated by the green star and its appeal for Wenny, she is nonetheless unnerved by its attraction: "For an instant all her life palpitated hideously with the star. She turned. Her lips almost brushed Wenny's cheek" (p. 38). Her anger with herself after the men leave, her futile attempt to lose herself in her music are both essential steps toward the long morning sequence in which Dos Passos effectively presents Nan's conflict. Despite some overwriting, the scene is moving–Nan scrutinizing her naked body, her conflicts made graphic in the repressed features of "thin New England lips" and "scarcely formed breasts"–and reaches an erotic culmination:

> Somewhere at the end of a long corridor of her mind she
> ran through the dappled shadow of woods, naked, swift, chased
> by someone brown, flushed, goatfooted. She could feel in her
> nostrils the roughness of the smell of Wenny's damp homespun
> suit. Aprèsmidi d'un Faune, the words formed in her mind,
> Music by Claude Debussy, Choreography by M. Nijinski.
> . . . (p. 44)

In this and subsequent passages, Dos Passos makes so clear Nan's ambivalence that Wenny's and Fanshaw's conflicts are also clarified. (Dos Passos gives similarly introspective passages for them, but later in the novel.) This reliance on psychological motivation may be the greatest weakness of the novel, because the embroidery comes to outweigh the design. Instead of revelation, each subsequent scene brings only repetition. Even Wenny's suicide, which occurs relatively early in the book (leaving room for Nan and Fanshaw's relationship to change), brings little that is new to the themes already presented. His suicide could be viewed positively as the antithesis of Fanshaw's inaction; it could also, more maturely, be considered a totally ineffectual act, only another kind of postponement. Had we been prepared psychically for it (the relationship between Wenny and his father seems paramount but is scarcely mentioned), Wenny's death might have confirmed his difference from Fanshaw (witness Quentin Compson's similarly motivated death in *The Sound and the Fury*). As it is, occurring in the same atmosphere of hysteria that colors his leaving college and proposing to Nan, it seems more contrived than necessary, a deus ex machina to free the plot for the development of Fanshaw and Nan's relationship.

Similar as they are psychologically, the central difference between Nan and Fanshaw lies in motivation. Dos Passos implies that Fanshaw's romantic life has no meaning at least partly because his professional life has none. For Fanshaw, his work (teaching art history) is only another social convention; he has little passion for or even interest in what he does. In fact, when he thinks about his work after the war, it seems to be only one part of his social round: "Exit to Massachusetts Avenue and the College Yard and the museum and tea with professors' wives" (p. 309). In striking contrast is Nan's impassioned defense of her career as a violinist:

> "That's where my music comes in," Nan was saying, her voice grown suddenly tense as Wenny's. "By living it, by making myself great in it, I can bust loose of this fearful round of existence. What a wonderful phrase that is, the wheel of Karma! I understand why women throw themselves head over heels at the most puny man. They have got to escape, if only for a moment, from the humdrum, all the little silly objects, pots and pans and spools of thread that make up our lives. I've got to get that in my music. Nothing else matters." (p. 89)

Dos Passos presents Nan's dedication to her music as energetic, life-giving; it is Fanshaw's defensive stance about his work that seems affected. Nan's art is creative; Fanshaw only observes. That Dos Passos uses the free-living persona of Mabel Worthington in conjunction with Nan has caused some readers to find an antithesis between Mabel's passion for life and Nan's reluctance to live sexually. But by using a third woman, Fitzie Fitzhugh, who represents the conservative outlook, Dos Passos can use Mabel as focal point instead of contrast. As Fitzie tells the Worthington story with horrified glee, Nan can see beyond the conventional stigma. Nan admires Mabel and for that reason Dos Passos ends *Streets of Night* with Nan's interviewing her. Mabel has been "successful"—she has married, had a child, gone into business. There is, however, no mention of her music. While Nan by no means glories in her lonely career, as the scene of her turning to the supernatural suggests, we do know that she has chosen to break the meaningless engagement to Fanshaw and that her life remains more than a compromise with convention.

Nan's kind of strength—whether or not it can suffice alone—is

evident in her sense of direction, and the imagery connected with
Dos Passos' title further emphasizes her strength. Fanshaw dreams
of "long streets of blind windows, dark, cold under arclights," himself lost, searching for his mother, or else alone with Wenny and
Nan, the three of them losing their way. Wenny, similarly, saw
each street as an image of his life, each avenue leading to the conviction, "No more dreams, I'm going to live tomorrow." Only Nan
sees the streets literally, for what they are.

In Dos Passos' most effective interior monologue for Wenny, the
streets figure prominently. Again Dos Passos uses the Noah's ark
and the toy images from Wenny's boyhood, complete with the contrast between the loving aunt who reared him and the prescriptive
father who abandoned him, but this time he insists on a fusion between Wenny and his father: "Panic terror swooped on him all of
a sudden; it was not his face. The face was thinner, the upper lip
tight over the teeth, the hair smooth and steel gray, the jowls pink-
ish, close-shaved, constricted by a collar round backwards. My face,
my father's face . . . my father's voice is my voice. I am my father"
(pp. 197, 199). Similarly, Dos Passos creates the parallel between
Wenny's whore, Ellen, and his idealized vision of an "Ellen of Troy,"
forcing him to equate death with sex in the final lines of his monologue;

> I have nerve for this, why not for the rest; for shipping
> on a windjammer, for walking with Nan down streets unac-
> countable and dark between blind brick walls that tremble with
> the roar of engines, for her seagrey eyes in my eyes, her lips,
> the sweetish fatty smell of Ellen's lips. Maybe death's all
> that, sinking into the body of a dark woman, with proud cold
> thighs, hair black black. . . . Spread out your bed for me,
> Nan Ellen death. (p. 201)

Some solutions to the psychological dilemmas that seem to dom-
inate Dos Passos' early fiction had been prefigured in "Seven Times
Round the Walls of Jericho," the unpublished novel that Dos Passos
and Robert Hillyer supposedly collaborated on during World War I.
Filled with the imagery Dos Passos was to use in his other early
novels—streets, moons, women's full skirts, flowers, rivers—"Seven
Times" is also a direct antecedent of his first play, The Moon Is a
Gong, first staged in 1925.

In both the play and the fiction, Dos Passos emphasizes self-cog-
nition, the stranglehold of various conventions, the necessity both

to dream and to have personal ambition. (Dos Passos seems to have been thoroughly American both in his adoption of the Horatio Alger myth, although in his view material success seldom indicated real personal success, and in his insistence that heroes could, physically, attain whatever they wanted: i.e., beating on the moon, finding a true love, winning against all kinds of plausible and implausible forces.)

Because the 1920 novel *One Man's Initiation: 1917* was originally the fourth section of "Seven Times" or was at least a later version of that section, Dos Passos' protagonist in "Seven Times" is also Martin Howe (nicknamed "Fibbie" because of his tendency to fib), who has a musician friend named John Andrews. As a child, Fibbie feels rejected by his family and dreams of herculean feats to win his mother's attention and love.

> And when he grew up big and strong he'd go up in a balloon and get on the edge of the moon and beat it and beat it. How fine it would be! Mother and Nurse wouldn't be able to get up there to stop him. . . . far up above their scoldings and their prohibitions, beating out tunes they had to dance to, beating such rhymes out of the drum of the moon that everyone would pile out of the dark houses, and fill the streets and climb on the roofs and on the zigzag chimney-pots to look at him.[8]

Martin's hero is his unconventional uncle, James Clough, a family black sheep whose play, *The Dreamer Wakes*, though a commercial failure, inspires Fibbie for the rest of his life. Although his uncle dies soon after the play closes, his life serves as model for the younger Fibbie, who now sees the old-time physical challenge of beating on the moon expressed in images from Clough's play:

> O we were going to take drums and trumpets, all of us, and shout down the tottering walls of Jericho, so that the wind should blow through the stinking streets and the idols should fall into the putrifying heaps of their victims. . . . And you say it is not the time. . . . The walls are tottering, I tell you. . . . we are afraid of getting hurt. . . .

"He would live freely, hughly," Martin declares, and for several years, before World War I, he does. He travels, he meets women—Suzanne Lavonniere, his uncle's lover, and the red-haired Mary West—but soon he is caught in the military system described so carefully in the war novels. Both *One Man's Initiation* and *Three Soldiers* have a greater poignancy when we see the protagonists as the much younger characters of "Seven Times." Transfered from the young romantics who will beat on moons, dream of "strange countries to travel in and wrongs to undo, and women beautiful as Helen to love, and great thrilling deeds," to men sobered by the perversion of authority no less than by death, John Andrews and Martin Howe depict the impact of modern warfare and culture on traditional romantic sensibilities. In light of this characterization, the image of Don Quixote and the windmills is viable for all three books.

What changes noticeably as a result of Dos Passos' own war experiences is his analysis of the causative forces in these characters' lives. In "Seven Times," Dos Passos used Fibbie's summary of Clough's play to represent the philosophy underlying the novel. What the dreamers in the play awake to is this central, romantic realization:

> In each act it had been the same; two spirits' really sincere struggling towards the utterest realization of life against a murky background of smallness and convention, first among the old aristocracy, the genteel people, then among the artists, the would-be free, last among working people, slaves of strange old superstitions; in all the same smallness of little egos struggling to maintain their self importance.

Large egos war against small—a battle not unlike Quixote's against his own unimaginative culture. But after World War I Dos Passos learned to identify larger patterns of causation, whether accurately or not. With new bitterness, he wrote that the challenge was more than that of self-fulfillment; the challenge was that of staying alive:

> World War I turned out to be the real world with a vengeance. After a couple of years of driving an ambulance, carting the mangled and dying out from under the sound of guns, I began to think I understood what the Socialists meant. The world we lived in, which they called Capitalism, was a bloody slaughterhouse; anything was worth trying to make it a place fit to live in. . . . What we hoped from socialism was the end of the war and militarism and the introduction of self government into industry. We thought producers were good people and the people who lived off the process of distribution were bad people.[9]

Again, perhaps, too-quick identification with ideology plagued Dos Passos, but at least he is far past the romantic stance of a character's trying to reach self-knowledge, independent of surroundings.

And if his panacea for the correction of social ills remained "romantic" in its own way, perhaps that was the continuing motivation for his characters. As he said near the conclusion of the unpublished essay quoted above, "self government and responsible participation by every man and woman in the business of the community" was his new social ideal. Martin Howe and John Andrews had scarcely been allowed "self-government" within the military; Fanshaw, Wenny, and Nan had each avoided the "responsible participation" that might have been possible. Dos Passos' earliest fiction had provided only failed protagonists but, in the process of this writing, he was himself finding out "how the world is." The fruits of that education became visible in his socio-political writing, the slant of his travel reportage, and his increasing concern with history—even within his fiction. As he was later to recall about this period,

> I found myself under a sort of compulsion to try to relate the lives of the people I knew to the panorama of history. The method was experimental. As I worked I used occasionally to reassure myself with the thought that at least some of the characters and scenes and feelings I put down might prove useful for the record.[10]

Whether "the record" was to be Dos Passos' own "contemporary chronicle" or a more objectively historical account of the times, accuracy and colorful detail—combined with a seasoned understanding of the patterns of history—would be his aim.

3. History as Travel: Dos Passos on the Road to America

. . . weary and faint with desire
For strange lands and new scents;
For the rough-rhythmed clank
Of train couplings at night,
And the stormy, gay-tinted sunrises
That shade with purple the contours
Of far-off, unfamiliar hills.
—John Dos Passos, *"'Whan That Aprille . . .'"*

From 1920 to 1928, the period of his first serious attempts to write innovative fiction, Dos Passos traveled in Portugal, Spain, France, Italy, Morocco, Austria, Asia Minor, Russia, and Mexico. (Between 1916 and 1919, during both his study of architecture and his service in World War I, he had visited Spain, Italy, France, and other parts of Europe.) His passion for travel, so evident in these years, continued throughout his life, yet never with such intensity. In the 1920s, Dos Passos seemed to be using his travels as a means of learning about the world, its cultures and its literatures, and also about himself in that world. For all the vivid physical detail of the travel essays he wrote, his attention even in that medium was frequently on the young American protagonist who was doing the traveling. This combination of quasi-autobiographical characterization with philosophical and literary emphases suggests that Dos Passos' travel writings played a significant part in his development as writer.

Dos Passos' writing during the 1920s—of whatever kind—repeatedly shows his interest in the theme of search. Martin Howe, John Andrews, Fanshaw, Wenny, and Nan are all searching for ways to live useful, satisfying lives. So, too, is Dos Passos. In his letters and essays, he plays the devil's advocate, questioning his friends' aims, their occupations, their marriages, their views on national policy, economics, and literature—and, repeatedly, his own progress as a writer. From 1915 to approximately 1920, Dos Passos' letters were filled with a confident, continuing set of principles for the modern writer. The almost cocky tone of his remarks to Robert Hillyer, E. E. Cummings, and, most often, Rumsey Marvin is modified during the 1920s to a somewhat defensive casualness about his own writing. There is no question that Dos Passos is writing a great deal, with his usual steady earnestness, but seldom does he set himself up as judge. He is likely to praise writing that he admires, but the tone of his comments about his own fiction is one of dissatisfaction. In 1921 he writes to Hillyer, "As to my possibilities in word-mongering, I have never been deeper in the dumps. Things I write become every day more putrid."[1] Rereading "Seven Times Round the Walls of Jericho," he exclaims, "Christ what raw juvenilia!"[2] His first play, according to Edmund Wilson, evoked the description "very infantile."[3] And about *Streets of Night*, Dos Passos recalled that it was "all redone after *Three Soldiers!*"[4]

Compared with his genuine excitement later over his accomplishment with *Manhattan Transfer* in 1925, these comments are fairly reliable indications that Dos Passos was pessimistic about his career as a serious writer. His persistent turn to travel and the kind of writing that grew from it may have been one way of avoiding a direct confrontation with the serious fiction that somehow managed, he then felt, to elude him.

Dos Passos' sense of personal depression during the early 1920s probably relates as well to what he frequently described as a disappointment with the promise of the postcollege, postwar years. Once out of the intellectual atmosphere of Cambridge, once supplied with the myriad of experiences from World War I, the would-be writer had both the freedom and the understanding to write great fiction. This, at least, had been the theory. As Dos Passos later recalled,

> Like many others of my generation I got most of my education from the first war.
> Some of the seeds sown in the course of this education have taken a lifetime to germinate. These were years of colossal hopes and colossal disappointments. Certain things held fast. Invention and discovery in science, and to some extent in the arts; and to much greater extent in technology, continued unabated. Civilization was torn and battered by every nightmare scourge out of the vision of John on Patmos, but at the same time the creative instincts showed a gift for survival.

Some minds met the challenge of disaster by an outburst
of invention and experiment.[5]

His disappointment with his own failure to meet that challenge is
clear in a 1921 letter that closes, half-mockingly, "O Robert the
years go by and the Thames is still unburnt and where are the mon-
uments aere perennius that were to be set up in rows along the
Hudson?"[6]

Yet the recognition of those "colossal hopes" runs side by side
with his own malaise, for just the year before he chastised Stewart
Mitchell for the January 1920 issue of *The Dial*—not so much for its
quality per se as for its failure to be dynamic, dramatic. "I was desperately disappointed," he recounts, and his instructions to Mitchell, for future issues, show clearly the direction of his own attitudes
about the purpose of modern literature. He demands (1) "a distinct
intellectual trend, that of the Chicago economic-social crowd, of
John Dewey and Thorstein Veblen and the rest"; and (2) a soft-pedal-
ing of an "arts-for-arts sake position" because

> There has never been great art that did not beat with every
> beat of the life around it. . . . this moment is so on the brink
> of things. Overpopulation combined with the breakdown of
> food has wrecked the checks and balances of the industrialized
> world. In ten years we may be cavemen snatching the last bit
> of food from each others' mouths amid the stinking ruins of our
> cities, or we may be slaving—antlike—in some utterly systema-
> tized world where the individual will be utterly crushed
> that the mob (or the princes) may live. Every written word
> should be thought of as possibly the last that humanity
> will ever write. . . .[7]

The apparently new awareness of the times, of the physical conditions surrounding the literati, made Dos Passos impatient not
only with the art novel but also with its customary protagonists.
Like his own first characters, many protagonists in the fiction of the
early twentieth century were well-meaning but naive—or misdirected, inexperienced, sometimes chauvinistic—people who could
not survive inimical social or political forces, often because they
did not understand them. They were people marked by self-pity-
ing attitudes (Wenny's blaming Boston for his isolation instead of
himself: "No place for love in the city of Boston; place for death
though")[8] and self-destructive acts (broken loves, social crimes, suicide). The chief weakness of these characters was that they existed

in such introspective vacuums that they seldom faced the real world; their stories, accordingly, could never comprise an art that "beat with every beat of the life around it."

In his travel essays of the 1920s, Dos Passos was able to explore and in some ways answer these essential questions about literature and its relation to the world. His first travel essays, those on Spain and Spanish writers, described his reactions to Spanish life and its implied philosophy—always set against his concept of American life and its implied attitudes—and located the aspects that are for him most valuable. The literary essays parallel the more general ones emphasizing that the strengths of such writers as Pío Baroja, Blanco Ibáñez, and Antonio Machado are their concern for the world and their effective yet innovative methods of re-creating it.

Faced in his own country with what he considered a stifling pressure to conform, Dos Passos was initially much attracted by the Spanish insistence on individuality, "the strong anarchistic reliance on the individual man"; he admired those who know "no feeling of a reality outside of themselves . . . except the God which was the synthesis of their souls and of their lives." Paying slight attention to his own acknowledgment that religion is important to the Spaniards he describes, Dos Passos continues, "This intense individualism . . . is the basic fact of Spanish life. No revolution has been strong enough to shake it."[9]

Because people take pride in themselves, in being themselves and not just faceless cogs in some modern machine, they have vigor, intensity, the conviction of private opinions. Dos Passos shows this clearly, and with amusement, as the Spaniards in "The Donkey-Boy" argue about the weaknesses and strengths of America. Even when "convictions" turn to outright stubbornness, Dos Passos enjoys the intensity of the Spanish emotion. One is reminded of a 1920 letter to Marvin in which he laments the "lukewarmness" of the typical educated American; as would be his habit during the 1920s Dos Passos compares his own culture with those he has known in his travels:

> Spaniards and Frenchmen of intelligence whom I know
> are tremendously awake, always doing a thousand things,
> throwing themselves vigorously into politics and archaeol-
> ogy and painting and music, as if they realized that we had a
> short time in the world and might as well make the best of it.
> But I know so many Americans, people of great talent and intel-
> lect, who are sunk continually in a faintly melancholy sloth.

Charming people to be with, who talk wistfully of novels that
may some day be written, or pictures that may some day be
painted, of things to be done in archaeology, of going to Europe
in the spring–who drift along and watch with well-modu-
lated dismay, the world going to barbarism about their
ears.[10]

More typical than the malaise of the American intelligentsia,
however, and more often the subject of Dos Passos' attention is the
frantic barbarism of fast-moving modernity. In *Rosinante* he speaks
lovingly of the contrastingly tranquil life in rural Spain: "It was all
so mellow, so strangely aloof from the modern world of feverish
change" (p. 52); and in 1921 he writes Hillyer, "This retirement into
the wilderness was highly salutary. I have no conceit left."[11] A similar tone dominates his letters to Marvin from Spain:

I feel quite come to life again after a long sojourn in the blue
infernal regions. . . . I had another wonderful walk, along the
coast of the province of Malaga, between the Sierra Nevada and
the sea. Superb burnt hills and irrigated valleys full of banana
trees and sugar cane and of the sound of water running through
irrigation ditches. A wonderful part of the world.

As he often does, Dos Passos follows such a statement with a specific image, by one example proving (or at least making vivid) his
contention: "The people in the towns hire a fig tree for the summer
and go out under it with their pigs and goats and cats and chickens
and eat the figs and enjoy the shade. Life has no problems under
these conditions."[12]

Without quoting Veblen or approaching the problem in statistical
terms, Dos Passos manages to propose economic explanations for
some of the differences between the cultures. Early in the *Rosinante*
collection, one Spaniard is outspoken in his condemnation of America. Although he admires the country's prosperity, he is quick to
point out, "It's not gold people need, but bread and wine and . . . life.
. . . in America they don't do anything except work and rest so's to
get ready to work again. That's no life for a man. People don't enjoy
themselves there" (p. 28). Dos Passos peoples his sketches of Spain
with characters who are willing to stop, enjoy, and share their en-
joyment, like the old mail carrier: "It's to enjoy. A moment, a *mo-
mentito*, and it's gone!" (p. 33) or Don Antonio: "On this coast,
señor inglés, we don't work much, we are dirty and uninstructed,
but by God we live. . . . nowhere in the world are the women lovelier

or is the land richer or the cookery more perfect" (p. 38). Dos Passos summarizes, "Far indeed were they from the restless industrial world of joyless enforced labor and incessant goading war" (p. 70).

A genuine epicureanism characterizes certain Spanish enjoyments, "the easy acceptance of life, the unashamed joy in food and color and the softness of women's hair" (p. 70), and Dos Passos appreciates that quality. He also is quick to point out the basic duality in the Spanish philosophy, that paired with this Sancho Panza sensuality is the completely nonphysical idealism of "the knight of the sorrowful countenance, Don Quixote, blunderingly trying to remould the world, pitifully sure of the power of his own ideal" (p. 70). For Don Quixote, his ideal became his own reality, and his belief in individual vision came to foreshadow Dos Passos' own mature philosophy:

> I have brooded too much on the injustice done in the world
> —all society one great wrong. Many years ago I should have
> set out to right wrong—for no one but a man, an individual
> alone, can right a wrong; organization merely substitutes
> one wrong for another. . . . (p. 75)

Repeatedly in his fiction, Dos Passos sets the single individual against the social agency, the organized force, and it is part of his dark picture of modern life that the individual loses so consistently. For the Spaniard in the early 1920s, however, his tenacious idealism, rooted in his avowed love of place, made some success possible. As Dos Passos describes the particular bent of Spanish idealism, "predominant in the Iberian mind is the thought *La vida es sueño:* 'Life is a dream.' Only the individual, or that part of life which is in the firm grasp of the individual, is real" (pp. 53–54).

Because each person believes in his own views, whether physical or philosophical, great variety exists in all areas of Spanish life, including its art. Dos Passos gives much of his attention in these essays to Spanish writers, stressing always the improvisational nature of their work, their ability to suit form to content, to allow their writing to reflect the temper and tone of the present. But his primary focus, as he discusses Machado, Ibáñez, and Baroja, is on the ways they have chosen to write about the present, the modern world, a world sometimes "dismal, ironic," its people caught in "the debris of civilization."

Dos Passos admires Baroja above most writers because he does not shirk the writer's responsibility to include in his work "all who have failed on the daily treadmill of bread-making" and to write about them without pity or sentimentalizing. Baroja's focus remains true; his art is a vehicle for neither romanticizing nor propagandizing. Here in 1920, Dos Passos is already aware of the fallacy of choosing "unfortunate" characters for their value as cheap emotional ploys, and he is doubly insistent that Baroja treats existing social ills as a novelist, not as an anarchist: "His great mission is to put the acid test to existing institutions, and to strip the veils off them. I don't want to imply that Baroja writes with his social conscience. He is too much of a novelist for that, too deeply interested in people as such" (p. 93).

The importance of this admiration to Dos Passos as a developing novelist himself becomes clear as one reads his comments about *La Busca* [*The Search*], Baroja's series of novels about "the drifting of a typical uneducated Spanish boy . . . through different strata of Madrid life." Long interested in the picaresque novel, Dos Passos has already used journeys and travels related to the developing of character in both *Three Soldiers* and *Streets of Night*; what Baroja achieved in the *La Busca* novels was a shifting context for his wanderer (a means of describing all types of society and culture) and a new kind of "hero." Neither the jolly, amoral peasant nor the wandering prince, the *golfo*—the observing commoner—has as his chief function learning about the world around him. It goes almost without saying that the character Vag in the *U.S.A.* trilogy and even Jimmy Herf in *Manhattan Transfer* are versions of Baroja's *golfo*.[13]

Dos Passos' enthusiasm for these novels runs high also because of their sociological accuracy: "Besides their power as novels [they] are immensely interesting as sheer natural history" (p. 98). The capturing and charting of contemporary reality (for nonpolitical purposes) was to become one of Dos Passos' aims in his own chronicles.

The same admiration for rich, sensual subject matter is apparent in Dos Passos' essays on Antonio Machado and Juan Maragall. Poets in the Whitman tradition, these writers emphasized the color and detail of common life; their verse "is taken up with places" (p. 147). The sense of tradition does not show in an inheritance of form, for the poetry Dos Passos admires is marked more by assonance, refrain, and word play than by stanzaic pattern. But Dos Passos admires this Spanish and Catalán poetry for its individuality, its presentation through imagery, its lack of commercial play. In contrast, he finds the writing of Blanco Ibáñez, for all its accurate detail and voracity for experience, to be aimed toward marketability, what people want to believe and read about Spain. Dos Passos views Ibáñez' early writing with respect, his later with sadness, and considers him inferior to Machado, Unamuno, and Baroja. Again, Dos Passos' essays about these writers provide insight into both his own developing aesthetic positions and his concepts about Spain.

The essays in *Rosinante* also show the origin of Dos Passos' later travel writing. Just as in a 1914 *Harvard Monthly* review of Jack Reed's *Insurgent Mexico*, he admired informality and a genuine sense of the country,[14] so here he chooses (or creates) interesting characters as representatives of the country and sets them in dialogue with each other. No matter what they discuss, the presentation can thus be–like Dos Passos' own writing–idiomatic. The heaviest of subjects can therefore be lively, couched in dramatic interchanges, described in the tones, colors, and physical details of the country. Dos Passos' narrative sense is also clear in *Rosinante* as he uses two travelers, Telemachus and Lyaeus (a Bacchus-like figure), instead of one of his narrative personae. The conflicts between the two young men as they discuss their experiences (in chapters headed "Talk by the Road") provide further narrative interest.

Dos Passos' use of the two personae also connects the Spanish essays with his earliest fiction, for Telemachus represents the stable, educated, somewhat repressed youth (complete with Penelope and Odysseus for parents) and Lyaeus the more spontaneous, fun-loving companion. That Dos Passos felt some need to change the quasi-autobiographical tone of the Telemachus persona seems clear because by the time the *Rosinante* essays were to be adapted for his longer collection of travel writing, *Journeys Between Wars*, he changed the names of both personae, omitted much of their discussion, and deleted the many references to both Telemachus' father and his mother. The original *Rosinante* is the journey of Telemachus-Dos Passos-questor, dreamer in the Quixote tradition (hence the title of the book): an account of a journey shadowed by the counsel of the sage but sometimes restrictive Penelope. The excerpts that remain in *Journeys Between Wars* are closer to conventional travelogue, with the narrators conveying their experiences as a means of sharing information, not developing a psychological portrait. The dynamics of the relationship between the idealistic and serious-minded Telemachus and the more practical Lyaeus are also omitted, so that the essays become much less dramatic.

Style within the revised excerpts is also less colorful. In the original *Rosinante*, Telemachus describes a bullfighter's gesture in terms of both color and motion: "'That gesture, a yellow flame against maroon and purple cadences . . . an instant swagger of defiance in the midst of a litany to death the all-powerful. That is Spain . . .'" (p. 17). Later, the scene becomes "a swagger of defiance in the midst of a litany to death. That is Spain."[15] Just as he had revised so as to omit all references to the *Odyssey*, so Dos Passos later deleted color words and images that formed patterns supplementing the search theme.

Another source of drama omitted from *Journeys Between Wars* is the juxtaposition of Telemachus' attraction for women, and the moral judgments of the waiting mother, Penelope. Telemachus is beset by the memory of his mother's maxims, which on occasion "popped up suddenly in his mind like tickets from a cash register" (p. 202). As his anger against these principles grows, he finally comes to curse them; but even at his most daring, Telemachus fails to act. The memory of Penelope is of a "vague inquisitorial woman-figure," inescapable even in the presence of "the dancer standing tense as a caryatid before the footlights, her face in shadow, her shawl flaming yellow; the strong modulations of her torso . . . burned in his flesh" (p. 19).

We have already seen that this kind of tension—between woman as moral force and woman as physical temptress—runs through much of Dos Passos' early writing, regardless of genre. What is most interesting about these changes from the 1922 *Rosinante to the Road Again* and the 1938 *Journeys Between Wars* is that by deleting lush descriptive passages and the Telemachus theme Dos Passos erased all reference to this early dominant pattern. The searching son, the disinherited, the timid young man afraid of and yet attracted to women—all such elements here disappeared in the excerpted version of the early essays.

In Dos Passos' second collection of travel essays, the 1927 *Orient Express*, he becomes more explicit about the relation between his aesthetic principles and the impact of the country described. Written soon after the *Rosinante* essays, most of these pieces contain the same colorful description, but Dos Passos' emphasis here is less on color per se than on other sensory details. Also his tone is less enthusiastic (a somewhat surprising shift since people were inclined during the late 1920s and 1930s to consider Dos Passos pro-Communist), and his imagery more complex. One of the key images in the *Rosinante* essays was the butterfly, suggesting beauty and promise, elusive but not impossible; in *Orient Express* the central image is the bee, a work-oriented, self-sufficient, and orderly insect. The practicality of Russia contrasts the ephemerality of Spain.

Colored by this bee image, the tone of the essays in *Orient Express* changes from excited expectation to a mixture of ennui and disappointment, culminating in several vituperative asides about travel itself. The opening image, typical of Dos Passos at his descriptive best, is positive: "It isn't a sound coming across the water, it's a smell, a growing fragrance beating against my face on a burst of warm air out of the east, a smell of roses and dung burst by the sun, a rankness like skunk-cabbage overlaid with hyacinth, pungence of musk, chilly sweetness of violets."[16] Soon, however, the smells become much less pleasant. In Venice he is beset by "the smell of tidewater, rotting piles, mudflats, a gruff bodysmell amorous like chestnut blooms, like datura, like trodden cabbages" (p. 4). Dos Passos' own reaction to this contrast between the exotic sights and "the inexorable smell of the tide creeping up slime-covered steps" finds expression in the image of "chilly hands of the Adriatic groping for your throat" (p. 5).

Even though in these essays Dos Passos continues using faces as mirrors of the culture ("All life is sucked into the expressiveness of faces"), the faces he sees in the Orient seem to convey more concern than comfort. Unlike his impression of the Spaniards, these people live in fear, frozen by the aftermath of 1917, selling their priceless possessions as if they were worthless. Their bleak visages reflect only despair at "the ruined dynasty of things," and the picture is intensified by Dos Passos' focus in detail on such characters as the "poor old woman who sits hungry in her bare room looking out through a chink in the shutters . . . an old woman looking out through the shutters with the eyes of a cat that has been run over by an automobile" (p. 44). Yet, in keeping with the antimaterialistic attitudes he expressed in *Rosinante*, Dos Passos insists that the country can turn this material poverty to good use: freed from modern culture's obsession with "things," the Russians can instead concentrate on the development of their inner resources.

That he can speak so firmly in these 1921 and 1922 essays about the "cleansing" example Russia could set the West is some indication of his sympathy with the Communist experiment. Because logic alone cannot dismiss the unpleasant images he has already presented, however, Dos Passos turns to a quasi-surreal narrative method and describes an urgent "wind out of Asia," blowing over his table, upsetting his chair, blowing our cities clean of the Things that are our gods, the knick-knacks and the scraps of engraved paper and the vases and the curtain rods, the fussy junk possession of which divides poor man from rich man, the shoddy manufactured goods that are all our civilization prizes, that we wear our hands and brains out working for; so that from being an erect naked biped, man has become a sort of hermit crab that can't live without a dense conglomerate shell of dinner-jackets and limosines and percolators and cigar-store coupons and egg-beaters and sewing machines, so that the denser his shell, the feebler his self-sufficience, the more he is regarded a great man and a millionaire. (p. 45)

Dos Passos is in no position to predict, but the fact that he gives such a glowing image of this possible "thingless" future is important.

This passage is one of the few positive impressions in the book, however, because Dos Passos alternates between vignettes of poverty and depression and censure of all travel per se. Contrary to his usual love of the travel experience, his sense here seems to be that travel, like material wealth, is only a glorified escape, a drug, in fact, the dosage of which constantly needs increasing. Another passage from *Orient Express* links travel more explicitly with culture's other "tin gods," pointing out that, for most people, none of this roaming about brings any kind of peace. Dos Passos' closing image for himself as traveler is in no sense ambivalent: "Huddled in a knot, hard and cold, pitched like a baseball round the world. . . . you meet yourself coming back and are very sick into your old black hat" (p. 181).

Some of Dos Passos' dissatisfaction with his role as correspondent and observer grew from his developing sense of the most interesting subject matter, as well as method, for modern writing. We have seen him use a surreal setting for his "wind of the East" image; in another *Orient* essay he juxtaposed quick segments of scattered dialogue in an ironic montage very close to the Newsreel sections of *U.S.A.* As he said in retrospect, "The artist must record the fleeting world the way the motion picture film recorded it. By contrast, juxtaposition, montage he could build drama into his narrative. . . . The narrative must stand up off the page."[17] Even the vindictive sections of the essays in *Orient Express* are studded with concrete detail and graphic imagery, just as much of Dos Passos' writing builds toward or away from key images. To his customary reliance on the image as structural device, Dos Passos has added a sense of timing that demands compression, intensity; the world is busy, and therefore he should be selective and choose only the most precise words and scenes. As he wrote to Marvin in 1920,

> writing to be any good has, in my opinion, got to be stripped naked. Like in good architecture, every inch must have something functional to do, must be an integral part of holding the building up. That doesn't cut out decoration at all, it just means that every bit of decoration must mean something. And yet it seems perfectly impossible to write things down as clearly as that. . . .[18]

A key essay in *Orient Express* pays tribute to the French poet and novelist Blaise Cendrars, a writer whose work was, in Dos Passos' phrase, "stripped naked." In "Trans Siberian Homer," Dos Passos explains that his attraction for Cendrars stemmed from his admiration both for the man's technical prowess and for his subject matter.

Cendrars wrote about the American South and West, about New York and Alaska and Florida, about the Panama Canal ("Travels with Seven Uncles"), about the California Gold Rush and General Sutter ("L'Or"), and about railroads ("Homeric Hymns of the Railroad–"). Dos Passos praises his immediacy, his ability to catch the real world, and the sounds of actual speech in poetry such as this:

> *I spent my childhood in the hanging gardens of Babylon*
> *Played hookey in railway-stations in front of the trains*
> *   that were going to leave*
> *Now, all the trains have had to speed to keep up with me*
> *Bale-Timbuctoo*
> *I've played the races too at Auteuil and Longchamp*
> *Paris-New York*
> *Now, I've made all the trains run the whole length of*
> *   my life*
> *Madrid-Stockholm*
> *And I've lost all my bets. . . .* (pp. 192–93)

In these relatively long poems, the personal details and reflections are balanced with sharply imaged passages like "women with half-hours for rent between their legs / that could also be used / For coffins."[19] In 1929, after Dos Passos had translated more of Cendrars' work than the snatches appearing in this early essay, he edited and illustrated a collection of Cendrars' poems and in the foreword spoke of the poet's "alive informal personal everyday poems" (p. 3). Dos Passos compares Cendrars' poems with the best work of the imagists, characterized by "virility, intense experimentation and meaning in everyday life," and mourns that during the past decade, "stuffed shirts" have once again taken over the literary scene. A brief image poem like Cendrars' "Sunday," for example, sounds a great deal like William Carlos Williams' work:

> It's Sunday at sea
> Hot
> I'm shut up in my cabin like a
>   lump of melting butter (p. 136)

Dos Passos thus offered Cendrars' work as a positive example of the way a writer should use his surrounding culture, describing him as "a kind of medicine man trying to evoke things that are our cruel and avenging gods. Turbines, triple-expansion engines, dynamite, high tension coils, navigation, speed, flight, annihilation. . . ." (p. 197)

Cendrars' work was important in the early 1920s because it showed Dos Passos that a writer could be immersed in what might seem to be trivia and yet from the composite detail might evolve a definitive observation about life in all its larger senses. Dos Passos praised Cendrars' "L'Or" as being "the swiftest leanest parabola . . . that cuts like a knife through the washy rubbish of most French writing of the present time, with its lemon-colored gloves and its rosewater and its holy water and its *policier*-gentlemen cosmopolitan affectation" (p. 197). Dos Passos' enthusiasm for Cendrars complements his earlier praise for Boccaccio ("It is wonderful what a picture he gives you of his time")[20] and for the Spanish writers already cited in this chapter and points toward both his own increasing use of the real culture surrounding him and a point of view that was seemingly more objective than any he had yet adopted.

In this early travel writing, as in his early fiction, Dos Passos had used the color and imagery of the physical world to an almost unprecedented degree, but the emotional center of that writing—whether fiction or nonfiction—was his personal view of life. Dos Passos' response to the war, his response to Boston intellectual life, his response to traveling in Spain and the East—his writing from 1917 to 1922, for all its accumulation of concrete detail, presented a largely subjective picture.

The changes Dos Passos felt were necessary when he republished the *Rosinante* essays—his omission of the Telemachus thread and the reduction of imagery—were symptomatic of his shift from a subjective orientation to an objective method. More like William Carlos Williams, who consistently employed images for their intrinsic effect and not for their connotations, than such realistic writers as Sinclair Lewis and Theodore Dreiser, Dos Passos came to rely on the power of the image, considered alone, to convey meaning. And like Cendrars he began to sense the scope—from humor to pathos to tragedy—of life in his own country, on its own terms, the immediate presentation creating the American image and legend. Borrowing from Cendrars, Dos Passos was content with noting a hot room, a boy selling potatoes, a fearful child.

Instead of choosing objects like the abbey and the green fire in *Three Soldiers*, for an incremental and eventually symbolic impression, Dos Passos packed so many objects and images into his writing that there was no way to give each thing larger meaning. Correspondingly, his chief mode of structuring his work came to be juxtaposition, the fusion of single images into collage. And the objective attitude, the swift-moving "Camera Eye" technique allowed him a degree of impersonality he had not achieved writing about John Andrews or Martin Howe, his own surrogate characters.

The product of Dos Passos' melding of technical concerns and thematic interests was his 1925 novel, *Manhattan Transfer*, a book that began as a collage of images from the contemporary scene and ended as a brilliant portrait of America.

Part II
The Mature Artist:
Dos Passos as
American Chronicler

4. *Manhattan Transfer*:
The Beginning of the Chronicles

I have spent my life wrestling with the problem of how to tell a story.
–John Dos Passos, 1968

Just as Faulkner found his subject when he first wrote about the South and its traditions in *Sartoris*, so Dos Passos struck a vein of pure and as yet unexplored subject matter in his 1925 novel about New York City. *Manhattan Transfer* became a popular success as well as a critical one, and for good reason. It conveyed American curiosity (and fear) about urbanization and technology and the gradual dehumanization of society. It was one of the first modern novels to try to capture realistically the flavor and tempo of a city (a subject usually treated with stereotypical innocence or malevolence). It created a montage of events that did not coalesce into cause-and-effect patterns implying traditional moral standards, and many of those events–the ones dealing with abortion, homosexuality, and some types of violence–were rare in modern fiction. Sinclair Lewis wrote enthusiastically that *Manhattan Transfer* was "a novel of the very first importance. . . . the foundation of a whole new school of novel-writing. Dos Passos *may* be, more than Dreiser, Cather, Hergesheimer, Cabell, or Anderson the father of humanized and living fiction." Lewis admired the novel's "breathless reality" and its use of "the technique of the movie, in its flashes, its cutbacks, its speed."[1] He also admired its richness, its panoply of characters, events, and detail that any reader could recognize and identify with. By so creating a veritable kaleidoscope of apparent "fact" about city life and then using those ostensible facts for his narrative purposes, Dos Passos took the first step toward his later contemporary chronicles. He led his readers to consider his novel "real" by using a pastiche of headlines, songs, and technological details that gave a sense of contemporary life; they responded by applauding his accuracy and perspicuity.

In terms of Dos Passos' own artistry, *Manhattan Transfer* was even more significant than its high critical reputation suggested. The success of the novel affirmed his feeling that American writers should write about American subjects. Reflecting his belief as well that fiction should deal with the immediate, this novel was set within his own lifetime: reader response ratified that belief also. The social attitudes portrayed, and sometimes criticized, were still current; the book thus caught the tone of prevailing discussion about social problems. And on the most personal level, *Manhattan Transfer* did depict that "snarl of human events," did provide an accurate record of the time, and did show Dos Passos' deep involvement with the *âme nationale*, the sense of a national culture—all of which he was to suggest as worthy purposes for the best fiction.

Stylistically, too, *Manhattan Transfer* was the perfect answer to the consciously American writer's dilemma: it treated purely American subject matter, characters, and themes, yet did so in innovative ways and in a tone that was brusque, teeming, even "flip"—i.e., typically American. E. D. Lowry, Blanche Gelfant, and David Sanders have accurately described Dos Passos' use of techniques borrowed from futuristic art and the films and drama of Eisenstein, Meyerhold, and Griffith.[2] Much of the force behind both *Manhattan Transfer* and the *U.S.A.* novels is their quick-paced movement from one story to another, movement achieved largely through the juxtapositions of Dos Passos' collage-like (or skein-like)[3] format.

Manhattan Transfer's narrative collage is comprised of short scenes from a variety of stories. More accurately, they are scenes about key characters, because often the action is not plotted in any conventional pattern. Since this method is difficult to follow, reader interest has to be caught immediately. Unlike *One Man's Initiation: 1917*, *Manhattan Transfer* does little rambling. Scenes begin quickly, and each scene presents a central character in action. Dos Passos uses description, but because of the rapid progression of visual details, even descriptive sections move quickly. "Simultaneity" he termed the method and identified its antecedents in "the Italian futurists, the Frenchmen of the school of Rimbaud, the poets who went along with cubism in painting," describing his interest in artistic innovation as an outgrowth of his experience during World War I:

> Everything looked different in the light of what was
> happening in Europe. After the armistice, while still in

the army, I had managed to get myself inducted into what was known as the Sorbonne detachment. An early form of the GI bill of rights. . . . This was the Paris of socalled [sic] modern painting which was really modern in those days: Modigliani, Juan Gris, Picasso. This was the Paris of futurism, expressionism in literature, of new schools of music: Poulenc, Milhaud, Stravinski, Diagheleff's Russian Ballet.

Though I was never in Paris more than three months at a time I went home with my interest in experimentation–already whetted while I was in college by the Armory Show and the Imagist poets–enormously stimulated. I felt compelled to set down in new terms what I saw in New York and then, making my way around under various pretexts, in the country as a whole. . . .

Why not write a simultaneous chronicle? A novel, full of popular songs, political aspirations and prejudices, ideals, hopes, delusions, crackpot notions, clippings out of the daily newspapers. . . . *Manhattan Transfer* was an attempt to chronicle the life of a city. It was about a lot of different kinds of people.[4]

For these various stylistic reasons, *Manhattan Transfer* acquired a speed consonant with the tempo of the times. As announced by its title, the novel's pattern emphasized the rapid transit, the subway, its interchanges filled with rushing people, almost disembodied faces (like Ezra Pound's famous "petals on a wet, black bough"), apparitions caught in split seconds of time and then relinquished, some lives touching, most not.[5] As Dos Passos wrote several years after the novel: "It was always the same in the subway, the echoing passage stinking of elevatorshafts and urinals, the scattering people in overcoats on the platform, hurried eyes that looked at you but never into yours (when eyes meet on the I.R.T. the airbrakes go on, the train stops with a crash), jostling bodies packed together through the long tunnel under the river, and the whiff of grit and burned gas in your face."[6] In addition to being an important image of modern isolation, the subway and its transfers represented the archetypal circumstances of meeting by chance at the crossroads, as well as the full-to-the-brim kaleidoscope of color and character.

Central as an image for lives touching and diverging, the subway is just one of the images of modern invention that permeate *Manhattan Transfer* (along with skyscrapers, steamrollers, trains, and mechanical doors). The subway is especially important thematically in relation to Ellen Thatcher; Dos Passos introduces the image

on the occasion of her honeymoon with the bisexual John Oglethorpe. Once the Oglethorpes have changed trains at Manhattan
Transfer, Ellen hears the wheels rumbling "Man-hattan Tran-sfer.
Man-hattan Tran-sfer,"[7] a refrain that punctuates her desperate inner rejoinder, phrased with obvious self-irony, "I'll be feeling gay . . .
I've got to be feeling gay," and the counterpoint lyric, "*Oh it rained
forty days . . . And it rained forty nights.*" The montage is hardly
joyful.

The flux and speed of the subway in this early scene set the pattern for Ellen's life. Looking for gaiety and success yet aware of
the unhappiness both surrounding her and inside her, Ellen Thatcher claims to travel alone, although Dos Passos clearly shows that she
joins whatever man she feels obligated to (Oglethorpe for his theatrical experience, Stan for his youth and sexual prowess, Jimmy for
his proximity and stability).

Instead of being aggressive herself in choosing a suitable lover or
husband, Ellen is the female continuously acted upon. Not whimsically did Dos Passos list as a possible title for the novel "Tess of 48th
Street or The Story of a Pure Woman,"[8] for in many ways Ellen is
clearly a victim of the rapidly changing moral values in this century,
and most of her scenes in the first half of the novel depict her victimization. Just as Hardy's Tess Durbeyfield begins as "a mere ves-
sel of emotion untinctured by experience"[9] but eventually is driven
to murder by a conflict between unfulfilled love and social censure, so Ellen begins as an ebullient child and learns, through loss,
that genuine love is more valuable than success or social position,
and also more rare.

Dos Passos' suggestion that Ellen is in some ways the same kind
of victim as Tess—misused by a first lover (Oglethorpe), misjudged
by her real love (Stanwood Emery), and left to become the prey of
whatever man fancies her—is naturally modified by conditions of
twentieth-century life, but the two women's motivations are surprisingly similar. The inexperienced Tess succumbs to Alex d'Urberville but then renounces her submission to him: he is her superior in fortune and position but not in pride. Ellen, a stagestruck
eighteen, marries Oglethorpe at least partly because of his position,
but her sexual awakening comes with Emery, a man who attracts
her because of his youth and joy. Her acceptance of Stan despite
his drinking problems parallels Tess' devotion to Angel Clare,
despite his unjust application of a hypocritical double-standard
morality. Early in the novel Hardy questions "why so often the

coarse appropriates the finer thus, the wrong man the woman, the wrong woman the man" (p. 101). The fact that people often use and misuse others provides a dominant theme for many modern novelists, but the social issue where women characters are concerned is the matter of visible guilt. Angel Clare confesses his sexual experimentation to Tess, expecting to be forgiven. He is. Tess, reciprocally, then confesses her forced experience with d'Urberville, but because that intercourse led to pregnancy and the birth of a child, Clare banishes her from his life. Tess with candor asks a religious fanatic, "suppose your sin was not of your own seeking?" (p. 108). The problem, culturally and socially, is one of definition (guilt or innocence, virgin or whore), the same problem that Dos Passos explores in telling Ellen's story.

That Dos Passos' sympathy lies with Ellen is clear in that he creates many poignant scenes to show that her affection has been repeatedly misappropriated. Used by Oglethorpe as a disguise for his homosexuality, Ellen comes to know genuine love for Stan. (The description of that affair from its early states of joyful excitement and later tenderness to Ellen's eventual separation from Oglethorpe reinforces the quality of her love.) Yet in society's eyes Ellen has wronged Oglethorpe. All virtue is on his side as he screams at her through Herf's apartment window, and she becomes a fallen woman after her divorce. The culmination of Ellen's emotional education, however, an education presented in detail to show her real vulnerability, comes after she receives that divorce, when she learns but a few hours later that her lover has—accidentally but no less irrevocably—married someone else:

> "Ellie this is Pearline. . . . Isn't it a fine name? I almost split when she told me what it was. . . . But you don't know the joke. . . . We got so tight in Niagara Falls that when we came to we found we were married. . . . And we have pansies on our marriage license. . . ."
> Ellen couldn't see his face. The orchestra, the jangle of voices, the clatter of plates spouted spiraling louder and louder about her . . .
>> And the ladies of the harem
>> Knew exactly how to wear 'em
>> In O-riental Bagdad long ago . . .
> "Good night Stan." Her voice was gritty in her mouth, she heard the words very clearly when she spoke them.
> "Oh Ellie I wish you'd come partying with us. . . ."

"Thanks . . . thanks."

She started to dance again with Harry Goldweiser. The roof-
garden was spinning fast, then less fast. The noise ebbed sick-
eningly "Excuse me a minute Harry," she said. "I'll come
back to the table." In the ladies' room she let herself down
carefully on the plush sofa. She looked at her face in the
round mirror of her vanitycase. From black pinholes her
pupils spread blurring till everything was black. (p. 193)

Once she has lost Stan—first to Pearline and then, quickly, to death
—Ellen begins to take on the qualities of the chic automaton she
later becomes.[10]

While the details of Tess' later life and Ellen's are not parallel,
there grows in each woman a desiccation, a deadness, that appears
to result from her bitterness after having lost the great love of her
life. After Angel Clare leaves her, Tess lives alone, enduring poverty
and eventually becoming a murderess—all for some strange concept
of her "love" for Clare:

I never loved him at all, Angel, as I loved you. You know it,
don't you? You believe it? You didn't come back to me, and I
was obliged to go back to him. Why did you go away—why did
you—when I loved you so? I can't think why you did it. But I
don't blame you; only, Angel, will you forgive me my sin
against you, now I have killed him? I thought as I ran along that
you would be sure to forgive me now I have done that. It came
to me as a shining light that I should get you back that way. I
could not bear the loss of you any longer—you don't know
how entirely I was unable to bear your not loving me! Say
you do now, dear, dear husband; say you do, now I have
killed him! (p. 407)

Taking Ellen's story as the primary narrative thread of *Manhattan
Transfer* seems consistent with the amount of attention Dos Passos
gives her and with his obvious sympathy for her as character. It
also allows the reader to give more definite meaning to the chapter
titles, often read simply as images of modernity, cultural bits of
color having little meaning in themselves. Connections between
titles and Ellen's story line do, however, exist. Her birth opens the
"ferryslip" chapter, with Dos Passos carefully treating her arrival as
being as undistinguished as that of the migrants he describes in the
epigraph to the chapter. Chapter 2, "Metropolis," opens with Ed
Thatcher's realization that New York has become the "world's sec-

ond metropolis." Images of gold and glitter, skyscrapers and light, and steel, glass, tile, and concrete color Ellen's father's reveries and lead to a final devastating image of Ellen, near the end of the book, "made of gold foil absolutely lifelife beckoning from every window" of a skyscraper (p. 284), a true product of the metropolis that created her. It is at the end of Chapter 2 that Dos Passos pictures Ellen as a child left alone at night, crying not for her mother but for her father, afraid of the dark and the loneliness of this city setting. Dos Passos carries this seemingly isolated image into the characterization of Ellen as a mature woman when he describes what begins as a euphoric breakfast-in-bed the morning she runs away from Oglethorpe ("She lay laughing with her legs stretched wide in the cool slippery sheets"). The tone of the scene, however, quickly darkens to emphasize Ellen's real, innate dependency: "She felt hungry and alone. The bed was a raft on which she was marooned alone, always alone, afloat on a growling ocean. A shudder went down her spine. She drew her knees up closer to her chin" (p. 133). As both child and adult, the fetal position comforts her.

In Chapter 3, "Dollars," Ed Thatcher asks Ellen a central question ("You wouldn't like your daddy any better if he were rich would you?"), only to receive the answer he has fostered, "Oh yes I would daddy." "Tracks," the title of the next chapter, implying a change in social status, shows Thatcher becoming wealthy through the stock speculation he has undertaken when a friend commands him to "think of your little girl." Chapter 5, bearing the title "Steamroller," gives us Ellen's despairing marriage to Oglethorpe, shadowed from the start with her nausea of self-disgust and Bud Korpenning's suicide.

The first part of *Manhattan Transfer* accordingly ends with Ellen's victimization through matrimony, without, ironically, the defilement that closes Hardy's first section of *Tess*. (Just as E. D. Lowry has pointed out in his comparison of *Manhattan Transfer* with *The Waste Land*, lack of sexual fulfillment carries the greater stigma for modern characters.)[11] Tess is trapped by both her pregnancy and the knowledge that results from her experience; Ellen is trapped by the legality of her sexless marriage.

The second section of each novel—Hardy's and Dos Passos'—focuses on the heroine's attempts to escape unhappiness. Dos Passos' chapter titles in the second part of *Manhattan Transfer* relate more directly to Ellen. (She is even glimpsed in Oglethorpe's room as the book opens.) "Great Lady on a White Horse" and "Long-legged Jack of the Isthmus" are both nursery rhyme images relating to Ellen's visibility and endurance (only Long-legged Jack will outlast the forty days and forty nights of rain in the refrain introduced during the Oglethorpes' honeymoon journey). "Nine-Days Wonder" shows Ellen succeeding in a new show but also helping her "innocent" friend Cassie to locate and finance an abortionist, surviving a scene with the irate Oglethorpe, and pacifying her father: she is beset, characteristically, by people who need help and turn for that help to her. In the climactic chapter "Went to the Animal's Fair," the successful George Baldwin threatens Ellen with a gun, for leading him on—and the innocuous nursery song used as chapter title and refrain comes to have sinister connotations:

> The birds and the beasts were there,
> The big baboon by the light of the moon
> Was combing his auburn hair.
> The monkey he got drunk,
> And fell on the elephant's trunk;
> The elephant sneezed and fell on his knees,
> And that was the end of the monk,
> the monk, the monk, the monk. The monk.
> The monk.

"Five Statutory Questions" heads the chapter that so quickly grants Ellen her divorce and then presents her with the fact of Stan's unexpected marriage. "Rollercoaster" continues Dos Passos' ironic use of amusement park imagery and creates a Joycean montage of Stan's half-conscious agony, punctuated with lines from all the rhymes and songs of the earlier, happier chapters—implicit references to Ellen—as, drunk and unhappy, he sets himself afire. The second section of *Manhattan Transfer* ends with the chapter titled after the recurrent mourning song "One More River to Jordan." Ellen finds ostensible success in "The Zinnia Girl" and survives her mourning for Stan, first resolving to have and rear his child but then deciding on the abortion that leaves her, suddenly, "a wooden Indian, painted, with a hand raised at the streetcorner."

If these first two sections of *Manhattan Transfer* have been dominated by Ellen's story, the third gives her history less emphasis—partly because, for Dos Passos, her coldness (from whatever cause) has now been firmly established and marks her as a progressively less interesting character. His attention moves instead to the panoramic spread of New York, marred by the events of World War I, under the chapter title "Rejoicing City That Dwelt Carelessly." Back from the war, soldiers flaunt venereal disease and flout prohibition, and business executives see only rocketing profits. But another load of homeless deportees leaves New York, and the promise of the "new land" is once again nullified.

"Nickelodeon," title of the second chapter of the last part, echoes Dos Passos' earlier emphasis on pleasure through the amusement park motif, but the chapter itself depicts a down-and-out veteran who turns desperately to robbery, a passé actress, and Ellie and Herf at the end of their marriage. "Revolving Doors" emphasizes the reversal of fortunes—Congo Jake now wealthy from bootlegging, the Merivales tainted by a bigamous marriage, a working girl murdered behind a Spearmint sign.

The novel closes with two chapters titled to refer to earlier images. "Skyscraper" echoes Stan Emery's wish to be one but carries here an ironic epigraph about a legless man seen on a New York street—not only superior height but even normal height here assumes the guise of mystery. Human beings are more likely to be deformed in some way than they are to be "normal." The tone of New York and its activity is caught in the phrases "Pursuit of happiness, unalienable pursuit . . . right to life liberty and. . . ." Dos Passos does not include the word *happiness* in the refrain, for in his 1925 presentation of New York there is little. Herf has quit his job and left Ellie and in the last chapter, "The Burthen of Nineveh"—an echo of the Biblical refrain warning of destruction—he leaves New York. Ellen agrees to marry Baldwin, amid the laments of a blind beggar with "bloodyrimmed eyes," Dutch Robertson and Francie are sentenced to twenty years in prison, and Anna Cohen burns in Madame Soubrine's dress salon, "a little blaze in a pile of rubbish." At the close of *Manhattan Transfer*, there is no question of Dos Passos' anger at urban inhumanity, the waste of human life and potential. Early sections of the book illustrate economic and social pressures and the sad effects of the mass media on the modern mind, through Ellen's story, but *Manhattan Transfer* eventually encompasses a wider scope. In one way, perhaps Dos Passos' concern with all of twentieth-century culture was a kind of ironic reversal of Hardy's absorption with tradition, ancestry, the lineage of family. Instead of tracing his characters' ancestry, Dos Passos rather stresses the absorption with the present so evident in the modern world: the legacy of this century is, for him, represented by scraps of newsprint and lines of songs.[12] There is scant mention of family, and even more rare is the notion of an extended family. Ellen has learned only from her father, Ed Thatcher, and all she has learned is that success and money mean power. Yet, given the perversions of modern life, perhaps this inheritance becomes her curse as surely as Tess Durbeyfield's passion became hers.

Dos Passos' notes for *Manhattan Transfer* also suggest that the novel was to be Ellen's story, with Jimmy Herf's life juxtaposed internally. (Another alternate title was "Confessions of a Cub Reporter," suggesting some analogy to Sherwood Anderson's use of George Willard as narrator in his 1919 *Winesburg, Ohio* stories.) One outline for the novel, appearing on the front of a notebook used for an early draft, implies that Herf paralleled Dos Passos' early male protagonists, all young, inexperienced, groping:

> I. *Elaine Oglethorpe's stage career*
> II. *Jimmy Herf's Coming of Age*
> III. *Jimmy Herf's Education*
> IV. *Elaine Oglethorpe*[13]

For Dos Passos to open the novel with Ellen's stage career, after her marriage, and then juxtapose Herf's immature state shows that the discrepancy between Ellen and Herf is intentional. Like Dreiser in *Sister Carrie*, Dos Passos was writing about an actress as a highly visible and recognizable image of glamour, sexual and financial freedom, independence. Dos Passos' choice of Ellen's career is partly realistic, but it also implies the superficiality and volatility of modern fortunes and values, a volatility that Joe Hayward's career in the business world echoes. By opening an early draft of the novel with a relatively long scene at Ellen's birth, Dos Passos places the main narrative interest with the Thatchers: his use of juxtaposition came later, but even then Ellen's story appears to be primary throughout the process of composition. Clearly, Ellen Thatcher Oglethorpe is meant to be a character like Nancibel Taylor, except that by 1925, Dos Passos' women characters have learned to love— perhaps too well. Confident in their own sexuality and freedom, these women view men, at least part of the time, as adolescent; and their chief weakness, as modern women, is overindulgence of that immaturity (as, for instance, in the scenes between Stan and Ellen). Confident and poised, Ellen achieves stage success and, later, literary success, while the men of *Manhattan Transfer* mark time. Even Jimmy Herf, in the course of the book, only begins to come to terms with his life.

A number of other modern novelists during these years had written about women protagonists, however, so that Dos Passos' interest in Ellen Thatcher was perhaps less distinctive than were his portrayals of blue-collar workers like Bud Korpenning and the nameless men who sleep in the Seaman's Union and forty-cent flophouses. When such figures had appeared in earlier fiction, they usually filled stock roles, appearing as either unlettered and unrefined or generous and simple in a pastoral sense. Dos Passos was interested in such characters rather as people who had chosen to do this kind of work. As he explained in 1926, "people are formed (much more) by their trades and occupations than by their opinions."[14] The kind of work a person does is seminal to his development—or lack of it—and gives validity to Dos Passos' descriptive ploy of providing information about each character's profession or job experience, sometimes in lieu of other kinds of description.

For Arthur Mizener, the key to Dos Passos' concept of character lies in the importance of occupation. Mizener compares him in this respect with Ben Jonson and Swift, who also saw characters as "representative cases, each of whom contributes in his way to our understanding of the drift of the community's life." Characters were interesting, not for their distinctive selves, but because of the lesson they might suggest about one element in the social context. Mizener argues convincingly that for Dos Passos choosing characters from different strata of society and different work areas is one effective means to his central purpose in fiction, attacking "with satire the institutionalized corruption and the disintegrated private lives produced by the two mighty opposites of our society —industry and politics."[15]

Drawing from a wide selection of occupational "types," then, best suited Dos Passos' purpose of giving an accurate picture of the American milieu in operation. "Successful" business moguls like Blackhead and Densch, scoundrels like Jake Silverman, men who bent laws only a little like Gus McNiel, James Merivale, and George Baldwin—Dos Passos paints each financially successful character with some obvious moral taint. His sympathy goes instead to the characters for whom financial success has become a psychological necessity, people who often began as workers: Congo Jake and Ed Thatcher, who manage to achieve partial success; Dutch Robertson, Bud Korpenning and Joe Harland, whose lives end in blatant failure, victims (at least as Dos Passos presents them) of capitalist economics. For Herbert Marshall McLuhan, this range of attitudes on Dos

Passos' part confirms his philosophical interest in Jeffersonian democracy, an interest that came to dominate much of the last thirty years of his writing career: "In wandering from the Jeffersonian ideal of a farmer-craftsman economy in the direction of Hamiltonian centralism, power and bigness, Dos Passos sees the main plight of his world. Hamilton set up the false beacon that brought shipwreck." What McLuhan sees, correctly, is that Dos Passos' need to slant his portrayals of these characters also reflects his own innate optimism. Dos Passos believed that society could change, that American culture could be taught to help, to cherish individuals and their aspirations:

> But out of that shipwreck, which he depicts, for example,
> as the success of Henry Ford's enterprise, we can recover the
> dream and create a reality worthy of it. That is an unfailing
> note. For those who are critically aware he prescribes the duty
> of selfless dedication to the improvement of the common
> civilization.[16]

Dos Passos' point of view is clear in a 1920 essay, in which he praises the back-to-the-soil movement in Russia, looking forward in his optimistic way to "a life bare and vigorous without being savage, a life naked and godless where gods and institutions will be broken to fit men, instead of men being ground down fine and sifted into the service of things."[17]

No matter that his personal inclination was to hope that people would be strong enough to fight debilitating institutions, Dos Passos' strongest portrayals in *Manhattan Transfer* are of characters "being ground down fine." When Bud Korpenning asks the old violinist how to get to "the center of things" in New York, the reader shudders with the foreboding that this country hick, complete with straw hat, will never succeed.[18] He is too ragged, too inept, too ugly; as the lunchwagon cook reminds him, "It's looks that count in this city." The second piece of advice Bud gets (from a sixty-five-year-old man who has worked since he was five and never held a good job) is to get a union card. Instead, Korpenning washes dishes, and the refrain "the center of things" takes on more and more irony, intensified later as Ellen Thatcher uses the phrase once she has secured her divorce and decided to abort Stan's child (p. 204). Needing to remain anonymous because of the murder of his father, Korpenning runs to different locations (all farther and farther from that romantic center), until he ends up at a flophouse. In one of Dos Passos' first attempts at stream-of-consciousness presentation, the ironic refrain that punctuates Korpenning's thought here is "don't matter where I go; can't go nowhere now." His last daydream, however, is, perversely, of being in that elusive "center." This is the way Dos Passos creates that dream:

> In a swallowtail suit with a gold watchchain and a red
> seal ring riding to his wedding beside Maria Sackett, riding in
> a carriage to City Hall with four white horses to be made an
> alderman by the mayor; and the light grows behind them
> brighter brighter, riding in satins and silks to his wedding, rid-
> ing in pinkplush in a white carriage with Maria Sackett by his
> side through rows of men waving cigars, bowing, doffing
> brown derbies, Alderman Bud riding in a carriage full of
> diamonds with his milliondollar bride. (p. 98)

Counterpointing Korpenning's story, which ends with his suicide at the end of Book I, is that of Congo Jake's. Interested mostly in women, Congo moves to the top by luck and opportunism—and by never caring too much. As a successful bootlegger, renamed Armand Duval, he is married finally to Nevada Jones, George Baldwin's former mistress.[19] To this "success" outside the law, Dos Passos contrasts the tale of Dutch Robertson and Francie, man and woman in love with little means of supporting themselves. After trying repeatedly to find work, faced with eviction from his single room, Robertson attempts a robbery. Working from real-life accounts, Dos Passos presents the two people as victims of their culture. When Dutch and Francie, now pregnant, are sentenced to twenty years in prison, we are conscious of the double irony; their crimes bring them not only severe punishment but effectively end their life as family. Congo Jake, in contrast, motivated largely by pleasure, not only goes uncensured but finds reward after reward.

Dos Passos' heaviest censure, however, falls not on the Congo Jakes of this prohibition era but rather on those socially approved citizens who work inside the law—who, in fact, control that law. George Baldwin begins his career with several lies, one misrepresenting his legal career to the McNiels, a second misrepresenting his intentions to Nellie McNiel. His successes, and lovers, accumulate, but without integrity. Extramarital affairs undermine his marriage; professional honesty is never a consideration. The final irony of Baldwin's life—and of *Manhattan Transfer*—is that his reward for all the years of corruption is, not punishment, but Ellen, the woman who has been educated to revere money and position at the expense of personal happiness. In some ways, at least as contrast, Baldwin's story dominates the novel; and, while he is not a direct antagonist of any of the characters in the book, he and his opportunism are antithetical to Dos Passos' stance in life. As the author had written to Arthur McComb the year before he started work on this novel, he was planning a book "about New York and go-getters and God knows what besides."[20] George Baldwin is the prototype of the American go-getter.

George Baldwin's greatest sin is not his acquisitiveness or his misplaced energy, however; it is his self-serving. In Dos Passos' hierarchy of evil, such complete disregard for the feelings and values of others is a cardinal crime, and many of the episodes in *Manhattan Transfer* seem to have been included to illustrate people's inhumanity to others rather than the plight of people in a technologically sophisticated world.

Bud Korpenning's story, for example, is sometimes cited to illustrate Dos Passos' feeling that genuine concern is impossible in a city, but it also shows that humanism has managed to live even within poverty and stress. Repeatedly, Bud does receive sympathy; except for the woman who pays him in old food, everyone he talks with understands his situation–that of the untrained, nonunionized laborer–far better than he and tries to explain reality to him. In terms of common humanity, too, Bud fares better in Manhattan than he has at home on the farm. Kept in servitude till his mid-twenties, beaten regularly and brutally by a hypocritical, penurious father (or guardian), whom he finally killed, Korpenning has hardly had an idyllic pastoral life.

Joe Harland is an even more important character for emphasizing Dos Passos' theme that inhumanity exists needlessly and inexplicably, often in places of greatest financial security. Once eminently successful in the market, Joe has now lost position, family, and health yet, as an alcoholic, receives neither pity nor charity from any of his former acquaintances. That his own family, the Merivales, considers him only a social embarrassment is Dos Passos' blackest charge against them (the scene young Jimmy Herf witnesses as they turn Joe away confirms Herf's later decision not to accept Merivale's help in finding a job). Though comparatively inarticulate, Harland serves, too, as Dos Passos' spokesman for the problems of financial success: "funny things get into a man. . . . You get kinder disgusted" (p. 164). Told about Baldwin's early attempt to kill Ellen, Harland replies only, "it gets them all sooner or later" (p. 187). The malaise, the world-weariness that begins to infect Jimmy Herf, before he realizes that he must leave New York, is fully depicted here in a character who appears regularly throughout the book as a focus for other characters' sympathetic reactions.

In some respects, Jimmy Herf's weakness as a modern urban man is his ability to sympathize, to understand. Herf shares with John Andrews and Martin Howe, and Dos Passos himself, the sensitivity, the awareness that makes his personal education difficult. The reader understands that Dos Passos intends Herf to be a protagonist, yet in *Manhattan Transfer* perhaps more noticeably than in the earlier books, this character is shaped by his ineffectuality rather than his compassion. Narratively, Dos Passos erred in making Herf a reactor instead of an actor. Herf resists: he resists his uncle's attempts to form his career; he resists following his cousin's example in the banking world; he resists accepting the values of Baldwin, O'Keefe, Densch, and Blackhead, and even Ellen.

What is needed, dramatically, to balance Dos Passos' portrayal of Herf as absorber of action is more attention to the things he does manage to accomplish. Perhaps had Dos Passos included the war years, when Ellen and Herf worked together, married, and had their child, Herf would have emerged a vigorous character. As it is, Herf's career choice (to work for the admittedly corrupt *Times*) does not satisfy him; his performance during the later stages of his marriage does not satisfy Ellen (and we are given so little information that we cannot feel sympathetic toward either character); and his reality as character does not satisfy the reader. Because Herf's boyhood experiences are given so much attention, the reader tries to make connections between them and Herf as adult, but often such links seem inconsequential (at least as they are handled narratively here) or misleading. Dos Passos, in creating the character of Jimmy Herf, has been guilty of the autobiographical fallacy for one of the few times in his career. By the time he began writing *U.S.A.*, however, he found in the Camera Eye technique a new method of portraying his own introspective reminiscence without interrupting major narrative strains.

The most likely explanation for the heavy emphasis on Herf's childhood and his relationship with his mother is Dos Passos' interest in the then-innovative Freudian patterns. Stressing the developing boy's relationship with his lonely, convalescent mother, Dos Passos implies a too-ready explanation of women and their problems as they enter Herf's mature life; i.e., his acquiescence in Ellen's complaints and suggestions; his self-defeating compliance with her request that he take a separate room and, later, that they divorce. Taken by itself, Herf's characterization would point less directly to Dos Passos' interest in this theme, but the emphasis on Ellen's devotion to her father is a parallel motif. Her childhood refrains "I want to be a little boy" and "Ellie's goin' to be a boy, El-lie's goin' to be a boy" (p. 19) change in maturity to "I hate women. I hate women" (p. 149), and her normally aggressive behavior bears out the masculine identification. That Dos Passos includes fairly specific scenes concerning Tony Hunter's trying to become bisexual and Ellen's marrying Oglethorpe—as well as her later abortion—also suggests his chafing under the restraints of writing about only conventional subjects. "Proper" writers did not choose such subjects; neither did nice people acknowledge their existence.

Dos Passos' attention to these subjects was relatively unconventional and seems highly appropriate in view of his enthusiasm for the breaking of traditions within *Manhattan Transfer*. One of the admitted heroes of the novel is the Philadelphia man who was killed for wearing a straw hat out of season. "By God if I was starting a new religion he'd be made a saint," Herf says: "talk about the Unknown Soldier. . . . the golden legend of the man who would wear a straw hat out of season—Saint Aloysius of Philadelphia with a straw hat on his head instead of a halo and in his hand the lead pipe, instrument of his martyrdom, and a little me praying at his feet" (pp. 310–12). The character dominates Herf's thinking as he leaves town at the end of the novel. Dos Passos' use of the defiant if martyred man places Herf's own weakness in clear view; if anything, Herf has been traditional in his quasi-liberal, dissatisfied attitudes and in his very inaction. Perhaps his greatest tragedy is this inability to break convention. Herf's leaving New York appears to be a positive act: Dos Passos' notes indicate a parallel with what he calls "the flight of Joseph."[21] Herf's earlier attempts to blame New York for his and Ellen's unhappiness are less than convincing, however, because we have seen too few examples of independent strength on his part to believe that he has repeatedly been victimized by the city. Herf finally assumes the same kind of remote identity as Vag, the wandering observer who serves as frame for the *U.S.A.* novels to come. For Dos Passos, who thought of himself as "Observer,"[22] such an identity would be, at worst, ambivalent.

In *Manhattan Transfer*, however, Dos Passos seems to be implying more than that the ideal role for an American man is to observe. This novel does more, narratively and structurally, than return us to the limitations of Henry James' great but narrowly focused world – and no one has ever termed Dos Passos a novelist of manners, although perhaps that designation would not be inaccurate. *Manhattan Transfer* was to be many things: "In a great city there is more going on than you can cram into one man's career. I wanted to find some way of making the narrative carry a large load."[23] *Manhattan Transfer* was more than a story of the twentieth-century "pure woman." It was more than "a barbaric poem of New York," an "epic movie," "the zoom of the aeroplane flight over a city."[24] It was more than an economic treatise brought to life, though Dos Passos would persist in arguing that lives were generally determined more by economics than by tragic flaws. It was more than satire. It was not yet America–that was to come in *U.S.A.*–but it was at least a great part of America: it was–and is–New York. Late in life, Dos Passos reminisced, "New York was the first thing that struck me. It was marvelous. It was hideous. It had to be described. . . . rapportage on New York. . . . Fragmentation. Contrast. Montage. The result was *Manhattan Transfer*."[25] And it *is* a new kind of novel. Just two years after its publication, he had written, "The day of the frail artistic enterprise, keeping alive through its own exquisiteness, has passed. A play or a book or a picture has got to have bulk, toughness and violence to survive in the dense clanging traffic of twentieth century life."[26] There is no better way of evoking the dense clanging traffic of New York than to ride Dos Passos' *Manhattan Transfer*.

5. "Politics" and the New Drama

Somewhere along the way it occurred to me that the materialist conception just did not account for the way men behaved. I began to see the urge for power, the desire to climb on your brother's shoulders and if possible kick him in the face in the process as a more logical explanation of what I saw going on in the world. Ideologies and creeds began to seem to me to be masks for the elemental passions.
—John Dos Passos, *unpublished essay, University of Virginia*

Dos Passos' interest in portraying the contemporary scene quickly shifted focus from physical details to the causation of those details. Lines from popular songs, visual montage, human interest stories from newspapers were, in themselves, a colorful means to help an author re-create that feeling of immediacy Dos Passos so admired, but such a re-creation would be limited to only external views of a culture unless the writer structured his pattern to suggest causation. In *Manhattan Transfer*, Dos Passos' pattern—accurately or not—pointed toward the devastating effects of urban living; such a portrayal, however, as Mike Gold pointed out in his review of that book, might be more convincing if actual rather than stereotypical causes were ascribed. Gold's reservations about *Manhattan Transfer* were, finally, reservations about Dos Passos' personal attitudes as they were expressed in the novel:

> I feel in him a bewilderment. The hero of his book and of his recent play . . . is a baffled young middle-class idealist. This protagonist is tortured by American commercialism, and always seeks some escape. But Dos Passos does not know how to help him; and the result is not tragedy, which may be clean and great, but bewilderment, which is smaller. . . . Dos Passos must read history, psychology and economics and plunge himself into the labor movement. . . .[1]

Gold was later to push Dos Passos toward a more active role in the Communist experiment, through his writing for *New Masses*, but here his well-taken comment is less political than literary. By choosing a relatively objective method of presenting characters, by suggesting that these characters were somehow the victims of urban society's inhumanity, Dos Passos had avoided what Gold felt to be necessary personal decisions. The events of the next five years, from 1925 to 1930, were to involve Dos Passos (who in 1925 was "a baffled young middle-class idealist") in a maelstrom of social and political controversy and give him a kind of awareness he had yet to develop.

Between 1925 and 1930, Dos Passos published no new novels (*Manhattan Transfer* appeared in 1925; *The 42nd Parallel*, in 1930), but he did see produced and published his first two plays, *The Garbage Man* or *The Moon Is a Gong*, in 1925, and *Airways, Inc.* in 1929. He also wrote political essays, theater criticism, and *Facing the Chair*, his poignant account of the Sacco-Vanzetti arrests. His writing during these five years accurately reflects the interests of his life, for this was a period of social involvement for him: helping to revitalize *New Masses*, working and writing for the Sacco-Vanzetti cause and the David Gordon case,[2] and helping to direct the New Playwrights Theatre (a literary activity that came to have political ramifications and led to his 1928 trip to Russia, where he met Sergei Eisenstein and others). The period forced Dos Passos to make decisions about his politics; it saw his characteristic high enthusiasm for the power of art—here, drama—subdued and eventually ameliorated; it exposed him to the terrible disillusionment that only genuine optimists experience, in the aftermath of the Sacco-Vanzetti executions, an event that—like the death of his friend José Robles a decade later—colored much of Dos Passos' thinking for the rest of his life.

Dos Passos described clearly the impact of these events in the 1920s on himself and other liberals. He spoke often about the fact that World War I had been cathartic—horrible, yes, but leaving young Americans with only a "sanguine feeling that the future was a blank page to write on, focusing first about the speeches of Woodrow Wilson and then about the figure of Lenin."[3] The disillusion that quickly followed the failure of the Fourteen Points and the League of Nations led to what Dos Passos saw as the naive acceptance of alternate political philosophies:

> Looking back it is frightening to remember that naive
> ignorance of men and their behavior through history which
> enabled us to believe that a revolution which would throw the
> rascals out of the saddle would automatically, by some divine

order of historical necessity, put in their places a band of benign philosophers. . . . we easily fell prey to the notion that by a series of revolutions like the Russian the working people of the world could invent out of their heads a reign of peace and justice. It was an illusion like the quaint illusion the Christians had. . . .⁴

This reminiscence, from Dos Passos' 1945 introduction to the reissue of *One Man's Initiation: 1917*, parallels the remarks he wrote even later, in 1968:

In my disillusionment I began listening seriously to the Socialists. Their song was that all that was needed to abolish war was to abolish capitalism. Turn the industrial plant over to the people who did the work and Man's aggressive instincts would be channeled into constructive efforts. . . . In the end we were to discover, nearly all of us, that Marxism, hardened into a crusading quasi-religion, turned loose more brutal aggressions than the poor old capitalists ever dreamed of.⁵

Letters and diaries from the year 1920 forward indicate that Dos Passos was intrigued by the Russian experiment and that his attempts to visit Russia were motivated as much by political interest as artistic, but it is equally clear that Dos Passos, even then, would make judgments for himself. No coercion from the Mike Golds or the Max Eastmans would ever be successful. Dos Passos proceeded carefully, usually slowly, toward his own kind of acceptance of new ideas. His customary stance was to keep an open mind, to try to gather as much genuine information as he could, on his own terms.⁶ And genuine information frequently meant knowing the people involved, being a part of the lives of people who believed certain philosophies, to see how they practiced their humanity; and that meant, of course, seeing Russia. His definition of "politics" throughout his life was much less abstract than many dictionary definitions: it was based on Gouverneur Morris' remarks to George Washington in 1790: " 'I mean Politics in the great sense, or that sublime science which embraces for its object the Happiness of Mankind. . . .' "⁷ For Dos Passos, any system that fostered inequity and fear needed changing: what he had yet to learn was that change was not always improvement and that complex situations demanded complex methods of alleviation.

Similarly individualistic was Dos Passos' notion of "history," which he came to formulate in his 1927 *Facing the Chair*. Again, his own ideological progression bears out his explanation that "history is made up of those sudden searchlights that for a moment make gigantic the drama of a single humble man."[8] In his lifetime, Dos Passos was most often moved to make philosophical decisions after he had been involved personally in a frustrating or unjust social situation. Had Sacco and Vanzetti not been executed, he would probably never have traveled to Russia (and *U.S.A.* would have been a different trilogy); had Robles not been murdered in Spain, the *District of Columbia* trilogy would also have differed greatly.

Dos Passos' developing political awareness can be clearly charted from his writing during the years in question. In June, 1926, he wrote the first of his political essays for *New Masses*, titling it ironically with an actual newspaper headline, "300 N.Y. Agitators Reach Passaic." His account of the textile strike was, as might be expected, sympathetic, and his use of the satiric headline was the beginning of a pervasive strain of satire in both his fiction and his nonfiction.[9] In *The Theme Is Freedom*, Dos Passos recalled that his support of the revived *New Masses* hinged on its support of the working class:

> Only the bankers and businessmen had profited by the war. Merchants of death. . . . With the working class in power, peace would be assured. . . . we launched the *New Masses* to throw our weight behind the working man's struggle to organize trade unions. In the meetings of strikers we saw new organs of self-government. The class war must be reported. (p. 4)

Dos Passos' method of throwing his weight behind the strikers, in the *New Masses* essay, is to emphasize their antagonists. He mentions the strikers only twice, each time describing them as stolid, dignified, stonelike: "standing still, saying nothing, looking nowhere, square hands hanging at their sides, people square and still, chunks of yellowgray stone at the edge of a quarry, idle, waiting, on strike."[10] In contrast, both of the antagonists (the sheriff and police and also the supporting liberals) are satirized in some detail. Dos Passos' methods avoid the tendency of so-called protest journalism toward maudlin or sentimental evocations; his writing holds his reader's interest, even though we know, essentially, where his sympathies lie. The contrast between the stonelike passivity of the strikers and the aggression the headline suggests ("agitators reach") is also masterful.

Dos Passos' journalism during the late 1920s tends to reflect the techniques of *Manhattan Transfer*—a fast-paced narrative focus on a single person or group, heightened or stylized detail (different in intention from objective detail), elliptical constructions (based on the selection of essential details, structured in sentences that catch an idiomatic tone instead of a formal one). His writing is also, for perhaps the first time, infused with a not-always-intellectual passion and consequently carries a tone of conviction. Other of his essays during 1926 deal with the promise of *New Masses* (to serve as "a highly flexible receiving station that will find out what's in the air in the country") and, most important, with the trial of Sacco and Vanzetti.

The incantatory rhythms of the prose Dos Passos had used in the Passaic strikers essay reappear in "The Pit and the Pendulum" and again in the prose-poem " 'They Are Dead Now–,' " which opens

> *This isn't a poem*
>
> *This is two men in grey prison clothes.*
> *One man sits looking at the sick flesh of his hands –*
> *hands that haven't worked for seven years.*
> *Do you know how long a year is?*
> *Do you know how many hours there are in a day*
> *when a day is twenty-three hours on a cot in a cell,*
> *in a cell in a row of cells in a tier of rows of cells*
> *all empty with the choked emptiness of dreams? . . .*[11]

Details, rhetorical emphasis made through repetition and contrast, rhythmic incrementation–Dos Passos' techniques in his poem to the martyrs are much like those in his prose account of their imprisonment and, most important, much different from his usual tactics in formal poems. The fusion of necessity, passion, demanding subject, and a changing concept of effective form seems to have led Dos Passos into a rhythmic shape which he could scarcely distinguish as either prose or poetry but which he used often throughout his career–in the Biography sections of *U.S.A.*, the prefaces of *Midcentury* and *Century's Ebb*, and many of his essays. It was clearly as if the intensity of his feeling during these years had carried him past his former aesthetic concerns.

Some of the same incantatory rhythms appear in *Facing the Chair, Story of the Americanization of Two Foreignborn Workmen* in the impressionistic sections that describe Sacco and Vanzetti as human beings (as both "jailbirds" and martyrs):

> Affidavits, affidavits read alternately by counsel in the
> stillness of the yellowvarnished courtroom. Gradually as

the reading goes on the courtroom shrinks. Tragic figures of
men and women grow huge like shadows cast by a lantern on a
wall; the courtroom becomes a tiny pinhole through which
to see a world of huge trampling forces in conflict. (p. 24)

For the most part, however, the pamphlet shows Dos Passos' attempt to let the "facts" of the arrest and trial influence the reader;
his style is therefore quiet, reasonable, steady. His method is chiefly
to include texts of affidavits and statements from the participants,
building a montage of quasi-evidence that, he hopes, speaks for itself. In one way, because the writing is so simply declarative, much
of *Facing the Chair* suggests his style for the narrative sections of
the *U.S.A.* novels to come.

There is also, obviously, the important thematic connection between *Facing the Chair* and his later writing, because here he sees
Sacco and Vanzetti as part of "the unending fight for human rights
of oppressed individuals and masses against oppressing individuals
and masses" (p. 21). Making the individual central is Dos Passos'
means of counteracting what he sees, with irony, as the process of
"Americanization": convincing someone that "making good" means
achieving financial success, regardless of methods. He uses the
negative subtitle to describe the education of Celestino Madeiros
(the prisoner who confessed to the crime for which Sacco and Vanzetti were executed), who had "learned Americanism all right, he
suffered from no encumbering ideas of social progress; the law of
dawg eat dawg was morbidly vivid in his mind from the first" (p.
24). One of Dos Passos' themes throughout the pamphlet is that
minority groups are apt students of these bitter lessons—they start
with nothing but prejudice against their origins; they learn to fight
only for some semblance of livelihood. The real lessons of American
democracy have been lost to them and their children:

> Sacco and Vanzetti are all the immigrants who have built
> this nation's industries with their sweat and their blood and
> have gotten for it nothing but the smallest wage it was possible
> to give them. . . . They are all the wops, hunkies, bohunks, fac-
> tory fodder that hunger drives into the American mills through
> the painful sieve of Ellis Island. They are the dreams of a saner
> social order. . . . (p. 45)

Dos Passos was far from alone in his impassioned stand for Sacco
and Vanzetti's freedom. Although he recognized their plight rather
late (they had been arrested in 1920 but were not executed until

1927), the intensity of his response is clear in his published writing from 1926 and 1927 and in his letters from the autumn of 1927.
Evidently, just a few weeks before their scheduled execution, Edmund Wilson had invited Dos Passos to a party, and Dos Passos'
refusal to come was, for him, abrupt and bitter. Several weeks after
this interchange, and after the execution, Dos Passos wrote, "ter-
ribly sorry to have been rude about your kind invitation to a party at
Provincetown—but you can't imagine how queerly your wire jangled
my nerves—Jesus X Columbus—man didn't you realize that we were
all virtually mad up in Boston—You try battering your head against
a stone wall sometimes. . . ."[12] As Wilson himself explained in a
1928 letter to John Peale Bishop,

> You were too far away at the time to appreciate properly
> either its [the case's] importance or its interest. It revealed
> the whole anatomy of American life, with all its classes, pro-
> fessions and points of view and all their relations, and it raised
> almost every fundamental question of our political and social
> system. It did this, furthermore, in an unexpectedly dramatic
> fashion. As Dos Passos said, it was, during the last days before
> the executions, as if, by some fairy-tale spell, all the differ-
> ent kinds of Americans, eminent and obscure, had suddenly,
> in a short burst of intensified life, been compelled to reveal
> their true characters in a heightened exaggerated form.[13]

The Sacco and Vanzetti case was to be an important reference point
for Americans—and particularly for anti-Americans—for decades to
come. Because its impact was so wide, one may fairly attribute to
it many of the modifications in Dos Passos' philosophy and aesthetics during the late 1920s: at least it had some bearing on his definition of Americanism, which became, for the next few years at
least, more negative than it had ever been and led to his inquiry
into alternate modes of government, socialism and communism.

Realizing that 1926 and 1927 were highly emotional, and highly
exploratory, years for Dos Passos, one can understand why his notion of the direct power of the theater became compelling to him.
Dos Passos had known John Howard Lawson's excitement about the
possibilities of innovative and socially important drama for years,
since they had served in Europe together during World War I. Lawson insisted on an emotional thrust to drama, demanding that plays
return to "richer story value, emotional connection; to create a the-

atre which touches some electrical crowd nerve"; and Dos Passos echoed, "the theatre more than anything else welds into a sentient whole the rigid honeycomb of our pigeonholed lives. Since religion has failed humanity, the theatre is the focus of mass emotion."[14] The idea was to excite viewers, to make them respond to drama emotionally instead of only intellectualizing about it.

Clearly, both Lawson and Dos Passos came to see contemporary theater as a means of effecting outright social reforms, a more direct method of communicating than the printed word. As George Knox and Herbert Stahl show so well in their *Dos Passos and "The Revolting Playwrights,"* a large part of this attitude reflected the German expressionists' concepts of drama, but had social conditions in America not seemed repressive, the aesthetics of expressionism would probably have had less appeal.[15] As Dos Passos wrote in his preface to Lawson's *Roger Bloomer* (1923), "The continuously increasing pressure in the grinding engine of industrial life will force other safety valves than baseball and the movies and the Ku Klux Klan." If people do not use the arts as a means of developing and expressing their humanity, says Dos Passos, then they will become "robots instead of men." The role of the theater, accordingly, was to "become a transformer for the deep high tension currents of history."[16]

From this rather easy romanticism, Dos Passos' view darkened and became more explicit, so that by 1927 he could attack the remote "art theatre" and demand instead that "vigor and imagination must take the place of expensiveness and subtlety."[17] More than aesthetic and technical qualities, contemporary drama must have an important theme, something the audience cares about having expressed. And if many such themes were political, Dos Passos defended that emphasis much later by remarking, "In an ideal state it might be possible for a group to be alive and have no subversive political tendency. At present it is not possible."[18] "After all, politics in our time has pushed people around more than anything else."[19]

Dos Passos' view of theater was not bitter, however, nor was it exclusively political. He, again with Lawson, emphasized the need for a return to entertaining forms of theater–circuses, vaudeville, burlesque, melodrama, because in those forms lay "the real manners and modes of the theater. There is in the extraordinary skill with which vaudeville performers put themselves over individually to the audience in the short time allotted to them, in the satire and construction you get occasionally in burlesque shows and musical comedies, in the brilliant acting and producing it takes to get across trick melodramas and mystery plays, raw material for anything anyone wants to make."[20] Lawson's *Processional* was a great success, wrote Dos Passos, because it used the techniques of vaudeville "with passionate seriousness."[21] And he said that his own first play, *The Garbage Man*, had succeeded, at least in the Edward Massey production, because it

> was an attempt to bridge the horrible chasm between the "serious" play that takes itself seriously and thinks that it's ART and the regular Broadway show that everybody is ashamed of, but that manages to keep a houseful of people sitting straight up in their seats from eight-thirty to eleven-thirty six nights a week.[22]

Dos Passos could see nothing objectionable in providing "magic rather than verisimilitude" and opted for serious drama as vivid and direct as musical comedy, with "as much entertainment value, too, as much stimulation and release by music, color, movement, laughter, a lump in the throat."[23] His personal excitement about the new possibilities for theater and the New Playwrights' production of some of these plays is evident in a 1927 letter to Hemingway:

> I'm in deeper and deeper in the drahma every moment. . . .
> Why don't you come out of these Parisian swamps, Hem—
> New York is getting to be just like Paris—only more exciting
> and really synthetic gin isn't a damn bit worse than Anis Delo-
> so—We even have Anthiel, and Pound and Max Eastman
> are slated to arrive.[24]

Reading Dos Passos' three plays without some comprehension of the exuberant productions they required can be a misleading experience. The fact that *The Garbage Man* was subtitled "A Ballet with Shouting" (and "A Parade with Shouting")[25] indicates that Dos Passos saw it as similar to Lawson's *Processional*; he also directed that it was to be presented in the best "musical comedy manner." *Airways, Inc.* is a more conventional drama, but the 1933 *Fortune Heights* is divided into forty-one separate, titled scenes, some of them focused on a stock tableau, suggesting vaudeville's rapid succession of changing acts, color, sound, and intensity. The conventions of vaudeville would have been familiar to Dos Passos' viewers; Russel B. Nye recounts in *The Unembarrassed Muse* that from 1820 to 1920 "New York had thirty-seven vaudeville houses, Philadelphia thirty, and Chicago twenty-two. Outside the cities, about two thousand smaller theaters also booked vaudeville. . . . between 14 and 16 per cent of the urban population attended vaudeville at least once a week."[26] Dos Passos' satiric use of popular dramatic conventions in "serious" plays would have been obvious to some members of his audience, just as the irony inherent in some of the titles he chose ("Detroit: City of Leisure," for an essay about un-employment) is clear to readers today. Reviewers who did not like the productions of the New Playwrights Theatre usually reviewed them erroneously, in the mode of "realistic" drama. In 1928 Dos Passos wrote an explanation of the innovative stage tactics in Lawson's *The International*, saying in part that the aim was not to create illusions of reality:

> An attempt was made in the staging and writing to go back to the simple popular forms of old melodrama and burlesque in which the actors are visibly actors. . . . "The International" is a broad cartoon of the dynamics of current history. It uses all the stock cartoon figures and ideas, warping them to its own purpose.[27]

Dos Passos also seems to have been interested in writing for theater long before he came upon expressionist drama. As early as 1918 he referred to a play he was writing called *Family Connection*, and internal evidence suggests that much of *The Garbage Man*, as it was later titled, was written earlier than *Three Soldiers*. Its theme is the familiar early one that breaking with familial and other traditions is desirable; the characters Jane and Tom manage to break out of stultifying family "connections" and finally reap romantic and material "rewards." The play's method is the charged, recurring image and quasi-surreal event pattern–heightened by outright fantasy–similar to that of *One Man's Initiation: 1917* and *Streets of Night*. There is also some use of the long-line incantatory rhythm that Dos Passos would use in the Biography sections of *U.S.A.* The most noticeable device is his reliance on jazz and dance routines.

Jane and Tom are the nominal protagonists, but New York is probably the central character. Dos Passos presents the city as a bleak wasteland (an image in *Manhattan Transfer* a few years later), caught here in the dialogue of a man who claims that he was "born in Brooklyn and raised in the Bronx and I know."[28] In a description reminiscent of Eliot's tone in *The Waste Land*, Dos Passos chants:

> Everyday they're tied tighter in ticker ribbon and type-writer ribbon till they can't move. . . . they don't have time

> to look at each other or in women's eyes and they've ground
> their lives little like sausage meat and crushed their lives in
> stone crushers and clanked 'em out into smudgy black picayune
> letters in printing presses. . . .

There is some social consciousness in one scene of robbery, when
financial standing determines justice: well-dressed thieves are set
free while innocent bums are arrested (in fact, one bum is killed
and promptly disposed of without regret). People are judged by appearance and arrested to satisfy the public demand for a scapegoat:
"We've got to get the guy we're looking for, see, because we bumped
off the other one and couldn't make any arrest. . . . Too damn much
publicity this burglary's getting. We've got to make an arrest or
there'll be hell to pay" (pp. 55–56).

Aside from this kind of indictment, *The Garbage Man* is hardly
a political play. In fact, in its theme of lovers running away from
convention and finally being able to reach their dreams (flying to
the moon together), this play is more romantic than socialistic.
The titular garbageman is not even a proletarian figure, an honest
workingman, but rather a clumsy symbol of Death. First appearing
as a physician when Jane's mother dies, Death later becomes the
New York garbage collector, carting off the society he appears to
mourn. Again, his presence returns us to Dos Passos' condemnation
of the city.

In contrast to the garbage of New York, Dos Passos sets the symbol of the moon, in Tom's eyes a "gong" to beat on and sound (as
in "Seven Times Round the Walls of Jericho"), and the pervasive
metaphor for living life to the fullest is beating on the moon. Moving between garbage and moons, death and life, Dos Passos gives us
a 1920s version of the carpe diem theme. Jane, innocent-turned-
star, cajoles Tom, "There's more than the treadmill. There's the
moon" (p. 69). In the finale, surrealistically, they make it to the
moon together. (In a manuscript version of the play, Tom's analysis
of the situation connects the play with Dos Passos' early novels:
"My fathers were afraid of life as yours were. The blood in our veins
is half gall.")[29]

Undoubtedly, the setting and production of *The Garbage Man*
compensated for its romantic and nearly apolitical themes. "The
whole play is done to music," say the stage directions for the first
act, and some effectively syncopated lines and funny non sequiturs
occur, especially in early scenes. Produced by Edward Massey in
Cambridge in 1925 and in Boston the following year, *The Garbage*

Man included many elements of musical comedy and was one of the New Playwrights Theatre's more interesting productions, despite its jejune philosophy and vapid characters.

Several years later, between 1927 and 1928, Dos Passos wrote a play that, politically, *did* belong on the stage of the New Playwrights Theatre. *Airways, Inc.* is not only his best play; it may also be, as Edmund Wilson suggested, some of his best writing.[30] Proletarian in sympathy and experimental in technique, the play foreshadows *U.S.A.* in its inclusion of events both past and present, act and motivation, and a wide panoply of American characters and cultural problems. In *Airways, Inc.* we see the almost innocent progress of an exploitative culture to its demise, as human values are exchanged for quick profits. The theme is not new, but Dos Passos' presentation of it is fresh and effective.

Using the Turner family as an apparently "common" American group (stable, moral, conservative, generous to its friends but also suspicious and prejudiced), Dos Passos identifies each family member with a different ideological segment. Dad Turner, the retired unsuccessful inventor, gambled on scientific discovery as a route to happiness. Losing, he became so embittered that even his children have difficulty living with him. Martha, the thirtyish sister, walks a tightrope between being the dutiful old maid, the slave of her family of brothers, and loving socialist agitator Walter Goldberg. Apolitical as she is, she has a firm sympathy for the underdog and compassion for Goldberg's struggles.

Martha's youngest brother, Eddy (named for Edison), is a shallow hedonist. Her oldest, Claude, is the most offensive of the three–a "dry positive man" whose self-righteous conservatism about his white-collar job leads him to condemn Martha for her affection for Goldberg, whom he refers to as a "damn kike," a "longhaired anarchistic agitator," "red," and a "damn sheeny." Aside from Claude, only the crude children whose voices serve as chorus during the play ever call people these names, so his use of them is a stern indictment. Of the four Turner children, it is Claude who finally does "make good," riding on the coattails of All-American Airways, Inc.

Dos Passos' most effective plot element is the creation of All-American, the corporation whose production of flight-related materials was made possible initially by Elmer Turner's record-breaking success as a pilot. Elmer, the middle brother and Martha's favorite, sees the corporation as a means of getting his own kind of plane produced. An inventor like his father, he wants to improve aviation. When his financial partner, Jonathan Davis, chooses the name "All-American" and describes the business as "a great scientific and patriotic duty," we are put on guard. Elmer's disillusionment when the directors care nothing about his inventions comes as no surprise; neither does the defection of his girlfriend, Mae.

To broaden the impact of this single family's experience, Dos Passos uses as observer Professor Raskolny, a close friend who has survived the Russian Revolution. At first he is a pair figure for Dad Turner, whose usual role is to lament his lack of recognition as both inventor and patriarch of the family. The two old men commiserate with each other. But, once Turner hangs himself (a happening that could well have been modified, if not omitted), the professor's comments relate more and more often to Goldberg's position, that of the revolutionary in a repressive culture—even though Dos Passos identifies Goldberg's kind of revolution as the mildest possible: "it's not charity we want but a sane arrangement of society."[31] Raskolny in his Tiresias role becomes a key means of gaining an immediate yet historical perspective on the conflict between change and a fearful yet profit-seeking normality. As he says in the play, "All history seemed unrolling in my head" (p. 96).

For, finally, *Airways, Inc.* is not a play about the varieties of belief so much as it is a condemnation of capitalism. The play was originally titled *Suburb*, a designation that suggested some urban-suburban difference.[32] Place, however, was not the issue for Dos Passos: *The Garbage Man* is set largely in New York; *Fortune Heights*, in a tiny crossroads community. Dos Passos had seen that the same kind of thinking existed everywhere. What he gained by choosing the title *Airways, Inc.* was an emphasis on the power of business, the profit motivation, coupled with suggestions of the glamour of flying (viz., Charles Lindbergh as national hero) and of flight as an archetypal image of freedom, a commodity none of these characters has enough of. Dos Passos succeeded in locating the blame for American greed squarely where he thought it should lie, with business (and the paper empire of the owners of Fortune Heights in his third play is a further example of his anger at the power of corporations). The opening dialogue of *Airways, Inc.* sets the depressing, forbidding tone:

> Yes sir, I think you'll find this a very interesting development, something new in suburban developments. . . . You see we combine here a residential section on the garden city plan with a teeming industrial center. This, sir, is the model city of

the future. You see behind these streets of lowpriced, artistic onefamily houses you can descry the sterner buildings of the Hartshorn Mills, the Swastika Refrigerator Company. . . .
(p. 82)

It is the plight of the American factory worker that he never escapes his job, and this setting of "Home, sweet home" clearly catches that sense of life as an "endless factory."

The theme of buying—merchandise, property, business—runs throughout the play, always to the dissatisfaction of the purchaser. Dos Passos shows the ways human considerations are buried under the pressures of finance, whether high or low; money is the pivot for action throughout *Airways, Inc.* As Dad Turner laments,

> Everywhere they're building ramshackle houses for young folks . . . Ozone Park, Crystal Meadow, Joyland, Fortune Heights, Coral Gables. . . .
> they think they'll buy acre lots of happiness where the fountain of youth was in Florida
> they think they'll buy a nickelplated future with monogram engraved to order like I did
> and what they buy is being old and having your kids hate you because you're old and being an old man without a job.
> (p. 98)

In Dad Turner's eyes, the capitalistic ethic, that buying a house in the suburbs will lead to "prosperity," "happiness," "success," has led to self-interest of the most inhumane sort: "They'll come home all busy thinking what they've been doing, what they're going to do tomorrow. They won't notice me. I can't get 'em to talk to me any more. Haven't for years. They're like people drunk with some terrible new drink" (p. 112). The "terrible new drink" is left undescribed, but events within the play suggest that a get-rich-quick mentality dominates American culture and that repression awaits any person who threatens the status quo (the profitable present). Walter Goldberg's execution (reminiscent in many ways of the Sacco and Vanzetti situation) goes without notice in the largest sense, because the very people who are well off and might support his defense, on strictly idealistic grounds, ignore the case. Rewarded by capitalism, they adopt its morality in return.

Dos Passos' most effective method of presenting Goldberg's death more as an index of the weakness in his culture than as a simple political execution is his use of juxtaposition throughout the play.

In early scenes, he juxtaposes the voices of the neighbor children and Raskolny with speeches of the major characters, creating a kind of single-level irony. After Dad Turner complains about his children's ignoring him, for example, Raskolny says, "In certain savage tribes in New Guinea, they put the old people up in the trees and shake them once a year in the spring; if they don't fall out they let them live another year" (p. 88). Later in the play, more elements of the culture are aligned: in one scene, for example, Claude and Martha wrangle about their differing views of family responsibility, while Raskolny simultaneously predicts revolution and a Sunday radio church service repeats platitudes:

> *Martha.* But Elmer said he really would come. You know
>   he loves Sunday breakfast.
> *Claude.* Go ahead your own way. It's no use me trying to talk
>   in this house.
> *Radio.* Let us pray, O Lord, we members of this great invisible
>   audience gathered together each in our respective home far
>   from each other in actuality but brought near by the wonders
>   of science as we hope to be brought near in thee in the won-
>   ders of the spiritual life. . . .
> *Professor.* In a million cities they walk to work and back from
>   work, and the machines hum and whine and are silent and all
>   the while the thought grows in them. In the hearts of a mil-
>   lion men the thought grows, in the whirring of the machines.
> *Radio.* . . . that it may do its wonderwork not only in these lit-
>   tle groups of loved ones gathered together with prayerful
>   hearts over the length and breadth of the land but in the great
>   world outside. . . .
> *Claude.* Now look here. . . . This damn sheeny Goldberg . . .
> *Radio.* . . . making a great united family united in worship,
>   united in service, so that with joyful hearts. . . .
> *Claude.* It's got to stop. (pp. 116–17)

The insistence on the power of science, of the family, of the spirit of cooperation is set against the Turner family quarrel over Martha's love for the "sheeny" Goldberg, the authority within the family, and Raskolny's fears for the larger family in the face of revolution. Dos Passos uses intermeshed lines frequently, often in moments of the highest stress, more often toward the end of the play. He succeeds in combining a tragic foreshadowing—using Raskolny as prophet, whose own reminiscences of revolution and sabotage provide some of the most moving lines of the play—with a seemingly modern montage effect. There are also many passages where characters' lines fail to correspond chiefly because the characters are not listening to each other. They talk about only what they themselves are interested in. These passages of linked non sequiturs emphasize the self-interest of most of the characters.

Dos Passos also manages to give the reader some understanding of the community opinion, first through the voices of children—usually expressing the most vituperative of opinions—and then through the dialogue of walk-on characters, people moving past the house, talking among themselves, strikers, friends, strangers. It is a rich and swift panorama of suburban opinion, focused adroitly on Walter Goldberg, first as agitator and then as executed man.

During the third act, Dos Passos brings together all these types of dialogue—the children's rejoicing at Goldberg's death ("Oh, the kike Walter Goldberg lies amoulderin' in the grave"); Elmer's sensible suggestions for Martha's recovery from her loss; phone calls from different elements of opinion; Raskolny's benediction, devastating in its bitterness; and Martha's own laments. She berates the house and the culture it represents ("I'd like to burn this house down and everything in it") and mourns for Goldberg in terms of her own undefined loyalties and her limited self-knowledge:

> Now I'm beginning to feel it, the house without Walter,
> the street without him, the city without him, the future that
> we lived in instead of a honeymoon without him, everything
> stark without him.
> Street where I've lived all these years shut up in a match-
> wood house full of bitterness.
> City where I've lived walled up in old dead fear.
> America, where I've scurried from store to subway to church
> to home, America that I've never known.
> World where I've lived without knowing.
> What can I do now that he is gone and that he has left me
> full of scalding wants, what can I do with the lack of him
> inside me like a cold stone? (p. 157)

Considering *Airways, Inc.* as a New Playwrights production, intent on some kind of political statement, one of its strongest achievements is that Dos Passos himself does little of the recriminating. The characters, in their quick-paced interaction, give us the analysis and the implied solution for the problems of prejudice, fear, isolationism, but the plot of the play keeps the reader from feeling that he is being subjected to a political treatise. Goldberg has his faults (one being an inability to live in the present), as does Martha (her unwillingness to relinquish her role as center of the family, to go with Goldberg)—no one is deified because of politics or position.

The main weakness of the play is Dos Passos' turn to violence when he runs out of uses for his characters. Dad Turner's suicide is more expedient than reasonable; Elmer's plane accident, while nicely ironic, is not necessary to make him see Mae's shallowness or the profit motive of American Airways. Dos Passos may have been influenced by his interest in melodrama, but his reliance on the macabre seems inappropriate for this particular play. *Airways, Inc.* does not pretend to be a comedy; unlike *The Garbage Man* and *Fortune Heights*, it draws its power from its tragic qualities—consistent tone, the threat of impending disaster, human resolution in the face of conflict that determines the action of the central characters, and an inimical and dangerous culture.

In his first two plays, Dos Passos had drawn upon a romantic plot structure. Tom and Jane survived the turmoil of modern success and were lovers at the end of *The Garbage Man*; Walter's death made *Airways, Inc.* a tragedy, as Martha recognized her loss at the play's conclusion (and there were the subordinate romances of Elmer and Mae and Eddy and Eva used to illustrate the tawdry quality of some loves). In the 1931 essay that prefaces *Three Plays*, Dos Passos explained that he had relied on this traditional romantic plot primarily because it was traditional in a particularly American way:

> Every theatre has at any given moment a basic myth that lives in the subconscious fantasies of the audience. . . . In America it's a boy and girl love song under the cheesecloth apple blossoms, and the boy's just made a million dollars, and they achieve Success, that mystic tabloid crown that hovers over the bright lights and skysigns of Manhattan. (p. xix)

By the time of *Fortune Heights* in 1933, however, Dos Passos' bitterness about "romance" and "success" was clear. The relationships that exist in that play are hardly "love songs"; they are more often sexual conveniences, with little concern for the other person's needs or desires. Impermanence is the mode and suggests that one person's dissatisfaction with another stems at least partly from an inability to separate fact from fantasy.

As to "success," even in his earlier plays, it appears that Dos Passos was modifying the myth by viewing the girl of this American pair as the more capable. It was Jane who was the money-maker. Neither Tom nor Walter Goldberg can be accused of having made a million; indeed, part of Claude's hatred of Walter is that he has so little money. And in *Fortune Heights*, Florence has made some money in San Francisco but has given up her success to come back to Owen; in this play, however, no one succeeds, because the Depression economy will not permit profits. Success is as far from the capabilities of the characters as love is, and all the quick juxtapositions of comic and stock characters used in *Fortune Heights* cannot alleviate the impression of disaster.

The manuscript collection at the University of Virginia contains a synopsis and a short opening scene for a play titled "Dream Factory," which shares the romance and illusion-reality theme with *Fortune Heights*. Two young Americans, Joe Wood and Fred Hammond, vie for the affection of Ella May Small, a girl who has been reared on movie and fashion magazines and is ill-equipped for anything but a fantasy existence. One of Dos Passos' interests is in presenting the difference between Joe and Fred: Joe is an enterprising young inventor; Fred, an aspiring actor not above using duplicity to succeed. That Ella May marries Joe but returns home to her ambitious, star-struck mother gives Dos Passos his primary theme: that fantasy has overtaken reality in modern American life, that many people live in what he calls "the dreamworld of the screen," spending their energies in "the big money luxury ritz reveries."[33]

The influence of the world of film—and the corporate intrigue responsible for it—was but a corollary to the pervasive American dream of quick financial success, so Dos Passos' interest in this particular dream world is not surprising. Always aware of the power of the popular media, he was fascinated with the possibilities of film as both an entertainment and a news medium. As *Dream Factory* suggests, the young American film industry only disappointed Dos Passos. In contrast to the aspiration of the New Playwrights Theatre (which had closed while producing his *Airways, Inc.* in 1929), American film was scarcely aimed at educating any audience: it was rather reinforcing the most dangerous of American myths. Dos Passos' disappointment in the lost possibility of this most dramatic of mass media is clear from his 1931 contention that the primary aim of good theater should be to create "a new myth. . . . to replace the imperialist prosperity myth."[34]

Fortune Heights attempted less to create any new myth than to debunk all the old American attitudes. It opens, under the ironic caption title "The Bull Market," on the site of a new glassed-in filling station decorated with the typically expansive realtor's promise:

Why Not Look Over Our Lots Now?

   FORTUNE HEIGHTS

We help
    U
      along the road

to ownership and independence[35]

The "road to ownership and independence," especially in 1933, was also the road to success, but from the beginning of the play Dos Passos shows us only lost opportunity. The people who are even temporarily solvent are morally impoverished, and that Dos Passos' condemnation of the American system is total is clear from the fact that the poor characters are not better—"Roadlice," he calls them. The similarity in their moral dimension between poor and rich seems to answer Raskolny's hope of finding a promised land in the United States: "After the collapse of the shining socialist dream, I came to America" (p. 93).

Fortune Heights is an uneven and unlikely mixture of propaganda and vaudeville. The play closes with a series of scenes in which farmers and laborers unite to try to prevent Owen's eviction from his filling station. Dos Passos' "solution" in 1933 to social crises is the action of common men, inarticulate in their rationale but moved by simple, genuinely humanitarian impulses ("I'm no kind of speaker but if you men'll listen to me for a minute I'll get something off my chest, as the feller said," begins Morry):

> Honest, it makes me feel real good to see you fellers crowdin' together to help another feller out. That's what we call co-operation. That's what's goin' to save us. . . .
> All over the country there's thousands of us.
> We stand on the Declaration of Independence.
> In school they taught us a citizen of these United States had unalienable rights. How can you have life liberty or the pursuit of happiness if you're thrown out of your job an' out of your home? A country where a man who wants to work can't earn his own livin' ain't the United States.
> We're out to find the United States. (p. 285)

This concluding theme, the "search" for the U.S.A., to find answers to the broken promises and the battered dreams, propels the play to an ending inconclusive in political philosophy. For, finally, co-operation does *not* work (Morry is killed, as senselessly as Rena was in the preceding act), and Owen and Florence and their child wander off into the world, alone.

The chief strength of *Fortune Heights* is Dos Passos' ability to build ironies, especially during the first two acts, through his use of titles for the forty-one separate scenes. Moving much like a vaudeville program, one vignette followed rapidly by the next, *Fortune Heights* develops an expansive structure. Signaled by the caption-like titles, the viewer can accept any kind of action, whether in direct sequence or oblique. "The Same Old Flivver" depicts the return of the derelict car the Meakins are trying to travel in, a pathetic scene in which the old couple discuss the plight of being unwanted and poor. "The American Home" is the eviction scene; "The Jazz Age" introduces the informer Ike Auerbach, who wants nothing so much as to seem a character out of a Fitzgerald novel; "The Economic Factor" presents Morry and Rena's discussion of the risk of pregnancy and their inability to marry. The play also progresses chronologically, but transitions and the inclusion of characters are not dependent on a strict plot sequence. Dos Passos achieves a doubly ironic effect by dividing the action into these titled short scenes: the immediate irony in relating title to content within each scene and the culminating irony of having an "entertainment," complete with comic scenes, like the circus car being emptied of passengers (in scene 6) or the blues dialogue (scene 8), deliver a serious message and even move unexpectedly toward tragedy with the deaths of both Rena and Morry.

Dos Passos' interest in various American myths is also evident in *Fortune Heights*. The romantic myth is debunked by the experiences of the couples and by the casualness of their pairing off. Even Florence, the most stable of the characters, is unfaithful to Owen, while Kay, Rena, and Mrs. Stead choose men for reasons of proximity rather than feeling. The myth of education as a means to success also takes its share of criticism: the most morally objectionable characters, Auerbach and Ellery, are the educated people, and the most flagrant crime, the robbery of Owen's station and the shooting of Rena, is committed by the "College Boy Bandits."

In addition to these somewhat peripheral myths, Dos Passos shapes *Fortune Heights* to establish the tyranny of the Poor Richard myth of hard work's leading to success. The aging Mrs. Meakin laments, in bewilderment, "I don't know what we're going to do. It's not as if we hadn't worked and saved and been thrifty and decent all our lives" (p. 214). A bum reminds Morry, "You work all the time and you're broke all the time," and the events of *Fortune Heights* prove the truth of his remark. Working, saving, helping others—none of the former middle-class values guarantees self-preservation (much less success) in the America of the 1930s. But because people could not accept reality and abandon the allure of myth, they were disoriented, bitter, vindictive. The song Dos Passos interjects throughout *Fortune Heights*, "I found a million dollar baby / at the 5 and 10¢ store," unfortunately remained plausible for too many Americans. It took many years of living in the "dawg-eat-dawg" world to bring even a character like Owen to the realization that what happens in life is not always deserved: "Funny this feelin' of having the whole country against you; I never did anything against it" (p. 266)

Dos Passos' last play succeeded in the scenes that show characters in such poignant realizations, but its melodramatic reliance on foreclosures and evictions, love affairs, robberies and murders as well as its use of a mock-comic speed and tone left its viewers baffled. Because of Dos Passos' technical innovation, the play certainly cannot be judged as part of the "realistic" theatrical tradition,[36] for all the realism of its Depression experience. *Fortune Heights* stands as an imperfect fusion of Dos Passos' interest in experimental theater and the use of American theatrical forms and his desire that drama express meaningful social ideas, a vestige of the New Playwrights era more interesting for its influence on his later fiction than for its own efficacy as theater.[37]

6. Dos Passos' Search for U.S.A.

A man can't discover anything, originate anything, invent anything unless he's at least morally free, without fear or preoccupation so far as his work goes. . . . This state of mind, in which a man is ready to do good work, is a state of selfless relaxation, with no worries or urges except those of the work at hand. There is a kind of happiness about it.
—John Dos Passos, 1936

In some respects the continuous search for America that Dos Passos was to emphasize at the end of *Fortune Heights* had been suggested in the themes and strategies of *The 42nd Parallel*. Begun in 1929, following his trip to Russia and his two years of work with the New Playwrights Theatre, the novel was an attempt to place in fiction the characters and themes he had been working with in the plays, particularly *Airways, Inc.*

Like *Airways, Inc.*, *The 42nd Parallel* explores the myths of equal opportunity, of middle-class values frustrated by various kinds of upper-class controls, of American promise stillborn. Dos Passos' characters are once again drawn largely from the people of middle or eastern America: Charley Anderson, an inventor-pilot somewhat like Elmer Turner; Janey Williams, an incipient Martha who never matures; J. Ward Moorehouse, another hypocritically ambitious Claude Turner.[1] Eleanor Stoddard's antecedents extend to Nancibel Taylor, but in this novel she is a midwesterner, as is Eveline Hutchins. Mac (Fainy) McCreary, the young labor agitator, moves from Connecticut to Chicago to the West Coast to Mexico; yet, no matter what his location, he remains the prototype of the disadvantaged but ambitious American. Dos Passos' intention of mocking the Horatio Alger image is suggested by his originally titling Mac's segment of the narrative "From the Ground Up."[2] To see these characters evolve, at least in some ways, from the characters in his earlier drama and fiction is to understand Dos Passos' rather apologetic comment to Thomas Wheeler that "a man's experience is horribly limited, a novelist has to start out with a few traits of people he knows when he's constructing a character. . . ."[3]

By 1929, however, as he began to write the first of his *U.S.A.* novels, Dos Passos' experience was much less limited than it had been during the postwar years. Then his range was bounded on one side by artistic naifs and on the other by advantaged Bostonians. Now he was familiar with the problems of the working class and the Left, through both extensive travel and what was for him an unusual involvement with political activities. The changes in his own life and attitudes paralleled the obvious, dramatic changes in the national economy,[4] and Dos Passos became increasingly concerned with the wider fictional purpose suggested throughout *Manhattan Transfer*: "I was trying to put across a complex state of mind, an atmosphere."[5]

In addition to these personal and cultural differences, Dos Passos' attitude toward the novel had also changed. He no longer saw it as a linear structure, moving by progression of character and incident, but rather as a montage of people and activity, no less an ebb and flow of happenings than the street scene outside a window on a busy day. That this aesthetic further complicated characterization goes without saying; in fact, the seemingly central characters in *The 42nd Parallel* were never intended to be the focus of the book as a whole. Instead of writing a picaresque adventure or a character study, Dos Passos' intention in *The 42nd Parallel* was to convey "atmosphere." Satisfied with some of his effects in *Manhattan Transfer*, he turned once more to montage, but a montage punctuated with spotlighted stills of the heroes of American culture (in the Biography sections). Dos Passos' vivid montage existed in the Newsreel (the external world) and the Camera Eye (the internal, autobiographical world); the biographies carried the moral and philosophical means for the *camera verité* sections; and the more conventional narratives of some representative "common" Americans presented lives intended to be illustrative, not necessarily exemplary. Dos Passos' comparison between the new novel structure and a tableau clarifies his intention:

> I have always paid a good deal of attention to painting. The period of art I was very much interested in at that time was the 13th and 14th centuries. Its tableaux with large figures of saints surrounded by a lot of little people just fascinated me. I tried to capture the same effect in words.[6]

The "little people" who occupy the major part of the narratives—
Eleanor Stoddard and Janey Williams, Charley Anderson and J. Ward
Moorehouse—are intended to contrast, then, or at least to foil, the
more apparent "saints" of the biographies—Eugene V. Debs, Luther
Burbank, Bob La Follette (and the equally visible "sinners," also
drawn large—William Randolph Hearst, Henry Ford, Theodore
Roosevelt). The relatively aimless conclusion of the trilogy—aimless in terms of the outcomes of the narrative protagonists—was
necessary to effect the sense of tableaux, life in motion, life taken
at random, interrupted in its flux only by the stable and central
figures of genuine American heroes. Dos Passos' growing interest in
American history gave him one important new dimension for his
fiction.

Narrative method and authorial choice in the trilogy must also
be seen in light of Dos Passos' aim of creating a new kind of fiction,
one that drew on his already expressed desire to couple history with
fiction, to "keep up a contemporary commentary on history's
changes, always as seen by some individual's eyes, heard by some
individual's ears, felt through some individual's nerves and tis-
sues."[7] He envisioned historically based fiction as a montage: "Songs
and slogans, political aspirations and prejudices, ideals, hopes, delusions, frauds, crack-pot notions out of the daily newspapers."[8] His
inclusive list here may serve as a corrective, if we tend to think of
collages as composed of only visible or concrete objects—headlines,
newsreels, conversations, songs. Yet mixed with these visible details are to be those elusive qualities of a culture, "ideals, hopes,
delusions," that cannot be illustrated by a quick flashback to the
family Bible or a crinoline skirt but demand insights into characters who hold various particular beliefs. Because Dos Passos was
dealing with the larger reality of America between 1900 and 1929
—not merely with such things as the composition of sidewalks or
the kinds of table settings—he limited his descriptions of physical
objects to the few scenes necessary for character description, his
more significant interest. In The 42nd Parallel, as in the other two
U.S.A. novels, Dos Passos' choice of characters was his most express way of conveying authorial opinion. In a 1934 review, he
stressed that the primary duty of any novelist was "to create characters . . . and then to set them in the snarl of the human currents
of his time, so that there results an accurate permanent record of a
phase of history."[9] Even the external world is here described as "human currents." That Dos Passos' view of character was integral to

his belief in self-determination seems clear from his later comment that "if you want to find out what is happening to a society the thing to study is the behavior of the people in it and not what they say about their behavior."[10]

Dos Passos' attempts to create a wide variety of characters to voice all kinds of philosophies necessitated not only a long novel—three, in fact—but also some technical means of distinguishing the authorial perspective from that antagonistic to it. Since no single character was to represent the author, as Nick Carraway had in *The Great Gatsby* and Jake Barnes had in *The Sun Also Rises*, Dos Passos needed a means of identifying the sympathetic perspectives. The four-part segmented structure of the novels, so well described by various critics,[11] was one of his answers to the dilemma of diversifying his writing enough to permit some inclusive yet relatively impartial view.

Of the four kinds of writing in the trilogy, then, the Biography and the autobiographical Camera Eye sections were subjective, in that Dos Passos' attitudes and experiences were their bases. The Newsreels ("intended to give the clamor, the sound of daily life"[12]) and the narratives named for respective characters were more objective presentations, used "to distill my subjective feelings," to present "conflicting views" and therefore achieve some kind of objectivity.[13] In his pattern of writing types, Dos Passos found a way of using all he knew about his craft, while controlling the cumulative effect. Through his technical invention, he achieved the effect he desired, that of "historical panoramic painting."[14]

The Biography sections represent most consistently the central authorial voice. More than half of the twenty-seven biographies (at least fifteen) are clearly positive; the others verge on the satiric.[15] In writing the Biography sections, Dos Passos dropped his objective pose. His opinion of these people was directly stated; and revealed his own prejudices and attitudes. And he saw this gallery of portraits as crucial to his panorama; materials in the University of Virginia Collection labeled "Early Notes for U.S.A." include this comment: "Idea of the great / interesting people / people who do things."[16] Once Dos Passos began his writing, however, he expanded those qualities: the positive biographies in the *U.S.A.* novels do depict "people who do things" but they also more consistently praise people who do things for the good of the culture. J. Pierpont Morgan, Minor Keith, and Henry Ford were admittedly people who did things, but Dos Passos refused to adopt the general American criteria for success. Financial gain alone meant nothing to him; he repeatedly questioned the eventual social outcome of a person's efforts.

Dos Passos' heroes numbered inventors (the Wright brothers and Thomas A. Edison); populist political leaders (Eugene V. Debs and Fighting Bob La Follette); perspicacious and usually leftist writers (Randolph Bourne and Jack Reed); union organizers (Big Bill Haywood and Joe Hill); and economist Thorstein Veblen. Because Dos Passos' theories of an equitable culture appear throughout the trilogy to be those of Veblen, his summary of the economist's views is of special interest:

> he established a new diagram of a society dominated by
> monopoly capital,
>   etched in irony
> the sabotage of production by business,
> the sabotage of life by blind need for money profits,
>   pointed out the alternatives: a warlike society strangled by
> the bureaucracies of the monopolies forced by the law of diminishing returns to grind down more and more the common
> man for profits,
>   or a new matter-of-fact commonsense society dominated
> by the needs of the men and women who did the work and
> the incredibly vast possibilities for peace and plenty offered
> by the progress of technology.[17]

As all of *U.S.A.* shows so vividly, Veblen's final "hope" was also that of the author: "that the workingclass would take over the machine of production before monopoly had pushed the western nations down into the dark again."

Nearly all the Biography sections show the centrality of Veblen's thinking in Dos Passos' philosophy. Minor Keith (United Fruit Company) is presented as a villain because the lives of workingmen meant nothing to him—of seven hundred men needed to build a Caribbean railroad, "about twenty-five came out alive. The rest left their whiskey-scalded carcasses to rot in the swamps. . . . Minor Keith didn't die" (42, p. 258). Keith's accomplishments, in comparison with their human cost, mean nothing to Dos Passos. Andrew Carnegie, exemplary giant of American enterprise, is also satirized because his great wealth grew from industries that profited from war; even his "charity" was, finally, suspect:

> *Andrew Carnegie gave millions for peace*
> *and libraries and scientific institutes and endowments and*
> *thrift*

> whenever he made a billion dollars he endowed an institu-
> tion to promote universal peace
> always
> except in time of war. (42, p. 278)

Censure also falls on J. Pierpont Morgan, as Dos Passos objects to the family dynasty's accumulation of wealth and control through interlocking directorates.

Dos Passos' criticism of Theodore Roosevelt is aimed toward his bigotry, his definition of "the white man's burden," his patronizing all but the privileged elements of American society. Roosevelt's lack of awareness about genuine humanistic concerns damns him; his weaknesses anticipate those of Woodrow Wilson. According to Dos Passos, "Meester Veelson" was the captive of an ideational jargon that obscured any clear vision he might have had. Misdirected rather than Machiavellian, Wilson surrounded himself with the words he hoped would save the peace, "talking to save his faith in words, talking to save his faith in the League of Nations, talking to save his faith in himself, in his father's God" (1919, p. 255).

Dos Passos' deepest criticism throughout the trilogy is directed toward people who misuse America's institutions—capitalists, for gain that is entirely personal; industrialists, for the destruction of personal resources; those who demand freedom of speech, for irresponsible or repressive speaking or writing. Just as Dos Passos was disappointed in Wilson's failure to use his eloquence successfully, with integrity, so was he angry about William Randolph Hearst's comment, "When there's no news make news." "You furnish the pictures and I'll furnish the war," Hearst supposedly wired a friend in Havana, and the "emperor of newsprint" created an unsightly tempest in American foreign affairs, for little purpose except increasing his paper's circulation. As a writer himself, Dos Passos was particularly conscious of the immorality of Hearst's practices and set in opposition to him (and to William Jennings Bryan, whom he saw as equally guilty of propagandizing the American people) such writers as Randolph Bourne, Jack Reed, and Paxton Hibben. Bourne sacrificed what might have been a brilliant literary career to what he saw as truth ("War is the health of the state"); Reed and Hibben, sympathetic to socialism and communism, extinguished their promise under a barrage of anti-Red reaction. Dos Passos ends the Hibben biography with the scene of his Princeton classmates trying to lynch him during their twentieth class reunion and mourns,

no more place in America for change, no more place for the
old gags: social justice, progressivism, revolt against oppression, democracy; put the reds on the skids,
   no money for them,
   no jobs for them. (*1919*, p. 194)

This important emphasis underlies Dos Passos' bitterness about
J. Ward Moorehouse and Richard Savage, whose work in advertising
and the creation of public opinion might well have been a positive
force.

Another consistent target for Dos Passos' criticism is the agency
that refuses to understand human limitation. Steinmetz's exhaus-
tion in the employ of a company is contrasted implicitly with Edison's long lived productivity:

General Electric humored him, let him be a Socialist,
let him keep a greenhouseful of cactuses lit up by mercury
lights. . . .
and they let him be a Socialist and believe that human society could be improved the way you can improve a dynamo,
and they let him be pro-German and write a letter offering his
services to Lenin because mathematicians are so impractical. . . . Steinmetz was the most valuable piece of appa-
ratus General Electric had
until he wore out and died. (*42*, p. 335)

The impersonal use of men as machines is bad enough. Worse in
Dos Passos' eyes, however, are people like Frederick Winslow Taylor and Henry Ford, who use their talent to create an "American
Plan" for efficient production, with its resulting assembly-line. Both
Taylor and Ford saw people as commodities and insidiously assumed physical and moral authority over the workers they employed. Insisting on personal freedom, Dos Passos consequently
opposes these efficiency programs on several grounds, not the least
being that they disguise profit taking behind moral platitudes.

For Dos Passos to devote a full biography to Rudolph Valentino
may seem disproportionate but, just as he was fascinated twenty
years later with the career of actor James Dean, he saw in Valentino—and the public response to him—a pathetic image for the sensibility of mass American culture, banalized by the very use of language that might have educated it. Again, he is angered by the mis-
carriage of the power of words. As Dos Passos charts the rise of
Rodolfo Guglielmi to star status, he notes the kind (and position,

by page) of news coverage that accompanies each episode: what we see is Valentino as a literal product of the media. Half of the biography describes Valentino's funeral, an occasion for unbelievable physical injury and chicanery, but the hysteria settles quickly:

> In Chicago a few more people were hurt trying to see the coffin, but only made the inside pages.
> The funeral train arrived in Hollywood on page 23 of the *New York Times*. (*BM*, p. 209)

Dos Passos' positive biographies are not all politically oriented: he admires Luther Burbank, Frank Lloyd Wright, Thomas A. Edison, and the Wright brothers because they go through life motivated toward discovery that seems truly apolitical. Their personal lives, however, are as subject to censure by American power groups and the press as was Valentino's. Burbank is shunned by the religious because he believes in "natural selection," a principle on which his important scientific discoveries depend; Frank Lloyd Wright, because he does not fawn before big business. Burbank and Wright—and Isadora Duncan, whom Dos Passos admires because of her immense physical energy, her imperious will—illustrate all too clearly that becoming society's victims rather than its saints was the common fate for many "people who do things."

Many of Dos Passos' positive biographies, however, are of people who were in some way connected with fairly practical political issues. (The sense of *U.S.A.* as proletarian fiction probably stems more directly from these biographies than from the characters and events of the conventional narrative sections.) In the first biography in the trilogy Dos Passos establishes a key attitude by describing Eugene V. Debs as "Lover of Mankind." Reacting against postwar antisocialist sentiments, Debs was jailed in Atlanta in 1918 for speaking against war; even his long altruistic life could not counteract that scandal, and he died a lonely, almost forgotten man. Dos Passos closes his portrait with Debs' own words: "While there is a lower class I am of it, while there is a criminal class I am of it, while there is a soul in prison I am not free" (42, p. 52). Like Debs, Bob La Follette cared about American promise and accordingly was able to create a model state in Wisconsin. He met defeat in national politics, however, because he was a "willful man expressing no opinion but his own." Dos Passos describes his role in Washington as "struggling to save democratic government, to make a farmers' and small businessmen's commonwealth, lonely with his

back to the wall, fighting corruption and big business and high finance and trusts and combinations of combinations and the mias-
mic lethargy of Washington" (42, p. 371).

Big Bill Haywood, Joe Hill, and Wesley Everest all share the fates
of Debs and La Follette–ignominy, the burden of public disapproval,
and death, brought on, at least in part, by an unsympathetic press.
Haywood, who died on broken bond, was exiled to Russia; Hill was
executed for a crime he did not commit; and Everest was castrated
and hanged by a mob of respected Centralia citizens. Their most
heinous crime was to have organized for the I.W.W. As Dos Passos
concludes, "To be a red in the summer of 1919 was worse than being a Hun or a pacifist in the summer of 1917"–and to be a member of the I.W.W. implied anti-American sentiments, at least to the
popular press.

The martyrdom of these labor leaders builds toward the ironic
biography of "The Unknown Soldier," which provides Dos Passos
with an occasion to depict all the hypocrisy and perversity of American attitudes at their worst. "Make sure he ain't a dinge, boys /
make sure he ain't a guinea or a kike," say members of the selection
detail. Dos Passos juxtaposes the pasty verbiage of the patriotic
dedication ceremony with the enlisted men's vernacular and the
poignant refrain "Say buddy can't you tell me how I can get back to
my outfit?" The difference between real life and death and some
pretentious ceremony about them is caught vividly in this passage,
and, even though "Woodrow Wilson brought a bouquet of poppies,"
there is no question that the unknown soldier would rather be a
live doughboy than a dead hero.

Dead, the average doughboy was deified. Alive, however, responding to the American promise as Joe Hill, Wesley Everest, and Big
Bill Haywood had responded, he might well be executed. America
in the twentieth century was a strange amalgam of rigid beliefs
and fear-hardened conventions, its once vital language now pushing
humanitarian concerns only further into darkness. What Dos Passos
viewed as promise, his country labeled threatening and soon found
ways of punishing the offenders. America's hero, the average man,
had become her outsider: the Vag who wanders, apart from any
society, in the frame section of each of the novels, has learned to
be content with the only safe role for an independent spirit, that
of observer.[18] The difference is frightening between the Vag of the
opening passage–content with his observing, content to absorb the
American speech ("mostly U.S.A. is the speech of the people"), con-

tent with his role of questing after understanding—and the Vag in the epigraph scene in *Big Money*, who is starving and no longer physically able to listen to that speech. In the latter scene, Dos Passos gives half his attention to the vagrant, who desperately watches drivers' eyes as he waits for a hitch. His ambition has dwindled to getting away, getting a hundred miles down the road. The other half of the passage describes the well-heeled business-man, flying across America, surfeited with food and luxury. "We are two nations," and Vag was now a true vagrant. By the mid-1930s, the romance was gone. As Dos Passos wrote in 1933, in his essay about the Roosevelt administration,

> Where was the forgotten man in all these meetings, the citizen of Hooverville, the down and out guy you find wher-ever you look for a second under the thinning veneer of comfort and the American standard? Or is Al Smith right in saying he doesn't exist? Depends on what you mean by exist. Maybe a few of him went to stand outside and crane and boo at Hoover, but the people you rubbed elbows with in the campaign rallies were of the stiffest small respectability. The forgotten man didn't go to the socialist meeting, and he'd have been out of place among the Deserving Democrats. Where is he?[19]

It was these forgotten men who stood united at the close of *Fortune Heights*. But the question "Where is he?" was an honest one. Dos Passos gave the forgotten American one identity in Mac McCreary and another—a darker one—in Vag, but his search for a hopeful future for the young American of average promise was to dominate his fiction for the next two decades.

Dos Passos' choice of Mac McCreary for the first narrative seg-ments in *The 42nd Parallel* may have given readers further sup-port for their feeling that the trilogy was to be proletarian. Many of Dos Passos' essays during the late 1920s and early 1930s dealt with the subject he was keenly interested in, although not to the exclusion of other social problems. In 1932, when Malcolm Cowley wrote to ask where Mac as character had gone in *1919*, Dos Passos replied, with perhaps more condescension than was appropriate, "Mac stayed on in Mexico and died there some years ago of heart failure while playing hearts with a small party of friends. . . ." He went on, seemingly to discourage Cowley's thinking the trilogy a proletarian statement, "I don't know if there's any solution—but there's a certain amount of statement of position in the later Camera Eyes. I think also—if I manage to pull it off—the later part of the book shows a certain crystallization (call it monopoly capitalism?) of society that didn't exist in the early part of *42nd Parallel* (call it competitive capitalism?)—but as for the note of hope—gosh who knows?"[20]

Dos Passos' interest in Mac might better be seen as an outgrowth of his realization that the familiar American success story was sheer bunk. As the ending of *Fortune Heights* showed so vividly, the American myth that any person could become successful was not only misleading; in the present national economic circumstances, it was tragically false. Not every poor child grew up to financial wizardry or even financial stability. Not every American found contentment: most, in fact, found nothing but poverty and tedium. By creating Mac's story, Dos Passos had many of the elements for just such a success story. When the poor Scotch-Irish boy loses his mother and starts for a new life in Chicago with his unemployed father, uncle, and little sister, we see the rags-to-riches plot begin to develop. Instead, in Dos Passos' telling, it becomes a rags-to-rags story, with the addition of a labor-agitator uncle whose philosophy might seem to provide an answer, except that his own life—and that of Mac himself—is hardly "successful" on any terms. Despite the assurance of Tim O'Hara, the confident uncle, that his philosophy would succeed, lives of the laboring classes in America were seldom prosperous. Tim's analysis of the "system," however, is moderately accurate:

> it ain't your fault and it ain't my fault . . . it's the fault
> of poverty, and poverty's the fault of the system. . . . that don't
> give a man the fruit of his labor . . . The only man that gets anything out of capitalism is a crook, an' he gets to be a millionaire
> in short order . . . But an honest workin' man like John or myself
> we can work a hundred years and not leave enough to bury us
> decent with. . . . And who gets the fruit of our labor, the gaddam businessmen, agents, middlemen who never did a productive piece of work in their life. (*42*, p. 38)

Similar rhetoric pervades Mac's narrative—he and his friends "believe in" the cause of unionization, of the I.W.W. efforts, but their actions and statements are vague at best and ineffectual in execution. "But God damn it to hell, a man's got to work for more than himself and his kids to feel right" (p. 136) is the closest Mac comes to an explanation of his philosophy; and Dos Passos' portrait of his subsequent wanderings—to the West, to Mexico—stresses his vacillation, his choice of the easiest route, rather than any commitment to ideology. In the last section of Mac's narrative, as he flees with Concha from the Mexican overthrow, he is pictured as a directionless man who does not understand either political situations or personal ones. Mac's motivation for staying in Mexico has become his own comfort and prosperity, a clear echo of the motives of the capitalists he had scorned so many years before.

Dos Passos' final characterization of Mac is thus harsher than it might seem, for his most stringent criticism throughout *U.S.A.*, as throughout *Airways, Inc.*, falls on capitalists like Maisie's brother, Bill, a Los Angeles real estate developer whose sole aim is to make money. The suburban attitudes that Maisie expresses are, understandably, threatening to Mac: the consumption that is not only conspicuous but competitive reminds the reader of Dos Passos' admiration for Debs and Veblen (shown early in the short dialogue between Mac and Maisie's brother, when Mac refers to Debs—"Suppose a feller didn't want to get rich . . . you know what Gene Debs said, 'I want to rise with the ranks, not from the ranks,' said Mac. Maisie and Bill laughed. 'When a guy talks like that he's ripe for the nuthouse,'" [p. 138]). Caught in the vise of economic pressures that took him farther and farther from his own political tendencies and interests, Mac ran to what appeared to be more sympathetic company. Because the course of his life was one of reaction instead of action, however, Mac is presented as something less than heroic.

Once Mac has arrived in Mexico, Dos Passos opens the narrative of Janey Williams and, somewhat later, J. Ward Moorehouse and Eleanor Stoddard. His reason for creating Janey seems to parallel his interest in Mac: the oldest child of a poor family, Janey leaves home, takes a job, and lives her life according to the simplest middle-class principles. She works hard, buys nice clothes, maintains her virtue, and persists in judging people by their position and affluence, instead of by their character. Like many Americans, Janey is the dupe of cultural propaganda and ends, fittingly, working zealously for the master of American public relations, J. Ward Moorehouse. Her callous treatment of her brother Joe becomes the index for her distorted sense of values.

Mac's story, even in its aimlessness, overshadows Janey's at least partly because it is more interesting. His is also an independent fiction; Mac's life does not depend on that of any of the other characters. Janey's, in contrast, connects quickly with that of Moore-house—as does that of Eleanor Stoddard and, in 1919, Evaline Hutch-ins; the lives of these women characters seem tangential to the Moorehouse story. This structural dependence may be one reason for critics' tendency to consider all the women characters in U.S.A., except Mary French, as minor. Dos Passos manages to achieve some sense of autonomy with Mary French partly because her life does not depend economically on that of any of the male characters. The lack of interest in most of the other women in the trilogy results at least partly from the dullness of their lives as Dos Passos creates them, or, more accurately, from the dullness of the direction of those lives—the lack of options.[21] The manuscript versions show, however, that Dos Passos did try to make his women more explic-able and thereby more appealing,[22] but because he tried to avoid being didactic, many of the more introspective scenes were eventu-ally deleted.

Narratively, then, Moorehouse's story dominates the trilogy part-ly because it serves as a plot focus, partly because in it Dos Passos found a vehicle for his social criticism. Modeled substantially on H. P. Davidson, head of the Red Cross during World War I, and Ivy Ledbetter Lee, public relations expert who worked for the Rocke-fellers, the Red Cross, utilities and railroads, F.D.R., and countless businesses as he created a concept of advertising that was also liai-son, Moorehouse became—in the three novels of the trilogy—the kind of hypocritical opportunist Dos Passos abhorred. In the writer's view, Moorehouse's only product was the manipulation of people's thought, a manipulation that was to "level thinking to a lowest common denominator set pretty near the idiot level." As Moore-house grew more powerful, unfortunately, he was able to replace individual morality with that of collective interests: "Influence was his profession."[23] How demeaning a statement Dos Passos consid-ered this is evident in his The Theme Is Freedom, when he con-tends, "Men and women risk their lives daily in search of a moral order based on independent judgment and individual responsibility. The events of the last ten years have proved that a solid scheme of ethics is the most practical thing in the world."[24] That Dos Pas-sos' interest in Moorehouse, charting his rise to tremendous power and success, had more momentum than did his interest in Mac was partly a function of plot development—Moorehouse's office and business circle in New York were a more natural point of coales-cence for other characters than would have been some I.W.W. camp or Mac's Mexican retreat—but it also provided safer philosophical ground. In the late 1920s and early 1930s, Dos Passos' villain was big business. The entrepreneur system, and its supporting agencies, was not only suspect; it had been convicted: "Capitalism was the bogey that was destroying civilization. Cut the businessman's profits we said. Production for use. . . . Capitalism was the sin that had caused the war; only the working class was free from crime."[25]

> The knot which our society must untie is the problem of controlling the power over men's lives of these stratified corporations, which, whether their top management calls itself capitalist or socialist, are so admirably adapted by the pull of centralization to despotic rule. Machinery must be invented to control the power of the administrators not only in the public interest but in the interest of each private individual.[26]

Dos Passos' explanation of his reaction to American enterprise in the *U.S.A.* novels is expressed in his 1951 comment:

> In the course of my own life, I guess, I saw a good deal more of the class war in the "twenties" than I did before. The work I did in the thirties reflected such experiences as I'd managed to have in the twenties. I, as well as many of my contemporaries, went in for humanitarian socialism (very different from the triumphant Marxism of our day) as a mode of revolt against the conclusion (which I still believe was correct) that wars and militarism were tearing civilization to pieces. This state of mind had been part of the American climate for two or three generations. Our big bugaboo was naturally Big Business.[27]

As the various plot lines of the trilogy show, once a character lost his or her sense of individual purpose and became a cog in the wheel of large industry—whether as secretary or chairman of the board— life became a series of automatic responses, leading finally to many kinds of dissatisfactions, among them emotional bankruptcy. (That Dos Passos' censure was later to fall on any kind of bigness, union organization as well as corporate structure, made his supposedly changing political stance more consistent.)

By following Moorehouse's life, Dos Passos could show that collection and abuse of the corporate power that he sincerely felt was ruining America. *The 42nd Parallel* was written in 1929, *1919* in 1930, and *Big Money* in 1932–33—all years before Roosevelt's social reforms had had much impact. *U.S.A.* was, at least in origin, a depression trilogy; and, child of Veblen economics that he was, Dos Passos could see little hope for the workers of a capitalistic system besides some kind of unification. As he said in a 1930 essay, American society is divided into three strata, "the owning class, the business class and the working class," with the chief political effort of 1930 being a Red hunt whose real purpose was "to club American workingclass dissenters into submission."[28]

Sympathy for people suspected of being Communists was not, however, the same as sympathy for communism, as Dos Passos' frequent comments during the 1930s attested. After his trip to Russia in 1928, in fact, Dos Passos had been clearly relieved to leave the country. He felt that conditions there were more than ominous. As he wrote in 1932, "I don't see how a novelist or historian could be a party member under present conditions."[29] And, in 1936, when he declined to join a Communist writer's union, he spoke to the need for liberty ("First rate writing is hard enough to come by under the most favorable conditions. Without liberty it is impossible"). His statement is principled and consistent:

> A man can't discover anything, originate anything, invent anything unless he's at least morally free, without fear or preoccupation so far as his work goes. . . . This state of mind, in which a man is ready to do good work, is a state of selfless relaxation, with no worries or urges except those of the work at hand. There is a kind of happiness about it. . . . writers accordingly must not make of themselves figureheads in political conflicts.[30]

Once again, Dos Passos' first consideration for happiness is individual freedom. Throughout his writing, he criticizes any situation that limits the individual's choice or potential.

In this context, then, the evil of J. Ward Moorehead's occupation, and his admitted success, becomes even more insidious. Whether Dos Passos writes about Charley Anderson, Ben Compton, or Richard Savage, the younger generation of Americans has swallowed and digested the ethics and morality of prosperity. From people never in personal touch with Moorehouse and his firm to people like Savage who work closely with him, the corruption is pervasive and complete. (Dos Passos' choice of name for the character most like his own earlier autobiographical persona signals his sense of wasted promise. Richard Ellsworth Savage, in Johnson's famous biography, was an illegitimate child whose impetuous sense of honor brought him to jail for murder, and to ultimate death. He was also a writer.)[31]

The centrality of Moorehouse throughout the trilogy becomes both philosophical and geographical. That many of the characters of *The 42nd Parallel* were from the West or Midwest, but moved —during the course of the book—to New York, was one reason Dos Passos chose the somewhat obscure title for the novel. The "42nd parallel" referred to the path of storms across the country, moving from west to east. Similarly, the ambitious paths of Moorehouse, Stoddard, Hutchins, Williams, and Anderson brought them east and north to the New York Dos Passos had already drawn so clearly, and so negatively, in *Manhattan Transfer*; and the eventual results of these characters' early "successes" in the city provide the story line for the trilogy. Dos Passos used this climatological explanation as an epigraph to the novel in manuscript:

> alternate areas of high and low pressure . . . forming slightly
> north of the Canadian border, frequently in the vicinity of Med-
> icine Hat . . . cyclonic disturbances . . . Blizzards in winter
> sweeping east and south following a well-defined track approx-
> imately along the 42nd parallel.[32]

In keeping with this emphasis, it seems no accident that the informed, sensible views of the chaotic culture come from midwesterners who have not yet been tainted by urban success. These characters exist in contrast to the sophisticates who people the New York world "in which all goals are unattainable and the most powerful gods are corrupt." John Aldridge views Dos Passos' U.S.A. as a wasteland, doomed to disappoint both its champions and its critics: "the rebels are defeated by the system and the tycoons are corrupted by it."[33]

By the time Dos Passos began writing *The 42nd Parallel*, his disillusionment with the American dream had fairly well-articulated causes; therefore, events in the trilogy occur for clearly defined and plausible reasons. In *Manhattan Transfer*, New York stifled relationships and promise—and people—sometimes inexplicably. Dos Passos' method there was to present rather than to explain; because he was apparently more interested in presentation than in social analysis, *Manhattan Transfer* worked almost as a cabalistic paradigm: whoever crossed the city limits was headed for misfortune. By 1929, Dos Passos' increased political and economic awareness enabled him better to structure relatively convincing situations. As Alfred Kazin explained, between *Manhattan Transfer* in 1925 and *The 42nd Parallel* in 1930, Dos Passos had "begun to study seriously the configuration of social forces, the naturalism and social history, which were to become his great subject in *U.S.A.* . . . Dos Passos knew where he stood now: the old romantic polarity had become a social polarity, and America lay irrevocably split in his mind between the owners and the dispossessed."[34]

The shift in kind of title between *The 42nd Parallel* and *Export*, the working title for *1919*, is substantiation of Kazin's point. Within the first novel of the trilogy, Dos Passos seemed to consider his dominant theme the waste of human potential; and his analysis of the dilemma in which his characters found themselves was comparatively romantic, to use Kazin's term. Ambition, greed, the ethos of success moved his characters along the stormy paths of the forty-second parallel, depositing them in New York City where all kinds of instability defeated them. Though there is more emphasis here on economic influence than had appeared in *Manhattan Transfer* or any of Dos Passos' earlier writing, the stronger determination for a character's outcome still appeared to be personal choice, based on personal philosophy and taste.

The working title *Export* for the second novel, which was to have as epigraph a "quotation from latest report on trade–export," suggests that Dos Passos' view of the personal tragedy that had occupied his earlier attention was changing to a kind of economic determinism, a recognition of a "social polarity." Amorphous social evil was becoming more pointed yet not so simple as it had seemed to Mac's Uncle Tim in *The 42nd Parallel*. Because Dos Passos had come to realize that economic gain or loss underlay most world events—even wars, which might appear to have some ideological basis—he was able to decide ultimately on *1919*, a title which suggested not only World War I but also the year of postwar negotiation and disillusionment, products too of financial chicanery. The connection with the war was crucial because so many of the Newsreel elements and the Camera Eye segments related to war experience and because most of the characters in the novel were dramatically influenced by the war—Joe Williams as one obvious victim, Richard Savage as the tawdry initiate, Daughter and Eveline Hutchins as peripheral casualties, and Moorehouse as manipulator supreme. But the general tone of malaise and despair was not simply the result of death and destruction apparent in World War I; it was the legacy of the broken illusions, the unavoidable and accurate learning that followed the armistice—in 1919.

Another reason that *1919* is usually regarded as the most despairing of the three novels is that even the Biographies do little to alleviate the aura of despair. Instead of heroes, Dos Passos chooses the wealthy who have benefited from war prosperity, or antiwar protestors (Joe Hill, Wesley Everest) or writers (Randolph Bourne, Paxton Hibben, Jack Reed). Energy in living goes into fighting corruption; nothing is left for positive endeavors and—in the cases of Hill, Reed, and Everest—nothing is left except dishonorable death. For the book to end with the tribute to the Unknown Soldier, the last vestige of the "righteous Americanism" J. Ward Moorehouse was producing, seems wonderfully ironic. One passage from an early draft provides a cogent summary for *1919*: "In the war to make the world safe for Wilson's democracy, the bankers began to dream empire, America had stood at Napoleon's tomb and dreamed empire—the System woke up to its absolute power, everywhere wobblies were lynched or jailed. . . ."[35]

The booming economy which existed at least intermittently through much of the 1920s lured remaining skeptical Americans into the profit-oriented philosophies. *The Big Money* became everyone's god, and in his third novel, Dos Passos charts believably the subversion of human values to economic ones. The continued rise of the likes of Moorehouse and Henry Ford vaunts the perversion of language—people's greatest means of humanization—and the equally indefensible dehumanization of work. Stressing Veblen's theories from the beginning of *The Big Money*, Dos Passos juxtaposes vivid evidence of the misappropriation of human resources with his exposition of Veblen's theory. The biographies provide a largely retrospective view of heroic Americans: the 1920s supply many negative examples, definite antiheroes, as Dos Passos' narrative emphasizes the modern turn to quick and often sensual gratification as a replacement for ethical or humane behavior. His use of the Sacco-Vanzetti case both in the Mary French narrative and in the concluding Camera Eye episodes is a way of stressing the loss of humane values. To set the deaths of these men against Frederick Taylor's "American Plan" is to realize vividly the distortion in American values.

It is no accident that Dos Passos begins here to compare himself with Whitman. The prototype of the lone American (a Vag no less than Melville's isolato), Whitman also dedicated his art to defining and capturing the characteristics of America. The opposite of Moorehouse's easy solutions to moral questions, Whitman's aim in his role as creator of language—poet—was to confront his country-men with their qualities, both good and bad. As Dos Passos had written in 1932, "We have had a proletarian literature for years, and are about the only country that has. It hasn't been a revolutionary literature, exactly, though it seems to me that Walt Whitman's a hell of a lot more revolutionary than any Russian poet I ever heard of."[36]

Dos Passos' tendency to see himself in the same sort of conscious-ness-raising role as that Whitman filled becomes more evident in his later writing, especially his history, *Midcentury*, and *Century's Ebb*, where the entire novel is addressed to Whitman. But during the 1930s his metamorphosis from objective and largely passive observ-er to spokesman for social issues becomes evident in his disregard for conventional style. Like Whitman, Dos Passos felt the need for new forms. And it may well be that the most radical innovation in *U.S.A.* was neither Dos Passos' philosophy nor his choice of char-acters, but rather his fusion of formal literary categories, his mix-ture of "poetry" and "prose" for an unusual and effective rhythmic impact—speed, rush, the urgency that some sections of the trilogy convey. At its simplest, this is the montage of the Newsreel sec-tions; and George Knox has written pertinently of the comparison that should be made between the verbal effects here and twentieth-century paintings (and poems like Ezra Pound's *Cantos*).[37] Com-parison between the drafts of the Newsreel sections—many lines literally cut and pasted from the papers—and the finished versions in the novels shows that each phrase, and its position, was impor-tant to Dos Passos.

At its most striking, Dos Passos' meld of poem and prose creates the rhythmic coherence of the Biography and the Camera Eye sec-tions, passages that have more similarities than differences. Moving from the precious distinctions of his college days, when his letters to Rumsey Marvin were filled with aesthetic statements, to an in-terest in genre and form that was much more expansive—based as it was not on device so much as philosophy, Dos Passos' tone during the twenties as he discussed purely literary matters is often some-what impatient. "I wasn't much interested in the labels on these various literary packages but I was excited by what I found inside," he recalls about these years; "at times I would find it hard to tell you whether the stuff is prose or verse."[38] The imagery of "package" surfaces again as he discusses his turn from poetry to the various kinds of writing in the mature novels: "I got to a point where there was no particular reason for making separate little packages."[39] "I did quite a lot of that [poetry] but it took a different form . . . it got into certain rhythmic passages in *USA*."[40]

More determined by the influence of Whitman than of the imagists, the Biography sections from the trilogy are marked by the long-line movement, detail building on detail (often ironic), the passage at first punctuated by periods, but later moving cumulatively to the rising climax. Each has at least one repeated image, occurring at studied intervals. In the case of Debs' portrait, the continuing imagery is that of the plainspoken midwesterner and the brotherhood of like men. The biography opens with the recitation of facts:

> Debs was a railroadman, born in a weatherboarded shack
> at Terre Haute.
> He was one of ten children.
> His father had come to America in a sailingship in '49,
> an Alsatian from Colmar; not much of a moneymaker, fond
> of music and reading,
> he gave his children a chance to finish public school and that
> was about all he could do. . . .

and moves to longer units of description as Debs becomes the important labor leader, rising to the inclusion of his own words, with which Dos Passos so thoroughly agrees; then ending with what Dos Passos sees as his betrayal—catalogs, colloquially phrased and charged descriptions, the imagery of faith become the imagery of betrayal:

> But where were Gene Deb's brothers in nineteen eighteen
> when Woodrow Wilson had him locked up in Atlanta for speaking against war,
> where were the big men fond of whiskey and fond of each
> other, gentle rambling tellers of stories over bars in small towns
> in the Middle West,
> quiet men who wanted a house with a porch to putter around
> and a fat wife to cook for them, a few drinks and cigars, a garden
> to dig in, cronies to chew the rag with . . .

And they brought him back to die in Terre Haute to sit on his porch in a rocker with a cigar in his mouth, beside him American Beauty roses his wife fixed in a bowl . . .[41]

Judging from the drafts and early manuscript versions of *U.S.A.*, Dos Passos' chief problem in writing these biographies was to include accurate information within the heavily accented lines—the rush and tumble of impassioned speech that he was attempting to approximate also had to be factual. Included among his work sheets are notes and listing of the concrete—places, dates, events—for respective subjects of these profiles. Once he had absorbed the facts, one assumes, he could fit them into the rhythms appropriate to the entry.

At times, changes from early versions to published ones suggest that the final tone or form of a biography was unexpected. The profile of Andrew Carnegie, for example, seems to have been much less satiric in its early version, or at least less effectively so. As published in the novel, the piece is titled "Prince of Peace" and its central irony works because Carnegie is shown investing in philanthropic enterprises only in peacetime. The heavy irony of the ending is, however, absent in the early draft, which closes "whenever he had a billion dollars he invested it." As published, the ending reads

> whenever he made a billion dollars he endowed an institution to promote universal peace
> *always*
> *except in time of war.* (42, p. 278)

The manuscript draft also includes a heavy-handed couplet that Dos Passos, happily, deleted:

Andrew Carnegie lies a-mouldering in the grave
But his billions go marching on.

Written with a different intention than the Biography sections, Dos Passos' Camera Eye passages share the repetition of key details and the unification of an underlying rhythm. In these admittedly subjective and autobiographical prose-poems, however, Dos Passos drew on the most modern signals for stream-of-consciousness effects: he replaced traditional punctuation with spacing within lines, capitalized only thematically important words, enjambed single words, and used formal figures of speech that might have seemed too poetic in some idiomatic writing. The Camera Eye passages are short, even fragmentary, in their lack of explicit connections, and often powerfully evocative:

skating on the pond next the silver company's mills where there was a funny fuzzy smell from the dump whaleoil soap

somebody said it was that they used in cleaning the silver
knives and spoons and forks putting shine on them for sale
there was shine on the ice early black ice that rang like a
sawblade just scratched white by the first skates   I couldn't
learn to skate and kept falling down   look out for the muckers
everybody said   Bohunk and Polak kids put stones in their
snowballs write dirty words up on walls do dirty things up al-
leys their folks work in the mills
   we clean young American Rover Boys handy with tools
Deerslayers played hockey Boy Scouts and cut figure eights on
the ice Achilles Ajax Agamemnon I couldn't learn to skate
and kept falling down (42, p. 101)

Early versions of this moving recollection of Dos Passos' boyhood
fears show that the key statement, "I couldn't learn to skate and
kept falling down," was originally underlined whenever it appeared.
More important, the names of the comparative figures in the last
paragraph were added later: the words *Boy Scouts* and the Greek
heroes did not appear in the early version.

At times, changes from early versions were in the form of additions (and, as in this case, the additions attempted to make personal
experiences wider, farther reaching); again, Dos Passos deleted material from early versions (and that deletion pattern suggests that
he was again trying to stay away from detail that had only personal
relevance). Versions of the Camera Eye 25, re-creation of Dos Passos' Harvard (bellglass) years, illustrate the latter kind of change.
The published version reads,

   those spring nights the streetcar wheels screech grinding
in a rattle of loose trucks round the curved tracks of Harvard
Square dust hangs in the powdery arclight glare allnight till
dawn can't sleep
   haven't got the nerve to break out of the bellglass

In the earlier draft, however, spacing and line indentation played
more significant roles, as Dos Passos referred to authors whose lives
were contrasts to his own during these college years.

   those spring nights the streetcar wheels screech grind-
ing in a rattle of loose trucks round the curved tracks of Har-
vard Square.

   Byron!

Dust hangs in the powdery arclight glare allnight till dawn.

Shelley?

Can't sleep. Dostoyeffski? [sic] *Haven't the nerve to break out of the bellglass,*

  Browning (Paracelsus)

    Coperus (Small Souls)

      Ibsen (Emperor and Gallilean)

        Strindberg (The Dream Play)

          Compton Mackenzie (Youth's Encounter)

What remains of the earlier draft is the cohesive and evocative (and ironic) reminiscence ("grow cold with culture like a cup of tea forgotten" and "all the pleasant contacts will be useful in Later Life say hello pleasantly to everybody crossing the yard"), building to the staggered-line conclusion. In draft, Dos Passos adds specifics that he later deletes, probably because they clutter his tempo. The draft concludes

it was like the Magdeburg spheres the pressure outside
sustained the vacuum within
* and I hadn't the nerve (paralysis)*
* or the intelligence (amnesia)*
* or the knowledge (aphasure)* . . .[42]

whereas the published version reads more simply,

* and I hadn't the nerve*
*   to jump up and walk outofdoors and tell them all to go*
take a flying
* Rimbaud*
*   at the moon.* (42, pp. 311–12)

The verbal effects of enjambement, the differences in line length and arrangement—Dos Passos is playing with groups of words here, in ostensible prose, just as much as any poet ever contrived effects (one is reminded of the close friendship between Cummings and Dos Passos, from Harvard years on). Of interest, too, is the fact that in these Camera Eyes—and many of the others—the persona is the ill-at-ease, advantaged boy who envies tougher and usually uneducated people.

For all the brilliance of the *U.S.A.* novels, for all the innovation of Dos Passos' craft, perhaps the books are related thematically to his earlier work more closely than a casual reading might suggest. For the trilogy that appeared to be a search into American culture had come to include so many elements of the author's own sensibility that they were no less personal than *Streets of Night* or *Three Soldiers*. As Dos Passos himself explained later,

> The basic raw material is everything you've seen and heard and felt, it's your childhood and your education and serving in the army, and travelling in odd places, and finding yourself in odd situations. It is those rare moments of suffering and delight when a man's private sensations are amplified and illuminated by a flash of insight that gives him the certainty that what he is seeing and feeling is what millions of his fellowmen see and feel in the same situation, only heightened. . . .
>
> This sort of universal experience made concrete by the individual's shaping of it, is the raw material of all the imaginative arts. These flashes of insight when strong emotions key all the perceptions up to their highest point are the nuggets of pure gold.[43]

That Dos Passos could use those nuggets to shape a world of recognizable externals and, at the same time, portray a world of deep personal insight was, as Kenneth S. Lynn commented, "the source of our undiminished interest in an amazing career."[44]

Part III
The Late Artist:
Dos Passos as
American Interpreter

7. *District of Columbia*: Mecca or Dis?

Under any system you'll have just as much liberty as people
are willing to make sacrifices for. We certainly have made very
little headway towards any democratic taking over of the ma-
chinery of governmental and industrial bureaucracy: the tradition
does deter men in power from too brutal exercise of their power.
That's not much but it is something. I hope that tradition will set
us on fire for freedom all over again. Dammit a man's got a right
to hope.
—John Dos Passos, 1951

By 1937, the year Dos Passos began work on *Adventures of a Young Man*, his psychological frame of reference had once again been shaken. If we can agree with Dos Passos that the single most important event in his early life had been World War I and the most crucial experience during the 1920s, the Sacco-Vanzetti trial and outcome ("I had seceded privately the night Sacco and Vanzetti were executed"),[1] then it seems plausible that the 1937 death in Spain of his Loyalist friend José Robles—and the mysterious circumstances surrounding it—carried a similarly weighty impact. Robles' death, evidently at the hands of his own party, crystallized many of Dos Passos' already vehement anti-Communist feelings and strengthened his implicit belief in the moral supremacy of a system that championed the individual.

Dos Passos' growing aversion for Communist tenets (and a corresponding enthusiasm for Franklin Delano Roosevelt's version of American democracy) had been evident throughout the 1930s. As he reminisced in *The Theme Is Freedom*, "It was somewhere during the early New Deal that I rejoined the United States."[2] In fact, in 1934 Dos Passos had written to Edmund Wilson, with whom he shared much of his political thinking, that his "benefit-of-the-doubt attitude toward the Stalinists" had evaporated.

From now on events in Russia have no more interest—except as a terrible example. . . . The horrid law of human affairs by which any government must eventually become involved in power for itself, killing for the pleasure of it, self perpetuation for its own sake, has gone into effect.[3]

In 1935, also to Wilson, Dos Passos stated even more clearly, "I personally would prefer the despotism of Henry Ford, the United Fruit and Standard Oil than that of Earl Browder. . . . means can't be disassociated from ends. . . . Whether the Stalinist performances are intellectually justifiable or not, they are alienating the working class movement of the world. What's the use of losing your 'chains' if you get a firing squad instead?"[4]

In 1937, however, because of his commitment to the preservation of human rights, Dos Passos joined with Hemingway, Lillian Hellman, Archibald MacLeish, and Dutch (but Communist) director Joris Ivens to produce The Spanish Earth, a film about Loyalist Spain to be shown at money-raising benefits in the States. Once he was in Madrid, Dos Passos discovered that Robles had been arrested late in 1936 for unknown causes and that he had obviously been executed. Dos Passos' outrage at this senseless death was in definite contrast to the attitude of other Americans, who were content to allow the situation to fade into oblivion. After all, Robles was only one person; the total picture of the war to end oppression was the important consideration. As Dos Passos recalled the situation in "Spain: Rehearsal for Defeat,"

It wasn't till I got to Madrid that I learned from the chief of the republican counterespionage service that my friend had been executed by a "special section." He added that in his opinion the execution had been a mistake and that it was too bad. Spaniards closer to the communists I talked to said that the man had been shot as an example to other officials because he had been overheard indiscreetly discussing military plans in a café . . . Some of my associates in the documentary film project were disgusted with me for making all these inquiries. What's one man's life at a time like this? We mustn't let our personal feelings run away with us. But how in the world, I asked them, are you to tell what's going on except by personal experience? Sacco and Vanzetti were each just one man. Isn't justice one of the things we are trying to establish?[5]

Dos Passos' 1939 letter to The New Republic, which tries to correct an impression suggested by Malcolm Cowley, restates many of these points and recalls Dos Passos' anger in 1934 (again in *The New Republic*) when he feared that Cowley had jeopardized the safety of artist Luis Quintanilla by using confidential information. In that rebuff, Dos Passos said tersely, "After all a man's life is all he's got,"[6] a sentiment that was to underlie much of his later philosophy. If idealistic principles could not protect the lives and properties of individual human beings, they were worthless.

Two of Dos Passos' 1937 essays from *Common Sense* repeat that insistence. As he writes in the July "Farewell to Europe," the only real promise for the future lies in the United States and its political system:

> Not all the fascist-headed newspaper owners in the country, nor the Chambers of Commerce, nor the armies of hired gun-thugs of the great industries can change the fact that we have the Roundhead Revolution in our heritage and the Bill of Rights and the fact that democracy has been able, under Jefferson, Jackson, and Lincoln, and perhaps a fourth time (it's too soon to know yet) under Franklin Roosevelt, to curb powerful ruling groups.[7]

Without powerful ruling groups, individuals might reach some stage of self-determination. As he wrote in December 1937, "In my opinion the one hope for the future of the type of western civilization which furnishes the frame of our lives is that the system of popular government based on individual liberty be not allowed to break down."[8] Philosophically emphasizing the convictions that had already permeated his fiction was but another stage in the development of Dos Passos' disillusionment, which finally appeared without equivocation in *Adventures of a Young Man*. The bitterness of his mood during the late 1930s is clear from both the novel and his 1939 letter about the Robles murder:

> This is only one story among thousands in the vast butchery that was the Spanish Civil War, but it gives us a glimpse into the bloody tangle of ruined lives that underlay the hurrah for our side aspects. Understanding the personal histories of a few of the men, women and children really involved would I think free our minds somewhat from the black is black and white is white obsessions of partisanship.[9]

Dos Passos' insistence on the importance of the single person is germane to both his political beliefs (which are consistently against any ideology that promotes the well-being of the group rather than the person) and his artistic creed (which stresses reaching universals through particular characters, scenes, images). It also reflects what Alfred Kazin had seen as a pervasive interest in character throughout his writing, not the proletarian character and his outcome, but the "solitary": "The loner in America interested Dos Passos long before he became interested in the American as protestor."[10]

No matter how bleak his personal outlook, however, Dos Passos reacted to these years of tension in his characteristically positive way, by once again beginning a search for meaningful values and stability. If foreign philosophies supplied only partial answers and if present-day American culture was not entirely satisfactory, then he would explore earlier America. "I'm trying to take a course in American history," he wrote to Fitzgerald in 1936.[11] Another comment to Fitzgerald, from a brief trip abroad: "I'd hate to stay away from the U.S. long these days. Things seem a darn sight more live and kicking there than anywhere else in the world—my main pleasure now is just driving around the roads and looking at the damned American continent."[12] True to his enthusiasm, in 1937 Dos Passos and his wife Katy began their serious travels through the country, traveling that was to evoke his later comment to Hillyer, "My this is a big untidy soulstirring country we live in. I feel myself continually tortured by curiosity about it.'[13] These trips by car that were to furnish material for Dos Passos' 1943 series of "People of War" portraits for *Harper's*, as well as for *State of the Nation* and the prose-poems in *Number One* and other later fiction, played a significant part in Dos Passos' accurate understanding of the American people and culture from the late 1930s through the war years and probably added concrete personal identification to his intensive reading and research into American history.

The importance of his self-designed "course in American history" is obvious in both his later fiction and the nonfiction books that were the immediate products of his studies, *The Living Thoughts of Tom Paine* and *The Ground We Stand On*, as well as the near-dozen later books of either social commentary or history. (Dos Passos called them "historical narratives'—*The Head and Heart of Thomas Jefferson* and *The Ground We Stand On*—or "travel narratives'—which included *State of the Nation* and *The Prospect Before Us* as well as books on particular places. His use of the word "narrative" suggests that the storytelling element was still dominant, even if these books were based on factual information.) Besides

Paine, Dos Passos' subjects in his first foray into writing about historical figures were Roger Williams, Benjamin Franklin, Daniel Defoe, Samuel Adams, Thomas Jefferson, Joel Barlow, Alexander Hamilton, and H. H. Brackenridge. In each case, Dos Passos saw the man as having somehow accomplished an inordinate amount during his life, at least partly because of the environment in which he chose to live it. The portraits Dos Passos creates are of the person in the context of America; in fact, he contrasts Defoe with Franklin to show that the British environment was more restrictive:

> Americans had man for man more opportunity for growth and development than their blood relations in the crowded British Isles where every man's life was hedged into established paths by deeprooted privileges and interests. It was as if the air the Americans breathed were fresher and more lifegiving. . . .
>
> It is hard to overestimate the advantage Americans in the eighteenth century had in growing up with only the sky over their heads. The slumlife of London cramped and warped the great men of the rising business class in England like a ghetto. When they rose above their station it was only by conforming to all the preconceived deformations of the ruling squirarchy.[14]

At the heart of Dos Passos' comparison of the two cultures, obviously, is his enthusiasm for the concepts and attitudes of democracy, with special emphasis on the equality of humankind. Roger Williams, with his vision of religious freedom, therefore becomes for Dos Passos one of the most important early Americans, in that he helped the colonists to break with those firmly established patterns of British thinking. Ben Franklin, "who remained, as an American, all his life free from the sense of social classification,"[15] also profited from that freedom to follow his own inclinations and abilities, whether in science, writing, or politics. Joel Barlow's insistence on freedom to educate people in these "republican institutions" spoke well to the point, as did Thomas Jefferson's instructions that "politics" was worth studying only insofar as it influenced "the happiness of the people." What Dos Passos found in his study of these different people was a collective appreciation for variance and for a system that bound loosely enough to allow that variance.

He also saw these men as having the capacity both to think and to act. Never mere rhetoricians, for all their abilities with words,

Dos Passos' heroes were also men of physical action. As he wrote of Tom Paine, "the word and the deed were always very close with Paine";[16] and he chose as preface to the long essay on Roger Williams his own testimony, ". . . I know what it is to study, to preach, to be an elder, to be applauded and yet also what it is to tug at the oar, to dig with the spade, and plow, and to labor and travel day and night amongst the English and amongst the barbarians" (p. 22). Action was crucial, not only during the early days of the country; Dos Passos also, however, insisted on a certain kind of action, moral action geared not toward any selfish end but toward the betterment of American life. This "intellectual and moral tone" was the legacy of Jefferson, Franklin, Monroe, Adams, and Washington; it is that quality that Dos Passos seems to mourn in this earliest journey into history and its heroes. As he had said in the prefatory essay, as if in explanation of his own absorption in the past,

> Every generation rewrites the past. In easy times history is more or less of an ornamental art, but in times of danger we are driven to the written record by a pressing need to find answers to the riddles of today. We need to know what kind of firm ground other men . . . have found to stand on. (p. 3)

The Ground We Stand On was one attempt to locate that position and to translate its qualities into language appropriate to twentieth-century American readers. It was also an important step toward Dos Passos' evolving concept that a piece of writing should express some "firmly anchored ethical standard . . . [an] unshakable moral attitude toward the world we live in and toward its temporary standards."[17] That this attitude differed from the modernist tenet that an author was primarily a recorder, an observer, accounts in part for the shift in Dos Passos' writing from a mode of presentation, paralleling rapportage, to a mode of near-didacticism, more akin to instruction. Some of the differences between the *District of Columbia* novels and those of the *U.S.A.* trilogy stem from this shift in basic definition of the authorial role.

The changes in Dos Passos' writing after *U.S.A.*, then, appear to have evolved from his process of using his own experiences to "prove" his philosophical concepts. As he became less and less receptive to communism, his fascination with America—both present and past—intensified. Yet his being more genuinely pro-American did not blind him to the traits that angered and dismayed him: he never stopped criticizing power structures, whether they existed in business, unions, or government. Dos Passos' interest and sympathy remained with the individual and his or her chances—or lack of them—of finding happiness.

From the late 1930s on, each of Dos Passos' books confirms his interest in the loner, the independent or alienated American that Kazin had found important even to his early fiction. In *Adventures of a Young Man*, this emphasis is clear: Glenn Spotswood tries to live a good life, with an aim beyond financial prosperity. His readiness to believe high-sounding ideology, however, blunts his perceptions; and the notion of "brotherhood"—whether within or outside the Communist party—lures him to his bitter death. From the opening of the novel Spotswood's naive idealism gains the reader's sympathy:

> . . . what he really wanted to be doing was beat his way around the country living like working people lived. The whitecollar class was all washed up. It was in the working class that real things were happening nowadays. The real thing was the new social order that was being born out of the working class. Of course, some things had been real, there had been a girl named Gladys. But gosh, it was hard to keep your life from getting all balled up. What he'd decided was to hell with your private life. He'd live for the working class. That was real.[18]

Even though his good friend, Paul Graves (who has not abandoned private life, being married and a father) tells Glenn that his philosophy is all "hot air and came from associating with longhaired men and shorthaired girls up there in Greenwich Village," Spotswood continues his "adventures" and—like Don Quixote—continues to meet only failure. Relying on other people's judgments, as he tends to do, is disastrous. Like him, most other Americans have forgotten what Dos Passos feels are necessities, as the opening prose-poem states:

> *We had forgotten*
> *the anguish of emigrant ships,*
> *the hunger and strained muscles, the shirt soaked with*
> *sweat, the twang of the broadaxe and the blue smoke of brush-*
> *fires . . .*
> *the forest, the fear, the hostiles unseen behind treetrunks,*
> *the words spelled out of the Book by the firelight, the search*
> *for the still inner voice . . .* (p. 2)

Points of origin, roots, acknowledgment of sources—the American people need information before they can come to understanding. The Glenn Spotswood story is a pathetic illustration of the kind of well-meant but misdirected idealism Dos Passos spoke of in "The Use of the Past": "The history of the political notions of American intellectuals during the twentieth century is largely a record of how far the fervor of their hopes of a better world could blind them to the realities under their noses."[19] Spotswood's "hope" is genuine; but his actions are, ultimately, ineffectual. Worse, they harm others —the Mexican farm laborers who work for four cents an hour and the miners of the Muddy Fork local, particularly Pearl Napier. In Napier's case, the result of Spotswood's "help" is death.

In his 1944 *State of the Nation*, Dos Passos identifies himself with the same kind of Spotswood optimism. In the preface to that group of essays, he stresses again the unpreparedness of most Americans; yet his "conclusion" is cheerfully, if unreasonably, positive. "The test finds us far from ready to meet it. We haven't the leadership, the education, the theoretical background or the political formula we need. Still, in defiance of historical logic, I believe we are going to meet it" (p. 2). It was this consistent attitude that forced Edmund Wilson to write much later to Dos Passos, after he had espoused what Wilson saw as basically conservative politics, "I really don't think you are well equipped for this moral political editorializing."[20]

Yet Dos Passos had clearly intended *Adventures* to be a "completely new departure" for the course of his fiction.[21] Not only had he written Stewart Mitchell as early as 1935 that, once *The Big Money* was finished, he intended to write using only "simple declarative sentences, composed only of Anglo-Saxon words";[22] he also had described the Glenn Spotswood story so that the moral dilemma of the character was obviously a result of his American rearing:

> Adventures of a Young Man is the first of a series of contemporary portraits in the shape of stories. Glenn Spotswood has been raised in the tradition of American idealism. He suffers from a congenital sense of right and wrong. He grows up alone in the world of the twenties and thirties. He has a tough time.[23]

The story is assuredly Glenn's. By using a picaresque structure for *Adventures*, Dos Passos is able to keep Spotswood at the center of the narrative and still include many kinds of episodes. The most important are the stories of the Kentucky miners, of urban, liberal intellectuals like the Gulicks, and of the Spanish Civil War. In each case, the rhetoric says one thing; people's actions convey the opposite. Spotswood is repeatedly the victim of the discrepancy, yet his ideology does not change. By using an episodic narrative, Dos Passos also can include many different characters, most of them foils to Spotswood's naivete and many illustrative of the dangers of easy or fashionable thinking. Usually liberal, these peripheral characters are less than free despite their talk about freedom; and Spotswood's developing convictions are impressive in contrast with the malaise that Dos Passos presents as characteristic almost everywhere else in the book.

Through the entire novel, however, runs the consistent condemnation of the American Communist party. Expedient, interested only in its own well-being (and usually sensual satisfaction), callous about the deaths of mere workers, the party has no redeeming traits in *Adventures of a Young Man*. Other philosophies are presented and undermined in the course of the book, but none comes in for such devastation as communism. After the publication of *Adventures*, that any reader could have thought Dos Passos even slightly interested in the movement seems implausible.

Dos Passos keeps the duplicity of the party before the reader through a chain of events and also through Spotswood's continued affirmation of belief:

> he remembered the quiet lowering beaten look of the Mexicans on the pavement in front of the courthouse all looking one way at the cars going by full of hooded men, all looking one way without any expression like a bunch of cattle in a field staring at a stranger.
> "By God, Jed, we've got to do something to stop this kind of thing." (p. 178)

Several obvious betrayals later, Spotswood (although no longer a party member) repeats, "I still believe in the workingclass" (p. 299). And, finally, bereft of all party connection and personal dignity, he begins a mock will that ironically continues the travesty of belief (a travesty heightened because, for Spotswood, the words are literally true): "I, Glenn Spotswood, being of sound mind and emprisoned body, do bequeath to the international workingclass my hope of a better world. . ." (p. 337).

As he had in *U.S.A.*, Dos Passos uses the prose-poems that open each chapter to reinforce the moral intention of the narrative. The last prose-poem repeats the theme of the opening, that of American naivete, of being ill-prepared, of having forgotten

> *our primer of liberties:*
> *that every right entails a duty*
> *that free institutions cost high*
> *in vigilance,*
> *selfdenial . . .*
> *and that the freedom of one class of people cannot be gained*
> *at the expense of the enslavement of another; . . .*
> *and that only a people suspicious of selfserving*
> *exhortations, willing to risk decisions, each man making his*
> *own,*
> *dare call themselves free, and that when we say the people,*
> *we don't mean the proletariat or the salariat or the managerial*
> *class or the members of the fraternal order or a political party,*
> *or the right-thinking readers of editorials in liberal or reac-*
> *tionary newspapers;*
> *we mean every suffering citizen,*
> *and more particularly*
> *you and me.* (p. 342)

Number One, the second novel in the *District of Columbia* trilogy, was an exposé of the machinations of Huey Long (Chuck Crawford), governor of Louisiana whose misuse of power was already notorious. When *Number One* was published in 1943, Dos Passos had already written *The Ground We Stand On* and the introduction for the Paine collection and had begun the biography of Thomas Jefferson. What the example of Long was to show, at least in part, was the failure of the personal responsibility that *Adventures* stressed, failure in that only because so many citizens had abandoned the notion of responsibility could politicians like Long stay in office.

Crawford's rise to power is shown through the eyes of Tyler Spotswood, Glenn's older and more wary, but already corrupted, brother. Originally the victim of his own enthusiasm for Chuck Crawford ("Number One"), Tyler is to learn that Crawford is completely amoral ("He hasn't a thought in the world except for himself").[24] Crawford cares nothing for the feelings of his wife, his staff, his colleagues, or his constituents. He wants only power and plenty of sensual satisfaction (an index, as Dos Passos uses it, of some kind of personal corruption, especially in the forties when so much of national importance was at stake). Once Tyler begins to recognize the level of Crawford's ethics, he finds himself facing "sour darkness." And the chicanery of the State Park Bottoms deal, with its attendant rites of debauchery and sex, begins the climactic revelation for Tyler, as Crawford not only sells him out, but then speaks directly to the American people about his own innocence. Like the shrewd politician he is, Crawford turns other people's hardships to his personal advantage.

The new theme that Dos Passos explores in this, the most simple novel of the trilogy, is that the concept of the individual's worth must be at all times balanced with the concept of collective good. *Responsibility* is the key word for the wise citizen. Rather than identifying the powerful citizen as "Number One"—as his staff has identified Crawford—each person must come to realize, as Tyler finally does, that his or her rights are primary. Each person must consider himself "Number One." As Tyler meditates from his all-too-customary alcoholic fog, "We can't sell out on the people, but the trouble is that me, I'm just as much the people as you are or any other son of a bitch. If we want to straighten the people out we've got to start with number one, not that big wind . . . You know what I mean. I got to straighten myself out first, see" (p. 242). What has prompted Tyler's realization is not only Crawford's betrayal, but also the last letter from Glenn before his death in Spain. Coming finally to majority, Glenn impresses his older, cynical brother with his simple stability, as he speaks of the need for real experience before making important decisions and of his mature recognition that he can do without "party labels." "Getting the liver and lights scared out of me regularly once a day fills me with respect and tenderness for every man, woman and child I see, for anything that is alive" (p. 229).

The chief point in Glenn's letter is that actions are the only accurate means of judging people and situations; that words are, finally, inadequate (and Dos Passos plays with this mistrust of language throughout the trilogy, using it in *Number One* for comic effect by quoting long sections of Crawford's homey, flatulent rhetoric); that the true politician will keep democracy alive so that people will be able to both exist happily and to learn and change as circumstances change:

> Tyler, what I'd started to write you about was not letting
> them sell out too much of the for the people and by the peo-

ple part of the oldtime United States way. It has given us freedom to grow. Growing great people is what the country's for,
isn't it? So long as the growth of people to greater stature all
around is what we want more than anything, it will keep
on. (p. 230)

"Growing great people" can only make Tyler reflect—sadly—on his
colleagues and himself; and as he defies Ed James' urging to sell
Crawford out for a lucrative magazine deal, he remembers Glenn's
injunction, "After all it's what you do that counts, not what you say.
One thing I've learned in my life is that everything every one of us
does counts."

Tyler ends his connection with Crawford with a small measure of
honor and serves Dos Passos well as one of the representative Americans who figure in each of the chapter's prose-poems,

> When you try to find the people always in the end it
> comes down to somebody,
>   somebody working, maybe:
>   a man alone on an old disk harrow . . . (p. 1)

—a particular individual, a genuine person, the collection of many
of whom create the mass, population, "people," constituency. But
the accumulation is of single faces ("As they flow in a packed mass
out the gate . . . you begin to make out differences in faces. . . . As
the crowd reaches the sidewalk, it dissolves suddenly into brisk individuals").[25] The generality, people, does not exist except as a composite of individuals. Stressed in each of the prose-poems for Number One, the relation of the single person to a collective identity
comprises Dos Passos' closing section as well: "the people is everybody / and one man alone . . . each life taut in the net of lives . . .
weak as the weakest, strong as the strongest" (p. 248). Indicative
of Dos Passos' disappointment with at least parts of the American
experiment is the fact that much of his writing in the District of
Columbia trilogy illustrated the "weak as the weakest" side of the
balance.

Moving from a historical perspective that had found America's
earliest politicians—many of them—to be altruistic and idealistic,
Dos Passos would have been particularly concerned about the
abuses of a Huey Long/Chuck Crawford; and perhaps even more
worried about an uninterested public that allowed such abuses to
continue. As he wrote in 1944 in State of the Nation,

Whether this nation is going to continue to develop as a
selfgoverning community ruled by laws that depend on the
people's consent or whether it is going to be sucked back under
that rule by the club of a boss and his gang . . . depends on the
behavior of every American citizen alive today. . . . Miracles
only happen when enough people want them to happen.
(pp. 1–2)

"Every American citizen," in fact, gives Dos Passos the structure
as well as the theme for his book. *State of the Nation is* its people,
a collection of vignettes and profiles about the Americans that Dos
Passos had met in his travels through the states. There are ship
builders from Maine, an Alabama bus driver, an efficiency expert,
a Detroit piano player, southern farmers–white and black, Texas
migrant workers, a Washington streetcar checker, striking coal miners, servicemen, Iowa farmers–all of them puzzled about the "state
of the nation," but generally hopeful. That Dos Passos found in
these people much to admire is clear both from his treatment in
the essays and in his observation to Wilson that he had seen

more attractive and interesting people in the space of a
few months than I'd seen in years and came back with considerable confidence in the ability of younger and less important Americans to cope with the terrific problems that face us
everywhere. . . . Taken up in detail things are not at all discouraging. . . . But now when I get back and see more of the
overall political picture, I feel appalled again.[26]

What Dos Passos is able to achieve through his method of juxtaposing one profile with the next–presenting one person and showing his or her attitudes, then moving on to the next seemingly random choice–is an authenticity that his fictional characters sometimes lack. By relying on his impartial presentation of this gallery of
Americans, he implies his own willingness to define the state of the
nation in terms of its citizenry; and reaffirms Glenn Spotswood's
notion that "growing great people" is the primary duty of the country. His method also gives credence to his prefatory comment that
American democracy is great because "the ordinary run of men here
have had a better chance to develop and to live their lives as they
wanted to than during any other period we know about anywhere
else in the world" (p. 2).

In *The Grand Design*, the third novel of the *District of Columbia*
trilogy, Dos Passos brings his fictional focus to that "ordinary run

of men" presented so vividly in *State of the Nation*. Both Millard Carroll and Paul Graves, new members of Roosevelt's New Deal farm team, are common citizens with stable, humane value systems. Carroll, one of the few characters new to the trilogy, gives up running his own manufacturing business in the West to go to Washington as a member of Walker Watson's farm division because "we owe something to the country. . . . I might be able to help out."[27] Paul Graves, after spending several years in Russia, decides to devote his expertise as an agricultural scientist to American economy (his reminiscence of life in Russia was a part of the conversation between Glenn Spotswood and himself in *Adventures*). Both Graves and Carroll are dedicated men, happily married and devoted to their wives and children; their role in the novel is to represent the (small) element of Roosevelt's bureaucracy that was altruistic. The only narrative suspense that the years of *The Grand Design* can offer, so far as these men and their families are concerned, is whether or not the strain and uncertainty of the government position will break them, physically or mentally. In essence, *The Grand Design* is a story of ruin, the price in "great people" necessary to fuel Roosevelt's plans; and Dos Passos' most interesting characters illustrate what he views as a common modern tragedy.

Although the novel begins and ends with attention to the Carrolls and the Graveses, one of the most compelling personalities is that of their superior, Walker Watson. In Dos Passos' portrayal of Watson's megalomania, we sense the real cost of the gamble for power. Surfeit with platitudes that are ironic echoes of the convictions of Carroll and Graves, Watson relies for his personal guidance on the astrological predictions of Madame Arno and memories of the wisdom of his "little old mother." Dining on milk toast, heavily drugged, Watson cannot survive losing his nomination for vice president under Roosevelt; his abusive outburst when the choice is made reveals the depths of his instability. In an earlier *State of the Nation* essay titled "The Punishment," Dos Passos had outlined this kind of character and his eventual, dramatic decline:

> His hands and face were floury white. His cheeks had deep hollows in them and the skin round his eyes had the bruised look of sleeplessness. . . . As he pulled himself up to shake hands I hardly recognized the sturdy reserved man of slow decisive speech I had last seen a few months before. . . . Shaking his head as if to shake loose some painful tangle of thoughts he said that the main trouble was he couldn't seem to get to sleep any more; he was only getting two hours' sleep a night and

that, combined with being hammered by the congressional committee all day, was wearing him down. (pp. 158–59)

The symptoms of depression that Dos Passos presents here are more vividly drawn in *The Grand Design* where Watson's erratic decline, both moral and physical, shadows everyone in his department and creates corresponding anxiety for his subordinates, especially Carroll and Graves.

These three characters are the sympathetic protagonists of the novel (though Graves' casual affair with Georgia Washburn darkens his character, and what seems to be exoneration, his real grief after her death, does not quite convince). Many other characters are drawn negatively, however, especially the Red sympathizers and party members. "I learned that you had to hate the fascists so bad you enjoyed killing them . . . in my spare time I used to go out huntin' fascists like shootin' birds down home, except that I hated the fascists an' enjoyed seein' 'em die" (p. 393)–Jed Farrington's gleeful discussion of his role in Spain sets the tone for the philosophies of many of these characters. Whether the flaw is outright evil or depravity (as in the case of Winthrop Strang, whom Dos Passos pictures as a homosexual) or unthinking opportunism (as in the case of the Gulicks), most people have strayed far from the label of "great American," although the term is used in *The Grand Design*, ironically, to refer to Watson. And as the novel shows so clearly, most people succumb to the machinations of ambition, even Franklin D. Roosevelt:

> At the desk in the White House in front of the brightlit globe
> sat an aging man, an ill man, a cripple who had no time
> to ponder history or to find the Danube or the Baltic or Vienna
> on the map: so many documents to sign, so many interviews
> with Very Important Personages, such gloss on the young men:
> 'Yes Mr. President,' 'No Mr. President.' The decisions were his.
> He could play on a man like a violin. Virtuoso. By the modulations of his voice into the microphone he played on the American people. We danced to his tune. Third Term.
> War is a time of Caesars. (p. 417)

As in this image, *The Grand Design* continues to emphasize the dangers of rhetoric. Dos Passos' epigraph to the first chapter is "A man of words and not of deeds / Is like a garden full of weeds," and much of this story of the complicated, and complicating, bureaucracy under Roosevelt is punctuated with phrases from "Fireside

Chats" and other political speeches. The chief quality of the language used in those remarks is innocuous reassurance ("social values more noble than mere monetary profit," "leadership in these critical days"). One of the key interrelating characters—Herbert Spotswood—is crucial to the development of this theme. Glenn and Tyler's father has become a lion of Washington society in his role of radio commentator, a new kind of word manipulator. Influential at sixty after years of ignominy, the aging Spotswood grasps for exactly the same thing Chuck Crawford did—personal power and sensual gratification. Much of the novel concerns the travesty of Spotswood's influential position. His judgments are ill-founded (he has no comprehension, for example, of either of his sons' lives and thinks Glenn died in Spain for "a good cause"). His relations with people are hypocritical; he is so absorbed in his own self-image that he ignores Tyler, who needs him desperately. Even his position as news commentator has resulted from his technical skill rather than from his knowledge. His explanation as he begins his new broadcast position makes clear both his shrewdness and his understanding of the popular mind:

> Now I'm going to get a better spot, fifteen minutes of comment on the European news, the threat of war, the Hitlerite insanity. It's not so easy as it sounds. I've had to give myself a regular course in elocution. . . . speaking on the air the problems are rather different. It's not a question of being heard in a hall, you are talking to each man individually. Proper delivery has been the secret of the President's magic. I've studied him from disks. . . . I talk into this recording machine and it spouts my words back at me so that I can hear how they sound. . . . There are programs I've repeated thirty times before I was satisfied. (p. 90)

As this description suggests, the character of Herb Spotswood serves a purpose more important than as a means of connecting plot lines within the three novels. For Spotswood's career illustrates graphically the American tendency to rely on authority (here, a literal "voice"), and it is that tendency that increasingly alarmed Dos Passos:

> We read the newspapers. We listened to the radio. On
> commuters' trains our eyes followed the close columns of
> print. At breakfast we set down our coffeecups to listen
>   to voices
>   in the know

at the front
at headquarters
who had it from the very highest authority
that the old bad world from which our fathers fled . . .
London Bridge is falling down . . . falling down
(We were weak in geography. . . . We were weak in history,
We hadn't any use for history. History was
over. History was what our fathers came over steerage
to get away from. . . .

London Bridge . . .
But now we read the papers . . . is falling down
(pp. 113–14).

Dos Passos' consistent fears are captured in these few lines and in passages on pp. 387–88, as well as throughout the novel. *The Grand Design* is a novel about the susceptibility of Americans, about the power of the American language, and about the loss of American promise. And it is the resolution of the themes begun in *U.S.A.*, a more complete expression of the issue that Dos Passos even then saw as central.

David Sanders reminds us that the three books of *U.S.A.* had in manuscript been titled *Course of Empire*, *New Nation*, and *New Era*,[28] suggesting that the underlying philosophy was part of Dos Passos' motivation for writing the earlier trilogy. The titles would have been more applicable to the *District of Columbia* books, but the suggestion of an affirmative progression no longer worked. For as Dos Passos studied the practice of American democratic principles and their locus of execution in Washington, District of Columbia, a geographic area designated specifically to the administration of government, he became increasingly discouraged about the promise of his "Ship of State." He could give only ironic answers in the concluding sections of the last novel, under the title "The Power and the Glory." As the end of *The Grand Design* shows, there is little of either power or glory.

As the concluding novel of the trilogy, *The Grand Design* brings together many characters from the earlier two books—not only the Spotswoods but also Paul Graves, Jerry Evans, Jed Farrington, Irving Silverstone, Dr. Jane Sparling, Mark Burgess, Elmer Weeks, Ed James, the Gulicks, and others—and manages, in a set of coincidences less contrived than juxtapositions in *Manhattan Transfer*, to effect a reasonable conclusion for the bitter Spotswood chronicle.

Born and reared, as they had been, in Washington, both Glenn and

Tyler had as children lived with a sense of promise ("I used to see the dome of the Capitol at the end of an avenue of trees in the fall . . . high above the clouds"[29]); and perhaps their disillusion was all the sharper for that early familiarity. In the respect that the Spotswoods are the native Washingtonians, then, the trilogy is their story; for much of Dos Passos' interest is on the role the city—as an emblem for the American philosophy—plays in the governing process. Just as early in the century New York was the imaginative center of promise for many people, so Washington became the focus during the Depression and World War II: Dos Passos' picture of Washington at the height of New Deal bureaucracy is, thus, an embittered one of the city as "tar baby . . . You try to give it a kick and your foot gets stuck and you try to give it a punch and your fist gets stuck and you try to back off and butt it with your head and . . ."[30] Herb Spotswood's triumphal return—especially after Glenn's death and Tyler's imprisonment—is only another index of the city's instability. With his return, narratively, the circle is complete; as readers we know that opportunists can predict and use patterns of change. To the shrewd go the spoils, "the corruption of power," and Dos Passos has drawn a particularly effective paradigm of that corruption with *The Grand Design*.

In many ways, this third novel is more like *Manhattan Transfer* than like the earlier two books of the trilogy because Dos Passos had predicated his censure of the bureaucracy on the grounds that it has little reason for being. Its existence per se is its evil, just as the only actual evil in New York was the pressure of the urban structure. As Dos Passos describes the mushrooming of Roosevelt's staff,

> millionheaded multitude of multifarious needs linked
> into chains of businesses, trades, skills, occupations, trusts,
> cooperatives, combines,
> to make up the shape of the nation. (p. 24)

What had begun as a helpful force, an attempt to get "professionals" involved in policymaking, ended as travesty, with many of the professionals themselves the waste products: "They were packed into bureaus and offices, two at a desk, four and five at a table in conference rooms; some worked on folding chairs and cardtables in corridors. When the offices closed they hurriedly ate and went home and sat smoking in their shirtsleeves in hotel rooms" (p. 24). And, as the novel so carefully delineates, even the good decisions were blunted by the ridiculous number of staff levels they had to survive in order to go into operation. Very little was accomplished; even though Paul Graves' views on preserving the family-sized farm were perspicacious, no means of implementing them was ever executed. Men's capabilities were worn away on the treadmill of indecision and rancor; Roosevelt's customary tactic to get action was the simple one,

> to appoint a new administrator, arbitrator, coordinator,
> to improvise a commission, to implement an agency, to draft
> a directive
> or to request new powers from Congress. (p. 25)

Washington in the Roosevelt years had become a nightmare of well-trained and would-be-helpful people, caught in a morass of petty self-promotion and indecision: like the younger Spotswoods, Dos Passos was chagrined, appalled, at the waste inherent in the administrative system. In a late essay he speaks of his "considerable distress of mind" when he realized "the nature of the defeat my country had suffered in the aftermath of the second world war." Washington had become an echo of his 1925 Manhattan.

Much of the material in *The Grand Design* has a factual basis in Dos Passos' essays from the 1944 *State of the Nation*. Once again the writer works from what he had discovered as fact in his travels and interviews, given one kind of shape in the journalistic writing he called "travel narratives," and then changed in the substantiation of character and character interaction for a novel. *The Grand Design* is, in many ways, the best of the three books; part of its ability to convince comes from the scaffolding of fact that Dos Passos had accumulated—in method not unlike Hemingway's iceberg principle. In *State of the Nation*, he summarizes another kind of risk that the new bureaucrats ran, that of being slandered and rejected should they maintain their independence. If a person was somehow protected by a group sharing his interests, he was a ready victim for the acquisitive groups already in existence. As one jaundiced Washingtonian tells Dos Passos:

> Look at your idealist. Look what happens to him. He
> comes down here in the public interest. That's what he thinks,
> anyway. If he has any brains he's probably had theories and
> spouted them around at some time of his life. The Dies com-
> mittee gets on his trail. Right away he's a red. Maybe he's been
> a tulip fancier or gone in swimming without any clothes on.
> He's a nudist. The Kerr committee makes him miserable dig-
> ging up his past. He either runs to cover and stops trying to do

anything or else his boss puts him in cold storage. He's not a party man. Say he's just out to save the American people some money. The first time anybody needs to be fed to the wolves, out he goes on his fanny. What comeback has he? A letter to the *Nation*. (p. 225)

In contrast, the person who has vested interests protecting him or her survives the melee much more easily: "If he's a real conspiratorial Communist the party protects him. . . . If he's a crook he's got partners in crime. An unattached individual citizen has no more chance than a man trying to fight a tank with a croquet mallet."

For Dos Passos, convinced as he was that any promise for the future of the country rested with individual action, the lesson was discouraging. His disappointment with American government was abetted during these years by the grief of his personal life–the tragedy of his beloved wife Katy's death in 1947 and the loss of his eye in the same accident, coupled with the omnipresent act that his writing hardly supported him, no matter how much or what he wrote. Considering his personal depression during the postwar years, it comes as little surprise that the exuberant promise of the early trilogy–whether expressed through Glenn Spotswood's idealism or the irony of Crawford's "Every Man a Millionaire" campaign song–would dwindle into a picture of a morass of disappointed people and deflated dreams, whose sentiments are captured vividly in the speech of one American factory worker:

The workin' man's got to stick together.
The international workin' class, tell me that's where I swear my oath of allegiance.

I'm willin' to take a chance on it, Mister. A workin' man's got to be a citizen of someplace, even if it's Hell itself. (p. 98)

8. The Search for an American Hero

*The troubles that arise between a man and his friends are often
purely and simply the result of growing up. People who continue
to be happy together, a man and his wife, say, manage to culti-
vate between themselves a private region of perpetual childhood.*
–John Dos Passos, *The Best Times*

The *District of Columbia* trilogy is more important to Dos Passos'
development as a writer than might be readily apparent. In these
three novels he had presented his materials as simply and clearly
as he could, exchanging modernist objectivity for a presentation
that was more directive, even charged. There was no longer any
question about the moral stances of the characters or of their auth-
or's opinions of those respective stances. The moralistic mode colored both attitude and style; as Dos Passos later wrote to Edmund
Wilson,

> You complain of my use of "right" and "wrong." As a
> result of the somewhat varied experiences of a longish life
> I've come to believe–with Jefferson and the eighteenth century
> people–that these terms represent something definite in the
> human makeup–part of the equipment for survival built
> up over generations. . . .[1]

That Dos Passos' new moralistic method might have been more
appropriate for a philosophical prolegomenon than a fictional chronicle caused him little concern. The change had resulted because of
his personal urgency to do what he could to avert the national disaster that seemed to him imminent. Dos Passos continued writing
until his death in 1970 at least partly because he believed he *could*
effect some kind of change. His comment to Stewart Mitchell in
1956 is characteristic:

> The gears of self government just don't mesh into the ma-
> chinery of government. Even so I'm not ready to "curse God
> and die." That doesn't mean that they can't be made to mesh.

... Of course it's much easier to throw up the sponge with Justice Holmes and say "God damn them all"—but where would physics be if Newton had had that attitude towards his everlasting apple, or Einstein towards his long pages of mathematical symbols?[2]

The despair that permeates the *District of Columbia* novels indicates on the one hand Dos Passos' displeasure with his country during the 1940s; on the other, it suggests that he will take definite steps to locate the reasons for his displeasure and to devise some means of correcting what he sees as problems. Once again, Dos Passos' writing helps to clarify his ideas.

Dos Passos' writing career does, in fact, fall into divisions that roughly parallel his work on the various trilogies, both *District of Columbia* and *U.S.A.* and the earlier writing that culminates in *Manhattan Transfer* (at least one critic has seen *One Man's Initiation*, *Three Soldiers*, and *Manhattan Transfer* as a "trilogy").[3] As Dos Passos worked his way through the war novels and the New York novel, he was convinced that "know thyself" would suffice and that if the abuse of power in either a military or a corporate structure would not allow for self-determination, then a person had the option to leave. Because John Andrews fails to understand this premise early enough, he becomes a victim of the military machine; Jimmy Herf, however, even though he loses Ellen, does make it successfully out of New York—and the implication of the close of *Manhattan Transfer* is that Herf alone has some chance of survival.

Characters in *The 42nd Parallel* also operate under that assumption, led by the biographies of heroic people who went in private directions, often with an eye to the public good but without any intention of conforming. As we have seen, however, by the end of *U.S.A.*, the change in the character of Vag showed Dos Passos' disillusion with that premise of self-sufficiency. Throughout *U.S.A.* he explored the possibilities that actually existed for fruition of the individual American dream; but his narrative method suggested that the means of understanding that promise lay in a wider understanding of the country, of the United States as panoramic scope in geography, history, and personality. The result of that exploration was only disappointing, however, and Dos Passos was left with the admittedly colorful but still chaotic montage of the trilogy.

If staying outside the powerful American structures of business and government was not an effective answer, by the time of the *District of Columbia* novels Dos Passos chose characters who might more easily work from within those structures. Aside from Glenn Spotswood, the other protagonists of the novels—Tyler, Millard Carroll, Paul Graves, Walker Watson, and many others—are involved in government occupations. Even if values are askew and only opportunists find success, these men have nevertheless made the attempt. It is obvious throughout this trilogy that Dos Passos has tried to limit his canvas; Washington in no way compares with the United States, and his shaping of the trilogy, albeit loosely, around the Spotswood family, is an attempt to spotlight the development of an ethical rationale rather than a geographic one. These changes from *U.S.A.*, however, do not alleviate the censure of what seems to be Dos Passos' position at the end of the 1940s: *disillusionment* not only with the concept that an individual can become self-determining, but also with the notion that he might also affect the course of his country and its history; *despair* that the future of America seems to offer no brighter prospects than the immediate past; and a strangely pervasive *hope* that something remarkable—against all odds and any reasonable prognosis—would happen to change what he considered the downward spiral of history.

As his writing for the next twenty years, from 1950 to his death in September of 1970, was to show, Dos Passos tried to discount this personal anxiety by searching for solutions to the dilemmas of misused power and size in the American past. His study of American and Anglo-Saxon history both fascinated and convinced him; and because he turned naturally toward Carlyle's "great man" theory of history, his study provided him with his first early American heroes, heroes that were to dominate his writing during this last period and to serve as partial models for his fictional characters as well.

Partly because Dos Passos was an eclectic historian, if one could count him a formal historian at all, his use of history was at times both romantic and idiosyncratic. As John Diggins notes, Dos Passos was apparently oblivious to the problems inherent in his finding solutions to contemporary questions in eighteenth-century ideology, especially when many of the basic problems of his own age depended on the advent of a technology and mechanization of which the revolutionary colonists had never even dreamed. As Diggins—himself a historian—suggests,

> Dos Passos was in the awkward position of assuming that the past was both exceptional and exemplary, unique as well

as analogous. He was attracted to colonial America because it offered a milieu politically and morally superior to contemporary industrial America. . . . but he was hard pressed to demonstrate that the fundamental structure of the past was so economically and culturally the same as the present that we can learn anything from the Founding Fathers—least of all learn how man could "dominate" machines and institutions from those who deliberately built institutions and the "machinery of government" to check democracy and control man.[4]

Using Dos Passos' phrase "our storybook democracy," Diggins finds that when Dos Passos writes as a historian he operates as a "nationalistic" one, using a "clearly retrospective moral orientation" to comment on events both present and past. Thus he can praise Americans like Alexander Hamilton and John Marshall, "whose respective financial and judicial policies went far toward creating the corporate economy and centralized state so inimical to Dos Passos' social philosophy. Hamilton possessed 'a simple honesty' and Marshall 'the weight of character.'" As this example shows, Dos Passos' choice of the traits that he considered positive sometimes obscured the central character of a person. For him, history is often "an act of the imagination," and at times the results of his imagining a character or an event are embarrassing. As Diggins points out, "He would have us believe, for example, that Roger Williams was the torchbearer of the idea of toleration, the Milton of American democracy, when in reality the great dissenter's ideas about authority and equality are perhaps closer to those of Lenin than those of Jefferson" (p. 339).

That Dos Passos' vision of history was often "more willed than true" accounts for many of the distortions that exist in his historical writing; but his personal need to search for answers, to will order, illustrates one crucial dimension of his late aesthetic—the dimension that writing should reveal the author's moral position. Consistent with this need, and sometimes regardless of fact, Dos Passos' last writing was a conscientious but always hopefully idiosyncratic chronicle of the history—and its great people—that had given America its distinction as a "chosen country." Not incidentally, his fiction during these last years was a parallel search into the history of his by-now-pervasive protagonist—a well-educated male American of mixed blood and high energy, often named Jay Pignatelli, sometimes Ro Lancaster, whose views increasingly echoed Dos Passos' own.

Dos Passos' summary of his sense of purpose as an American writ-er in 1950, midcentury, forms the basic argument of his first essay in *The Prospect Before Us*. In "The Preparation of a New Society" he stresses the need for stability as well as change. The ideal person works from an "ethical setting" in order to adapt to new social situations. As he had in the *District of Columbia*, Dos Passos de-plores bureaucracy, the corporate structure and its insistence on conformity, the dangers of faulty or prejudicial communication, and personal apathy; he praises the fluidity of the American society and contrasts it with the more rigid British social structure that he explores in later essays. (His attention to the English culture reveals some interesting parallels with the premises of his father's 1903 study, *The Anglo-Saxon Century and The Unification of the English-Speaking People*, a book he speaks about several times in *Chosen Country*. One thinks of Dos Passos' 1934 comment that "it would be funny if I ended up an Anglo Saxon chauvinist–Did you ever read my Father's Anglo Saxon Century? We are now getting to the age when papa's shoes yawn wide.")[5]

The essay collection as a whole, however, is not revolutionary; for all its interest in origins, it becomes, characteristically, affirma-tive, as the mock-lecturer says at the close of the book, "The pros-pect before us, ladies and gentlemen, is not all black. . . . The life of a nation, like the life of a man, is a gamble against odds. It takes courage and persistence and skill to swim against the current that runs so fast towards destruction. . . ."[6] The current Dos Passos chooses to swim against, in *The Prospect Before Us* as in his fiction, is bigness:

> Decentralization would make it easier for co-operation be-tween the managements of industry, organized for production and profits, and of labour, organized for protection of wages and working conditions. At the same time decentralization would make necessary a revival of self-government in the medium-sized towns and rural districts. . . . We have a continent to re-make, a thousand cities to rebuild. New enterprises and new careers for thousands and thousands of Americans whose ener-gies are now frustrated by the pressure of the abject multitude would be opened up by such reorganization of national life. It would result in the greatest resurgence of opportunity since the opening of the west.[7]

In decentralization, Dos Passos saw the chance to make each per-son recognize again his or her responsibility, to take an active part in the country and the solution to its problems, to use those frustrated energies. Dos Passos' ideal American was a bustling, open personality, willing to take chances and make changes but always evincing strong moral direction. Because he had been working for nearly five years on the biography of Thomas Jefferson, it comes as no surprise that Jefferson's image and that of Dos Passos' ideal American have many traits in common, as he says of Jefferson, "At sixteen Thomas Jefferson was already a man who knew what he wanted to do with his time, with every minute of it."[8] Dos Passos admires Jefferson's scholarship and attention to detail, his devotion to his wife Patty, his stability and his trust in reason and virtue. He quotes Jefferson's "Everything is useful which contributes to fix us in the principles and practice of virtue" and defends his concept of use and choice by explaining that "freedom meant choice. A man knew how to choose good rather than evil because he had the God-given faculty of reason. . . . It was the light of reason that showed a man which of his impulses were virtuous and which were vicious" (p. 161).

Dos Passos also admired Jefferson because he was essentially a private person, "more the man of letters than the man of action" (p. 194). Disillusioned as he had become with Washington politicians, Dos Passos preferred to think that the role of writer and moralist was more natural to the third president than that of politician. Dos Passos' highest praise for the elder statesman emphasizes his "fellow feeling" for his countrymen: "he couldn't restrain his impulse to set younger men on the proper path" (p. 402). Accordingly, Jefferson spent much of his time planning not only the University of Virginia but also a system of public education for the state, a system including "at least three years of free primary education" and courses for the deaf, dumb, and blind; courses in practical arts and crafts, as well as in architecture and landscape gardening. Certain levels of education would also follow a classic curriculum.[9]

Jefferson appeared to be Dos Passos' mentor as well in his generally affirmative outlook, and Dos Passos quotes in detail his reply, at seventy-three, to John Adams' question, "Would you live your years over again?"

> "You ask," Jefferson answered, "if I would agree to live my 70 or rather 73 years over again? To which I say, Yea. I think with you it is a good world on the whole, that it has been framed on a principle of benevolence, and more pleasure than pain dealt out to us. . . . my temperament is sanguine, I

steer my bark with Hope in the head, leaving Fear astern."
(p. 294)

Dos Passos' identification with Jefferson is obvious throughout both
The Head and Heart of Thomas Jefferson (1954) and the later two
histories of Jefferson's years; and his ironic emphasis on the statesman's death as a pauper—being some $100,000 in debt—translates
his worship of Jefferson into a satiric observation about the country
that used so many of his talents and returned so little to him.

This deification of people he admired was not a new pattern for
Dos Passos but, as Diggins points out, his portrait of Jefferson was
hardly so complex as it might have been. It was, in fact, almost
completely devoid of those "contrary tensions" and ambiguities
that were the essence of Jefferson's personality;[10] and the conclusion
might be drawn, since this kind of admiring simplification was
characteristic of Dos Passos' later style, that one problem with
much of his later writing—both history and fiction—was its lack of
ambivalence. By becoming didactic, Dos Passos had learned to sim-
plify and in some cases to repress information that would mar the
portrait he was trying to present. In characterization, the problems
were less threatening than in his discussion of theme; when Dos
Passos tries to clarify ideology, he sometimes turns to platitudes:

> when Dos Passos discusses ideas there is no evidence of
> his having reflected upon their significance. Indeed, the pro-
> found political and moral problems the Framers wrestled with
> are turned into platitudes simply through the reification of
> words like "freedom," "self-government," and "happiness," con-
> cepts the authors of the Constitution themselves found diffi-
> cult to reconcile.
>
> Convinced that the Founding Fathers knew what they meant
> and meant what they said, Dos Passos was certain that the
> meaning of their ideas could be comprehended not by interpret-
> ing but simply by invoking them, as though the *Declaration
> of Independence* . . . provides the last word in American
> political theory. (p. 343)

Chosen Country, the 1951 novel, suffers from this kind of formula invocation. One of Dos Passos' premises about strong character
was that a knowledge and understanding of origins were essential;
accordingly, he opens the book—which is the story of his meeting
and marrying Katy—with prolegomena that describe both of his parents and Katy's father. The implication is that once we know the an-

cestors, we can better understand the protagonists of the novel;
"country" merges with "people" in Dos Passos' somewhat solipsis-
tic treatment of place and personal sensibility.

The pattern throughout the novel is a movement from past to
present. The characters in both the Prolegomena sections and what
Dos Passos calls "Footnotes," people who appear briefly in the
present-day narrative but whose "history" seems important, contrast and complement the main characters of the narrative—Lulie
and her family, Jay Pignatelli and his. Dos Passos' belief in the stability of values colors his picture of the central characters; the aber-
rant social attitudes contrast with the stories of the elitist Eliot
Bradford, the opportunistic Anne Comfort Welsh, and Elisha Croft
the lawyer. In the main plot, George Elbert Warner (Hemingway)
provides contrast in his consistently boorish behavior. The characterization in *Chosen Country* points to Dos Passos' 1959 definition of the great early Americans, people of action as well as
thought (the emphasis on Lulie throughout is on her capability to
act); as he explains in the Foreword to *Prospects of a Golden Age*,

> Government they considered the noblest preoccupation
> of man. The aim of government was the happiness of the gov-
> erned. Happiness to the eighteenth century Americans meant
> something more than an improved standard of living. It meant
> dignity, independence, self-government. It meant opportunity
> for the young, a serene old age and fearlessness in the face
> of death.[11]

Lulie and Jay evince firm and stable virtues; they maintain dignity
and independence; fittingly, according to Dos Passos' principles,
they find happiness. In fact, in some ways Dos Passos appears to be
writing his personal *Divine Comedy*, using Lulie as Beatrice: without the interference of the real and often crass world (particularly
the scenes of Zeke's marriage), Dos Passos' account of Lulie would
be completely saccharine. As it is, partly because of the mixture
of history with narrative, the structure of the main story line is
interrupted and, in one sense, relieved.

In some ways, *Chosen Country* also reworks the Camera Eye
passages from *U.S.A.* Its focus is on Jay Pignatelli, from his boyhood (with a chapter title that suggests a youngster's fascination
with masturbation) through his development to adulthood. Most of
that development is given through relationships with women. The
process is that of Dos Passos' returning to his poetry and his earliest
prose, choosing the scenes that touch lightly on women, and then

exploring those hints more fully. Pignatelli's hesitant character in *Chosen Country*, however, is set against the relatively complete descriptions of both his powerful father and his beautiful but dependent mother. His own adult personality consequently becomes much clearer.

Early in the novel, Pignatelli meets Lulie–the youngest girl at the dance–through mutual friends and earns then her nickname, "Don Modesto." Her view of him as a chivalrous man, a bit unworldly, carries throughout the story; most of his turmoil as an adult results from the same character traits. And while neither Lulie nor Jay consciously waits for the other, when they do meet again, years later, they recognize each other's values. Dos Passos emphasizes Pignatelli's search for a Beatrice through his oblique chapter titles, finally creating the congruence of many kinds of love–as Dante did in the white rose–with the last chapter, "O My America My New Found Land," in which Pignatelli and Lulie finally marry. "'Today we begin,' he said, 'to make . . .' 'This wilderness our home,' she said. The risen sun over the ocean shone in their faces."[12]

Dos Passos' sentimental ending almost succeeds, partly because of the rigidly controlled biblical pace he achieved in the conclusion, partly because the novel comes soon after Katy's tragic death and it is obviously Dos Passos' attempt to commemorate the wife he had loved so tenderly. Lulie, her family, their Michigan cottage, even her friend Hemingway–Dos Passos manages to create a more vivid picture of Lulie's family than he does of his own. His elevation of her into a modern Beatrice does not exactly convince the reader, but it also does not detract from the sincerity of his attempt. The use of the word *sincerity* suggests that the issue here is similar to the one John Abbott Clark described when he reviewed *The Prospect Before Us*: "To many of Dos Passos' critics, such sentiments appear stale and unprofitable, the language banal. Today, anyone whose prose sounds as if it had been written by a human being for other human beings is contemptuously written off as naive in our flossier intellectual circles."[13] Given the problems of oversimplification, in both language and idea, Dos Passos' later writing does suffer from his need to express values that may not have reflected the most pressing concerns of midcentury, at least not in the most immediate ways. Clark's warning is relevant, however, for fashion in letters can be as fickle as fashion in women's wear. Dos Passos himself, at this period, was conscious of the whimsicality of literary judgment and spoke often about it. As he said in defense of Hemingway,

he has his hunting license in the fact that nobody living
can handle the damn language like he can. . . . If you are
working in a trade it seems natural to admire and respect
the craftsmen in that trade who really know their business.
And working in a few Union Square phrases because they are
the style doesn't make a man a good writer or a good party
member. Wait till the style changes, you'll see all those little
inkshitters or others just like them piping about home and
country and the family like they always used to do. I suppose
they are all sore at H. because they think he's in on the big
money. If they had any professional feelings about the trade
they'd be glad to see one of the boys making good.[14]

Craft never stopped being one of Dos Passos' primary interests, but
his modification of technique to enable readers to understand his
themes became his most noticeable style during the last twenty
years of his career.

Chosen Country was an important novel to Dos Passos, not only
because of its re-creation of Katy's life, but also because it became
his chief fictional expression of the inherent identity between the
American person and his or her country. *Chosen Country* is, in
some ways, misnamed. It seems to be "about" his love for Katy/Lu-
lie, rather than for America; but in Dos Passos' aesthetic Lulie's
identity becomes that of America, at least the simple, proud, relatively provincial America that she and her people know. The novel
thus becomes the fruition of Dos Passos' earlier themes, that the
purpose of the nation was "growing great people" and that its future depended on "the behavior of every American citizen," a re-
ciprocal responsibility. Jay Pignatelli and Lulie as lovers of themselves and of the land are Dos Passos' image of the relationship he
has been suggesting throughout his political writings.

Chosen Country was important to Dos Passos as well because it
became, chronologically, the first of his "contemporary chronicles."
This novel and the next two that he wrote were prompted in part
by his desire to fill in some important missing years. Once he had
defined to his satisfaction that peculiar blend of history and fiction
—the basing of fiction on milieu and event that might also appear
in historical accounts—he began writing books about years that fit
between the periods he had already covered. The contemporary
chronicles already written by 1950 included *Three Soldiers, Manhattan Transfer, U.S.A.,* and the *District of Columbia* trilogy (ac-

cording to Dos Passos' list in the front matter of *The Great Days*).
Chosen Country was thus the chronological beginning of the series,
preceding *Three Soldiers*; *Most Likely to Succeed*, published in
1954, was meant to bridge the years covered in *U.S.A.* and those
in *District of Columbia*. With *The Great Days*, Dos Passos' *Across
the River and Into the Trees*, the author can provide a retrospective
view of World War II from the vantage point of sixtyish Ro Lancaster, who does little in the novel but remember his "great days"
and try to control his young lover.

Completing his coverage of his lifetime in the chronicles was of
great personal importance to Dos Passos, so the suggestion that he
was "filling in" years not already covered may be misleading. Working as he customarily did, with seriousness and purpose and attention to craft, Dos Passos achieved a wide range of tone in the three
novels that were written during the 1950s, a range that suggests that
his earnest didacticism in much of his later writing was a matter
of choice, not accident. The differences among *Chosen Country*,
Most Likely to Succeed, and *The Great Days* are intentional and
seem calculated to convince the reader that the "progress" of the
twentieth century had turned into a rout.

Chosen Country is idyllic not only in location. Its characters are
fiercely independent, and Dos Passos speaks often about the quality
of their "spirit." Characteristic of his sense of personal integrity is
Grandmother Waring's comment, "We never paid the federal government much mind in my day" (p. 75). Dos Passos' ideal world
of decentralization and a return to individuality is the world of
Lulie's family, the Harringtons, both morally (with the children re-
peating sayings from the elders in their conversation) and physically:

> As soon as they had pushed her off from the float and
> she felt the silky glide through the darkgreen water of the
> cove and the canoe veering true to the twist of her paddle,
> she felt outrageously happy. All the anxious feelings she'd had
> through lunch and while she was hulling the strawberries for
> fear she wouldn't get out canoeing that sunny Saturday after-
> noon slipped away. . . . Behind the Alexanders' place the
> hills rose into piny ridges against a slatyblue sky full of
> billowing northwesterly clouds. (p. 66)

Only toward the end of the novel, when George Elbert Warner uses
Zeke's marriage as the subject of a sensational story to further his

career as reporter, does the fabric of the idyllic Harrington life begin to tear; the assumption is, that in Lulie's marrying Don Modesto, she can regain those earlier values for herself.

The tone of *Most Likely to Succeed* is far from idyllic; in fact, it is more bitter than ironic. Returning to one of his common early themes, the American convention that any young man *can* "succeed" if he sets his sights high enough, Dos Passos questions the definition of success by following Jed Morris to a lucrative career in Hollywood, in the midst of a rubble of personal relationships and political beliefs. Jed is the least attractive of Dos Passos' protagonists, being introduced early with his egocentric praise, "this was his favorite role, he told himself happily: the slum child who wins the golden girl."[15] When he makes love to Jane Marlowe aboard ship, his need to have people know about his conquest is more important to him than any personal feeling: "Something made him want to explain to the steward that he was really traveling steerage, that he was a dramatist, an artist, a working man himself, and that he had crashed the first class bar and picked up a rich bitch. It was adventure on the high seas and he was planning to go to bed with her" (p. 11). Jed uses the pose of the artist as liberal (and Communist) because it works for him, but his knowledge of the party line is limited. Never another Glenn Spotswood, Jed had already been voted "most likely to succeed" by his college classmates; his life, as Dos Passos portrays it, is a rapacious trek toward all kinds of the sensual satisfactions that to Jed epitomize success.

There is no question about Dos Passos' opinion of Morris: the story of his rise to Hollywood is an outright condemnation of American ethics and values. If this is satire, it is hardly subtle; the vituperation of the highly visible lives of such characters leaves nothing for the reader's imagination. As history of social or moral values, the book might hold some interest, but as fiction it grows uninteresting in its predictability. Jed deserves nothing but the waste that comes to him, whether it be in a heart attack or in being left without Marlowe, even after his having decided that he did, indeed, love her:

> It would be a new life from now on, with Marlowe. Marlowe. She was throwing herself at his head. She needed him more than he needed her. He mustn't think of all these things, he must just think of Marlowe or he would never get to sleep. He rolled into bed, whispering "Goodnight Marlowe" into the pillow and closed his eyes. "The happy ending." (p. 269)

The irony of Jed's storybook concept of "happy ending" underlies his faulty notion of "success" and "need." In *Most Likely to Succeed*, Dos Passos has given us a double focus for our dislike—both Jed's own self-serving career and the party's manipulation of individuals—and very little positive focus.

This is not the case with *The Great Days*, a novel that must have been suggested in part by Hemingway's *Across the River and Into the Trees*. Ro Lancaster is a journalist rather than a military man but, like Cantwell, his glory lies behind him, and he searches for happiness in the love of a much younger woman. Unlike Cantwell's saintly Renata, however, Lancaster's Elsa is a brazen opportunist, whose short life of failure with men is already destroying her. Lancaster's gradual understanding in the course of the novel—that Elsa is not capable of caring for anyone but herself, that he has nothing to offer this kind of woman—is portrayed with convincing poignance. Ro catches our sympathy; we care about his attempts to write again, to live again, at least partly because he is candid about his realizations. For one of the first times in his fiction, Dos Passos uses enough interior monologue, enough introspection, that we have some comprehension of the characters involved. Here is a vignette about Lancaster, placed just before his realization that he cannot live with Elsa:

> *Blueprint for the Future*. Nobody read it. What's the use
> of writing things nobody reads? I guess I couldn't find the
> right words, the words Roger used to ask me for so pitifully.
> Maybe if Grace had lived we could have thought them up to-
> gether. All that was left of our hopes of those days was a night-
> mare, a nightmare often recurrent. In my dream I was tacking
> a small sailboat against an ebbing tide. In my dream I was tack-
> ing in a light breeze against a tide that poured around a pit of
> white sand. Beyond that sandspit was the harbor and other
> boats luffing up to their anchorage. Sunlight on sails. Blue se-
> cure coves . . . no matter how smartly I come about, no matter
> how carefully I trim the mainsail and jib—look she's making
> speed, she has a bone in her teeth, she's leaving a straight wake
> behind her—every time I come abreast of the sandspit I'm
> further out to sea. Tack and tack again. Gulls shriek derision
> overhead. Not enough wind. . . . sweeping me away, sweep-
> ing me to oblivion. . . .[16]

The peaceful waters of Lulie's canoeing scene in *Chosen Country* are here dark and implacable, but they reflect the changes in both

Dos Passos' outlook and in American culture during this half century. Contrived as it is, the passage does give us a great deal of information about Lancaster's state of mind; accordingly, even Elsa impresses us as a sympathetic woman, since through Lancaster we come to realize some of the torment of her life.

The Great Days is a novel about two people coming to understand their lives in relation to each other, even if that understanding separates them instead of bringing them to some kind of fictional happy ending that Jed Morris might have created in a Hollywood script. It is not a bad book, for all the simplicity of its narrative method and its unappealing characters; much of its interest lies in the flashback sections of Lancaster's life with his wife Grace and their World War II years in Washington. These passages give Dos Passos still another chance to use his Washington materials and, in the character of Roger Thurlow (James Forrestal),[17] to explore the tragedy of personal waste that American politics seemed to encourage.

The novel seems to be as well an attempt to outgrow the "storybook history" that Dos Passos had been working with for the past decade: here he did not succumb to the impulse to write "storybook fiction" that might have paralleled his romantic pictures of the past. *The Great Days* is a good antidote to the charge of sentimentalism that followed his creation of Lulie in *Chosen Country* and again impresses us with the fact that his characteristic themes and methods were chosen for each novel, that they were never a question of accident. As he emphasized in 1968, "The U.S.A. narratives were never supposed to end. They were followed by other chronicles from other points of view. Intermittently, and always trying to look out from the vantage point of style, to let the matter mould the style, the narratives have kept rolling."[18]

Because the twentieth century has been a period of immense technical innovation in all the arts, it has become natural to study literature as structure, style, epistemological construct. What is in some ways most surprising when Dos Passos' work—fiction as well as nonfiction—is studied from those perspectives is that his style throughout his career did remain relatively constant. At some points, most graphically in *Manhattan Transfer* and the *U.S.A.* trilogy, he used his basic techniques more flamboyantly, in more dramatic patterns, but his writing was based on four tactics that seldom varied.

1. Dos Passos was a character-oriented writer. Regardless of what he was writing, he searched for a person on whom to focus. In his reporting of the United States during World War II, in his coverage of Harlan County, of the Sacco-Vanzetti case, of unemployment in Detroit—his approach to history was consistent. Instead of a study of restrictive Puritanism, he describes Roger Williams as its antithesis; instead of a point-by-point discussion of the Declaration of Independence, he gives us Thomas Jefferson—in three volumes; instead of a political or military analysis of World War I, it becomes, in vivid outline, *Mr. Wilson's War*, an account laced with individuals who not only represent the common American: they are common Americans. Even the books that might well have become treatises in political science—*The Prospect Before Us* and *The Theme Is Freedom*—are built on portraits of individual people. More and more in his writing, Dos Passos illustrated the centrality of his notion that the primary duty of any governmental system was "growing great people." In parallel fashion, the primary duty of the writer was to capture those people—both great and not so great—as the only sure means of reaching the reader in terms he would be able to understand.

2. This extension of the modernist emphasis on the use of the concrete, the actual, as a way toward the universal occurred because of Dos Passos' conviction that people, characters, were the most important elements in any culture. (His final break with any sympathy for the Communists stemmed from their tendency to negate the importance of the individual in preference to "the good of the party.") But the emphasis on the concrete is also clear. At the opening of *The Shackles of Power*, for example, he uses the first few hours of Jefferson's New Year's Day as a means of showing the man's energy and intelligence. Following Jefferson through those brief but real hours is a more effective experience for the reader than would have been any amount of textbook eulogy. As Lewis Gannett wrote in 1962, "You have a wonderful knack for picking up the apparently irrelevant minor item—Mrs. Wilson's gowns at one point, for instance—and so dramatizing the whole."[19]

3. Because Dos Passos was at heart a skeptical modern no matter how much he wanted to become an eighteenth-century rationalist, he realized that no cause-and-effect arrangement of these details and characters from life would be convincing. Montage, collage, or less sensational forms of juxtaposition thus became his structural basis, and from the days of *Manhattan Transfer* and the *U.S.A.* tril-

ogy forward, nearly everything he wrote was arranged on a variation of that principle. At its simplest, it became the flashback to his life with Grace in *The Great Days*; at its most complex, it was the four-part pattern of *U.S.A.* or *Midcentury*; at its most didactic, it was the interlock of "message" poetry with narrative in the *District of Columbia* books; at its loosest, it was the vignette placed against vignette throughout *The Ground We Stand On* and *Tour of Duty*. Like a true camera (rather than the introspective Camera Eye of *U.S.A.*), Dos Passos' narrative method asks the reader to focus and absorb; then to break (often whimsically, without explanation); then to focus and absorb once again—and leaves the reader with the primary responsibility of assimilating all the information from those various shots into some kind of cogent whole.

4. As he had said in *U.S.A.*, "U.S.A. is the speech of the people . . . in his mother's world telling about longago, in his father's telling about when I was a boy, in the kidding stories of uncles, in the lies the kids told at school, the hired man's yarns, the tall tales the doughboys told after taps; . . . the speech that clung to the ears."[20] Dos Passos' choices in language often depended on the characteristic modernist belief that a person could be best described by using his own vernacular. From his book and chapter titles to his descriptions of people to his invectives against the media (first newspapers, then radio, finally—and most violently—television) for its abuses of language, Dos Passos worked from the idiom out. It was his "inside" view of the American character. "At that I had to crash-land . . . I was never proud of that one."[21] "I was taking a little run around Georgetown before supper. . . . Just wanted to say how-doyoudo to the baby and to have a few words with Paul."[22] "But you don't own 'em yet, Danny."[23] "Well, I'm goin' to make you an honest woman, ain't I?"[24] "Go it Kid . . . Bust his jaw Jack / you had him licked Jack it was a fucking shame it was."[25] "Well for about fifteen minutes I was getting ready to put the children on the bus and join my mother in California and then I began to smell the Slansky boys at the bottom of it. . . . It was a woman said she was a friend of hers. My she was a dirty talking girl."[26]

Dos Passos' unquestioning belief that a person's colloquial speech was representative of that person also led to a reliance, narratively, on dialogue. His structuring of narrative segments around scenes depends partly on the success of the dialogue of characters in interaction; when that dialogue works, he can avoid supplemental description.

Besides relying on idiomatic dialogue, Dos Passos also built a basic narrative style out of the vernacular. The language of the *U.S.A.* narratives came to dominate much of his prose, a workman-like composite of relatively plain American English, whose sentences were more likely to be groups of prepositional phrases than elegantly balanced or periodic constructions. The casualness of American speech had a pervasive influence on what had begun—in the days of *The Harvard Monthly*—as a fairly elaborate syntax.

In contrast to Dos Passos' plain-speaking narrative, which was appropriate for so much of his journalism and fiction, he also worked easily in his prose-poem voice. First apparent in the *U.S.A.* Biography and Camera Eye sections, the use of specific poetic techniques within ostensible prose was a contrasting method for expressing views the idiomatic speech could not convey. Visual space, incremental rhythms, conscious repetition, significant line divisions, assonantal language patterns—Dos Passos knew well how to use these devices but so long as he was writing as an average American, the use of these techniques would seem inappropriate. By being able to move—through his fabric of juxtaposed elements—to a section of such contrasting language, Dos Passos could signal the reader that this was the authorial voice. Because it was used sparingly and because, in both early writing and late, it often conveyed the more didactic kinds of expression, readers learned to read Dos Passos' prose-poem sections as important statements of theme. This was as true in the *U.S.A.* Biography sections as it was in the prefaces to the *District of Columbia* novels and *Midcentury*.

So pervasive were these techniques that Dos Passos used them no matter what he was writing. Even the last few books about places —Portugal, Brazil, Easter Island—are written with the same devices and style: focus on character rather than event; attention to physical detail; reliance on juxtaposition of segments; use of vernacular. The qualities of the early *Rosinante to the Road Again*, as well as *One Man's Initiation: 1917*, remain, although Dos Passos has become content with re-creating the randomness of real life instead of trying to impose a construct on events.

Brazil on the Move, in fact, opens with a vernacular retelling of a funny story (casually, "The Brazilians are great people for telling stories on themselves").[27] Dos Passos makes much use of quotation from letters and journals, as he had throughout his histories of America. One of the most impressive sections of *Easter Island*, for example, is "The Narrative of Don Felipe Gonzalez Y Haedo, Captain of the San Lorenzo," which opens

> On the 14th of November 1770 we found ourselves, at
> half-past seven in the morning, with very little wind, and
> made a signal to the frigate for her captain and such officers
> as could be spared to come on board of us which, however, they
> asked permission to defer until after they had breakfasted;
> when we all, from both vessels, assembled together in
> the chief cabin. (p. 24)

Dos Passos maintains his casual tone by mixing these accounts in other voices with observations recorded in his own first person (a more characteristic rapportage): "invited for a fishing trip on an official cabin cruiser we rejoice in the coolness of the air over the moving water."[28] And, repeatedly, the vehicle for Dos Passos' comments about the country is his experience with its people. "The chief asset of Brazil is the Brazilians" (p. 2).

> Back in Manaus, at the exhibit put on by the Association
> of Commerce, the face of the man in charge lights up when I
> ask him about jute. . . . Petroleum . . . he frowns when the word
> comes up. . . . Now jute. He is smiling again. It is suited to the
> soil. It is easy to cultivate and to process. The growing of jute
> will give Amazonas a breathing space while the exploita-
> tion of other products is being developed. (pp. 123–24)

Dos Passos' later books of travel share more than technical mannerisms with his late fiction and history. It is increasingly clear that for Dos Passos these books of place should also convey his moral principles, and his choice of characters and detail for his rapportage throughout the books about Brazil (1963), Portugal (1969), and Easter Island (1971) is determined as much by the integrity of their lives as by their color.

His narrative about Bernardo Sayão, the great Brazilian road builder, emphasizes his self-abnegation: "Sayão fought the Rio bureaucracy at every stop. The ministry kept demanding explanations and sending out investigating committees to plague him. They couldn't understand a man who worked for the sport of it with no thought of accumulating a fortune for himself and his family" (p. 59) and his passion for his task (the joy of work in and for itself): "Sayão became obsessed with the need for good roads to open up the hinterland. . . . [he] had the greatest quality of leadership of any man I ever met. Building roads was his hobby and his obsession" (pp. 58, 57).

In *Brazil on the Move*, Dos Passos' points tend to be implicit; by the 1971 *Easter Island*, his techniques remain similar but the application of his moral principles becomes more clearly didactic.

His chief interest in the debacle of Easter Island, for example, seems to be its parallel with what he saw as the disintegrative forces of American youth in the late 1960s. The fact that the islanders' energy turned toward destruction rather than building, unbalancing the social life of the culture, seems a prophetic example. As Dos Passos draws the application, the portent is clear:

> Twenty years ago, even ten years ago, the Easter Island
> story wouldn't have seemed so cogent to an American. We
> were still hopefully committed to the building of a civilization.
> It never occurred to us that we were breeding a generation of
> wreckers. . . . Today, again without any massive impulse from
> the outside, counterparts have appeared in our society of the
> wreckers who had themselves a time pulling down the silly
> old statues on Easter Island. "None of it is any good, let's
> make an end of it." (pp. 140–41)

From this whim, "The result was a hundred years of arson and famine and murder and the near extinction of a talented and effective community. . . . The more we study the record that vanished cultures have left behind them the clearer it becomes that man's capacity for creative work is almost infinite, but that it is matched almost evenly by the impulse to destroy."

John Diggins would criticize Dos Passos' easy extension from the Easter Island culture to the American, the willingness to find proof for his personal uneasiness in circumstances that bear no real relation to those of today; but his tenets throughout *Midcentury* and *Century's Ebb* are much the same. Dos Passos saw disintegrating around him the civilization that he loved and thought he had helped to nurture, and his recourse was to move beyond satire into invective in order to save it. Whether or not invective was appropriate was not the question; the only pressing question to Dos Passos at the end of his life was the survival of his culture. As he wrote to his daughter Lucy in May of 1970,

> It seemed to me that, instead of sobbing about how bad
> the system is, the people of your generation should be try-
> ing to develop themselves, physically and mentally and mor-
> ally into decent human beings. . . . The pathetic thing about
> the great wellintentioned mass of college and highschool stu-
> dents is that they have been so badly educated they have no
> knowledge or understanding of the complications of the world
> we live in. . . .
> There's nothing new about working for the pure pleasure

of it. That's been the motivation of first class people from the beginning of time. . . .[29]

When Ro Lancaster wrote in *The Great Days* that the kind of journalism he spent his life writing was "the kind of journalism that's between history and prophecy,"[30] he was defining Dos Passos' own mode of narrative. Drawing from the factual bases of history, using a keen sense of prediction and understanding—based largely in people, and alerting readers to the dangers that lay ahead: the astute writer would be more than an entertainer; more, in total, than a craftsman. He would be not just a chronicler; his expertise would also lead him to the crucial art of interpreting. He would give his culture its antennae. That his fate might also be that of a Tiresias or a Cassandra should have been obvious to Dos Passos from the beginning.

9. The End of the Search

. . . it is these private dedications that mold men's lives.
—John Dos Passos, *The Best Times*

The tone of bleak despair that dominates Dos Passos' writing of the 1950s continues throughout his last two novels, *Midcentury* (published in 1960, but written several years before that) and the 1975 *Century's Ebb* (which was more negatively titled *Century's End* in manuscript). But with his characteristic optimism, Dos Passos contrasted disillusioning portraits and scenes with vignettes of people and prospects in which he found promise. That one can view these two books as a unit, even though a decade separates them (*Century's Ebb* was finished in 1970) is proof once again of the stability of Dos Passos' attitudes. As he had written in 1948 to Edmund Wilson, "I don't see why people are so freshly horrified each time because it is the same line I've been pursuing since *The Ground We Stand On* to the effect that it's political methods and not political aims that count . . ." and, in 1958, "I still think we have something better to teach the world than the Russians have. The essential thing is the politics of balance and moderation."[1]

Among Dos Passos' essential things were the supremacy of the individual against the collective; immediate means being as important as eventual ends; the necessity for the protection of individual promise in a system that nurtures rather than coerces; the need for a basic system of ethics (religion, morality) so that culture does not destroy itself—Dos Passos' principles as evident in his late writing had been incipient from the beginning of his career. His fictional statement of them first appeared in *One Man's Initiation: 1917* and *Three Soldiers*; and none of his work negates or denies them. Even during the years when he appears to be most influenced by Veblen's economic theories, Michael Millgate suggests that "Dos Passos' attack on the power and corruption of business is essentially based on moral indignation. So, for that matter, is his whole presentation of American society in *U.S.A.* His rationale may have been economic and political, but his impetus . . . was moral and emotional."²

This is not to imply that Dos Passos' fifty years of prolific writing were repetitious, for they were not. His writing was often the means of testing alternatives to his basic tenets. When his friends were rushing to live in cities, he explored the actual scenes of urban life in *Manhattan Transfer.* The long-term fascination with communism among the literati prompted plays, novels, and essays, as Dos Passos tried to find solutions to the ideological questions that faced him from the late 1920s to the late 1940s. His correspondence with Edmund Wilson, whom he much admired, gives a vivid account of his willingness to be convinced, should what he considered adequate arguments be forthcoming.³ But his own pragmatic testing ground—the nexus of real experience, of knowing actual people— was his ultimate source of proof; that source kept him opposed to communism.

It is not his opposition to communism, but rather his disillusionment with labor unions that dominates his later fiction, however. Basing his hope for the survival of American democracy—or at least Jeffersonian democracy—on the future of the common citizen, Dos Passos had held special reverence for institutions that were geared, ostensibly, to help that person. Roosevelt's New Deal with its W.P.A. and welfare benefits won him to a president for whom he had originally had only suspicion; the labor unions kept his support for many years, long after the beginning of the abuse of the workers.

By the 1950s, however, when the McClellan Committee investigations were in the news and Dos Passos was collecting material for his 1958 article about unions, "Anonymously Yours," his anger at the perversion of the union system was at its height: "'It used to be the capitalist got fat off the working man's blood. Now it is the labor leader.'"⁴ Most of *Midcentury,* in fact, concerns the labor problem, with the focus only peripherally on Communist influence on the leadership. The tragedy for Dos Passos as he views labor is precisely the all-American quality of the corruption (throughout the *District of Columbia* trilogy, there was an assumption that Communist infiltration was causing much of the trouble: the devastating final party scene of *The Grand Design* shows known Reds mixing politely with the highest government officials). Dos Passos does not emphasize that kind of involvement in the corrosion of the American union; rather, the primary abusers are men like the Slansky brothers, who pride themselves on being "local." Unfortunately, fleecing the union and its membership is a way of life for them. The gangsters in the union racket are 100 percent Americans.

The union ideal of "brotherhood" permeates *Midcentury*, often ironically, so that the image of people's coexisting within the union becomes in effect an image of some possible harmonious existence in the free world. The union was for Dos Passos a microcosm of his larger philosophic ideal, and, as Thomas Wheeler concludes his study, Dos Passos' life as writer was "the history of a search, a continual quest for political systems in which man can partici-pate."[5] Unions, with their shop stewards, seemed to be one possible answer; and during the 1920s and 1930s, when the power of labor was being felt through strikes, the collective force of people organized for a common good had captured Dos Passos' imagination. He cheered their struggle against the owner, the privileged and elite classes, believing that the difference between "serfdom" in America and communism was that "here in America men can still hope."[6]

As Dos Passos pictures the union system in *Midcentury*, however, all the qualities he respected during the 1930s have changed. No longer is union leadership trained from within the ranks: the story of Terry Bryant illustrates that change. As steward of the rubber makers union, Terry believed that he could make some difference. Writing to his "honest" (comparatively) union president about the corruption of his field representative gets him fired. Then, the mockery of the union's own equitable system for settling disputes, arbitration, convinces him that he wants nothing more to do with the system. Ironically, when he goes to work as a cab driver, he gets involved in the Duquesne Taxi Cab War (the cabbies were not unionized; therefore the largest company in town drove out competitors), where he is eventually killed while fighting against the monopoly.

Terry Bryant's story is a paradigm for Dos Passos' disillusion with the union and capitalism. As a World War II veteran, Bryant tries to do his best for his country. He recognizes battle fatigue and spends six months as a staff member—not a patient—in the rehabilitation center (an experience that later is held against him). He goes to night school where he meets Tasha; their marriage (and resulting four children) becomes the only stable relationship in the novel. From then on, as he tries to live according to the rest of American middle-class values, he meets only unhappiness. Terry Bryant's only fault was believing in the American system.

The Bryant story is the basic narrative line for *Midcentury*, but many other narratives reinforce it. Using a modified *U.S.A.* structure, Dos Passos divides *Midcentury* into four kinds of presentations. The prose-poems that open and close each of the three sections of the novel present the basic themes of the book and the new identity of the writer as "interpreter":

> Walking the earth under the stars,
> musing midnight in midcentury,
> a man treads the road with his dog; . . .
>   I feel the gravel underfoot, the starlit night about me. The nose smells, the ears hear, the eyes see. "Willfully living?" "Why not?" Having survived up to now at least the deathdealing hail of cosmic particles, the interpreting mind says "I am here."[7]

The Newsreel segments, collages of headlines and excerpts juxtaposed with careful and ironic alignment, open each of the twenty-five narrative sections of the novel. These sections are themselves labeled "Documentaries," suggesting that not only the Newsreels but also the narratives are factual. Whether or not the implication is true in every detail, at least the narratives are based on what Dos Passos, at midcentury, saw as fact.

The third kind of writing in the novel is the biography. Occurring less frequently here than in *U.S.A.*, the style of the biographies is closer to prose than to prose-poem. These profiles—mostly of labor leaders like John L. Lewis and Dave Beck—are generally longer than comparable sections from *U.S.A.* There is also progression within them, a continuity that suggests the American hero has undergone some change. Dos Passos opens with a biography of General McArthur (his ostensible theme early in the book is that American heroes were military), followed by a profile of Harry Bridges. In each case, both the character and the culture whose influence shaped him come in for censure. These two portraits are followed by that of Samuel Goldwyn (immigrant who made good, American style) and John L. Lewis (poor boy who made good, another American fantasy). Later biographies include rank-and-file labor leaders—none of whom measures up to Lewis—and the decline into the suicides Robert R. ("Railroad") Young and the younger Bob La Follette. The book closes with a contrast between prisoner of war General William Dean and movie star James Dean, to emphasize what Dos Passos sees as the fault of the midcentury American culture, particularly its "younger generation":

These were the kids who'd been soaked in wartime
prosperity while their elder brothers manned the amphib-
ious landings and the desperate beachheads . . . of World
War II;
   raised on the gibblegabble of the radio between the family
car and the corner drugstore and the Five and Ten.
   Nobody had every told them anything
   except to get more and do less.
   Nobody had ever told them that to be an American meant
anything more than to look at the comics and to drive around
the roads in a new automobile. (p. 420)

These were the young soldiers. Set against them was William Frishe
Dean, mature, experienced, stable. Dos Passos uses the contrast in
cultural background to explain why Dean didn't break for the en-
emy, while the younger prisoners did:

   "One of the most difficult problems for a prisoner is maintaining his judgment," General Dean told Worden.
   For judgment read sense of right and wrong.
   No one had told these kids that right and wrong was the inner compass that points true north. When army discipline
broke down they fell to pieces, each poor devil by himself. . . .

That Dos Passos uses the factual situation to further his own sentiments about modern life is a relatively common tactic; *Midcentury*
provides wider opportunity to circulate the ideas he had already expressed to Lucy in letters, and to his readers in essays. The mood
of *Midcentury* is one of disappointment.

   The fourth kind of writing is the narrative segment, divided by
character, once again carrying the thematic weight of the novel.
The discrepancy between American promise and the actual fulfillment in living is the tragedy of modern culture, and Dos Passos
chooses several continuing "stories" to illustrate the tragedy. Terry
Bryant's tale opens and closes the book, but the lives of Blackie
Bowman and Jasper Milliron are equally important—Blackie's because he gets trapped in the pseudoliberalism of the O'Dywer family (torn between his wife Eileen's free-love jargon, the O'Dywers'
use of communism, and his own moral stability); Milliron's because
he becomes the dupe of a family-controlled business in which he is
only nominally an "equal." In all three cases, the characters believed
in their choice of work and their compromises with life. All had
served in the military; all had tried to marry people they loved; all

had worked hard for their living. The end result of their lives, however, is ameliorated bitterness, as Dos Passos returns to the image of Dante's hell to describe modern America.

Characteristically, too, there is some sense of promise in Milliron's happiness at the end of the book. He and his second wife, Lorna, have left the corporation to build a new business/life/house. They depend on no one but themselves and, by supporting Milliron's daughter and her husband in their fight for the Duquesne taxi business, win a moral victory over the very forces of monopoly and corporate power that were ruining their earlier lives. Once again, for Dos Passos, to succeed in America meant to create personal ideals based on established morality, following individual ideals separate from those of any party or group. And only the lucky, and the strong, succeeded at that, because America was spawning more and more groups, reinforced by more and more powerful media.

Dos Passos reinforces this theme by adding five unrelated segments throughout *Midcentury*. Titled "Investigator's Notes," each story is about a union member's attempt to tell his story to the McClellan investigators. Each story is a pathetic account of the waste of human potential as year after year, time after time, someone tries to improve or change the system and is hurt because of his attempt.

The sum of Dos Passos' juxtaposition of his various kinds of writing in *Midcentury*, then, is a unified presentation of theme: the Promised Land coming to fruition (at least technically), leaving disappointment and sheer disbelief at every turn because—for all its promise—only a few Americans are happy. The cause of their unhappiness, however, lies not in the country so much as in the human condition itself, and the fallacies the culture has both created and perpetrated. Dos Passos' emphasis on the narratives rather than the Newsreel montages helps to place the burden of failure consistently with the people. Like *U.S.A.*, *Midcentury* is a well-crafted piece of writing; it may in fact be stronger than *U.S.A.*, partly because the movement between various kinds of writing and the cohesion among the parts are consistently defensible. As Kenneth Lynn suggested,

> *Midcentury* is in its own right a fascinating book. By a
> similar diversification of narrative techniques, it evokes the
> period 1945–60 as effectively as *U.S.A.* summons forth an earli-
> er era. But *Midcentury* becomes even more fascinating when it
> is read in conjunction with the trilogy it so closely resembles
> —when it is listened to as if it were the coda to a great Ameri-

can symphony. For in doing so we gain a unique understanding of what has happened to us as a people in the course of a fantastic century. . . . *Midcentury* introduces us to a new kind of American success story, in which self-indulgence has replaced ruthlessness as the golden key.[8]

The tone of the fiction is admittedly bleaker, but much of the strength of *Midcentury* accrues from its texture of directed montage. The randomness of the arrangement of parts in *Manhattan Transfer* and *U.S.A.* tended to leave readers with a less-than-clear understanding of Dos Passos' attitudes, while the oversimplification of presentation in the *District of Columbia* trilogy and the novels of the 1950s created some relatively uninspired writing. In his combination of varied writing styles, a tactic he returned to in *Midcentury* and continued to use in *Century's Ebb*, Dos Passos once again found the means of presenting a wide range of characters and material so that his abstract ideas were vividly supported. But this time he also orchestrated his arrangement so that there was no confusion about meaning. Part of the clarity comes through his division of the book into three parts, the Documentaries being subdivisions of those parts.

The first division, "Your Place in the World," presents a variety of common attitudes in the United States in the 1950s. Dos Passos' emphasis falls on people's philosophies and the matrix from which they came; the early documentaries focus, correspondingly, on the war mentality, the turn to psychology as explanation for everything, the loss of religion, the myth of America as "Promised Land" (and the exploitive psychology that grew from that myth). Implicit in his presentation of these themes is Dos Passos' search for an American hero: both Terry Bryant and Blackie Bowman are introduced here, although both, eventually, are martyred.

The second part of *Midcentury*, "A Creature That Builds," presents the need to create both work and institutions. Unfortunately, Dos Passos sees the middle-class work ethic as warped, since modern people are seldom content to enjoy work for itself; they must instead amass power through their efforts (Frank Worthington and Walter Reuther are Dos Passos' examples of this need for reward). Dealing primarily with the institutionalization of unions, this section is the most bitter of the three. The "Investigator's Notes" begin here, as well as the account of the travesty of Terry Bryant's dismissal and his "arbitration" procedure. Yet the headlines in the Newsreels shout promise, achievement, American superiority.

The final part, "Systems of Enterprise," denounces the notion that a system is necessary and provides numerous examples of people who did live their own lives, working conscientiously from their own value systems. The stories of Milliron and Will Jenks dominate this section, two men who broke with the capitalistic system because they could anticipate health and satisfaction as the result of taking other directions. Like General Dean, Jenks and Milliron are morally strong enough to make their own decisions. They represent the few Americans who can manage to hear "the still small private voice that is God's spark in man." Regrettably, according to Dos Passos, there are too few such people living in America at midcentury. *Midcentury* becomes a warning rather than a panacea, for all the optimism in the Milliron and Jenks stories.

That Dos Passos' aim in the novel is to establish dichotomies is clear. There is William Dean, properly championed. As Dos Passos concludes Dean's biography, with the highest praise possible, "The American people were right to make a hero of him" (p. 425). Clear moral values and conviction are so rare in modern America that evidence of them makes a person heroic. But nearly all the rest of the characters in *Midcentury* stand in contrast to Dean, Milliron, and Jenks. Blackie Bowman and Terry Bryant, for all their conviction, are dead, as are most of the union members who told their stories to the labor investigators. The subjects of the later biographies have been either suicides or the object of public scandal (as in Robert Oppenheimer's being declared a security risk). The moral supremacy of William Dean is quickly subverted by the position of the story of his unrelated namesake, James Dean, whose life and death is a tabloid fantasy much like that of *U.S.A.*'s Rudolph Valentino. Even the Milliron story has a dour ending (the result of Dos Passos' authorial intervention and manipulation) because Stan Goodspeed, Lorna's nephew, steals Milliron's credit cards and sets off—not to seek his fortune on his own merits, as the traditional young American would—but to cheat, steal, pander, and above all, do in the blood relatives who had cared for him. This abortion of family love and responsibility sets the tone of Dos Passos' closing prose-poem, then, his despair at the Stan Goodspeeds and the culture that somehow spawned them: "Man drowns in his own scum."

> Overcast blots the stars. . . . The man,
>   shamed drags beaten strides, drained of every thought but
> hatred. . . .
> Evil is indivisible. By hate they rose to flashbulb glory and the
> roar of cowed multitudes, police sirens shrieking how great the

leader, how little the led: the abject mike ever waiting to receive
    the foul discharge of their power to kill. The lie squared, the
lie cubed, the lie to the power of x deals death like a torna-
do. By hate they live. By hate we'll see them die. . . . These
nights are dark. (pp. 495–96)

Recurring themes–opinion formed by media and "news," common
person a nonentity in a culture dominated by "success" and power,
technocracy serving to increase negative philosophies rather than to
promote life-giving attitudes–dominate each of Dos Passos' prose-
poems in Midcentury, but his changing context keeps the implica-
tions fresh.

The same tone shadows most of his writing, both fiction and nonfiction, during the last ten years of his life. Notes and manuscript
versions of Dos Passos' last novel, Century's Ebb, suggest that he
saw the book (at least in draft) as a continuation of Midcentury.
Even if single characters might have the qualities to become heroic,
modern American culture would surely thwart them.

The fact that Century's Ebb had been titled Century's End in
manuscript confirms the mood of his late work; similarly, the first
segment of the novel called "Strike up for a New World" in published form had been titled "Warnings from Walt Whitman" in draft.
The despair that closed Midcentury in the macabre credit card binge
pervaded the opening of Century's Ebb. But in the process of writing, or in some kind of summary recognition of people's strengths,
or in his rediscovery of Whitman's sense of promise in his poetry
and Democratic Vistas, Dos Passos managed to repeat his more
characteristic pattern, that of juxtaposing elements both positive
and negative in the matrix of the novel. This time, however, the
direction at the close–a description of the December 1968 moon
landing–is positive. Modern America survives because its people
still have the courage to dare; their curiosity extends past merely
technical concerns: "This was the day man proved his mastery of
matter, the day he wiped out the unhappy prospects of Hiroshima."[9]

Confronted as he had been during the last years of his life with
rampant materialism, perversion of the values he considered necessary, and campus unrest (not to mention television and credit cards),
Dos Passos grasped at the moon landing as a striking image for the
ultimate promise in people, the human "need to know." As he explained in the closing of this section,

In our century we have seen everything that is hideous
in man come to the fore: obsessed leaders butchering help-
less populations, the cowardice of the led, the shoddy selfinter-
est, the easy hatreds that any buffoon can arouse who bellows
out the slogans, public derision of everything mankind has
learned through the centuries to consider decent and true; but
now, all at once, like the blue and white stippled bright earth
the astronauts saw rise above the rim of the moon's grisly
skeleton there emerges a fresh assertion of man's spirit.
(p. 472)

The image of "Christmas on the Moon," in fact, loomed so large in
Dos Passos' imagination that it shadowed even the darkest of those
other dark images, those of assassination—not only of John F. Kennedy, Lee Harvey Oswald, and Malcolm X, but of the restraint
necessary for the continuation of human life. As he wrote in 1968,
"People are going to face up to the fact that there is a great deal more
evil than good in the human character and that the monster has to
be kept under control. This leads back to religion. People can't do
without it."[10] That the moon shot coincided with Christmas
seemed to Dos Passos fully appropriate.

The evolution of Century's Ebb, however, as suggested by the
manuscript and by the incompleteness of the published version, suggests that the positive ending of the novel may have come as a surprise to Dos Passos too.[11] Several elements of the variegated strands
comprising the novel are clearly affirmative; many others, however,
are not. The most obviously positive is the autobiographical narrative of the lawyer Jay Pignatelli, Dos Passos' "Don Modesto" from
Chosen Country, who seems an anachronism because he is, in the
words of Danny DeLong, "so scrupulous it makes you want to
throw up. . . . He honestly believes that if a few good men got together and spread the proper information, they could get rid of
crookedness and demagoguery in public office and put the poor old
United States back on the rails. . . . A lawyer with scruples in the
year of Our Lord 1962. Can you beat it?" (p. 407). Pignatelli's narrative sections are headed "The Later Life and Deplorable Opinions
of Jay Pignatelli," Dos Passos' defensive bow to the critics whose
arrows were full of barbs like "conservative" and "reactionary."[12]

Jay Pignatelli—for all his "deplorable" opinions and for all his being at odds with his culture (or perhaps because of his being at odds
with it)—is the American hero toward whom Dos Passos has been
working. A man of optimism and courageous spirit, who has lost

more than one position because he followed his own convictions, Pignatelli's personal affinity with Whitman should not be overlooked. His recalcitrance, his responsibility to care about people ("People are you and me")[13]—"an offhand downunderneath reverence toward the idiosyncracy of the divergent, various, incalculable men, women and children who make up the human race"—suggest Whitman's spiritual stance. For both men, "every human clod" might possibly contain "the incongruous splendor, the spark of God."[14] And they would know that spark by the way the person responded to other human needs—"The individuality lies in how you use it"—and to the direction and the achievement of the race: "As for allegiance; what I consider the good side of what's been going on among people on this continent since 1620 or thereabouts, has mine."[15] Cesare Pavese early saw the parallels between Whitman and Dos Passos,[16] and Dos Passos himself, before his treatment of Whitman in his fiction, made many references to him in letters and essays—for example, "The best immediate ancestor . . . for today's American writing is I think a dark star somewhere in the constellation containing Mark Twain, Melville, Thoreau and Whitman."[17] "I read over half of Democratic Vistas the other night and found it much more based on realities than Sartre."[18] And, in 1938,

> Thank you for your nice letter. Your remark about Whitman is very much to the point. I read him a great deal as a kid and I rather imagine that a great deal of the original slant of my work comes from that vein in the American tradition. Anyway, I'm sure it's more likely to stem from Whitman (and perhaps Veblen) than from Marx, whom I read late and not as completely as I should like. The Marxist critics are just finding out, with considerable chagrin, that my stuff isn't Marxist. I should think that anybody with half an eye would have noticed that in the first place—[19]

The progression in Dos Passos' prose-poem rhythms and structure also indicates that he read Whitman increasingly, not only "as a kid" but with renewed interest during and after the U.S.A. period; just as the structure of Century's Ebb unquestionably places Whitman at the center of Dos Passos' reference system.

Another relatively positive strain in the novel is that of Danny DeLong, "the Boy Wizard of Wall Street" who ends the novel imprisoned in Sing-Sing, the pawn of not only corrupt business but also a corrupt legal system. For all his correspondence to Eddy Gilbert and Bobby Baker, DeLong appeals to Pignatelli/Dos Passos, and the author's presentation of his story in his own vernacular is sympathetic.

The third narrative, which fades midway through the book, is that of Paul and Ginny Edwards, a couple whose success in the Farm Administration seems assured (the apex of their story comes with the dinner at the White House with President and Mrs. Kennedy), yet their children have turned to drugs and LSD and drift further and further away. Of the three main narrative lines, only the Pignatelli story ends happily, with his second marriage after his first wife's tragic death, reasonable peace of mind, and some prosperity.

The rest of the novel, however, poses a bleak answer to the initial question which Dos Passos asks of Whitman:

> You, Walt Whitman,
> who rose out of fish-shape Paumanok
> to go crying, like the spotted hawk,
> your barbaric yawp over the roofs,
> to utter "the password primeval,"
> and strike up for a new world;
> what would you say, Walt, here, now, today,
> of these States that you loved,
> Walt Whitman, what would you say? (p. 5)

For answer, Dos Passos juxtaposes glimpses of modern American culture and the lines in which Whitman recreates his America a hundred years earlier: the "century" of the book's title could refer to 1865–1965 as well as to the twentieth century per se, as *Midcentury* had. The prominence of Dos Passos' use of Whitman's poems and sections from *Democratic Vistas* (which was itself first published in 1867–68 in the *Galaxy*, then as an essay in 1871) indicates that Whitman's views of the American people are to establish the beginning for the century. In some respects, they stand as its apex. Whitman's exuberance saw only glory ahead:

> As I walk these broad majestic days of peace
> I too announce solid things,
> Science, ships, politics, cities, factories, are not nothing,
> Like a grand procession to music of distant bugles pouring . . .
> they stand for realities . . . years of the modern, years of the
> unperformed . . . (p. 11)

a glory rooted in the supremacy of the common man:

Successions of men, Americans, a hundred million. . . .
The average man of a land at last only is important. He, in
these States, remains immortal owner and boss, deriving good
uses somehow, out of any sort of servant in office, even
the basest. (p. 11)

As people came to recognize their worth—both individually and
socially—and their equality; and as they came to rely on love rather
than greed and hate, America would transcend its geographic boun-
daries and become a cosmic force,

Bridging the three or four thousand miles of land travel
Tying the Eastern to the Western sea,
The road between Europe and Asia. (p. 352)

Reading *Democratic Vistas* a century after it was written is in
some ways disheartening, for to Whitman democracy was more a
means of improving the American people than it was a political
system. In *Century's Ebb*, Dos Passos moves between the kind of
promise Whitman predicted and actual scenes and characters of
modern life, through his collage of news, vignette, and biography.
The novel opens in New Jersey, partly because of Whitman's later
life there:

Born of a rundown family on a rundown farm on the
high dry hills of Long Island,
  Walt could well lay claim to the title
of average man—less than average:
bottom of the heap—;
  but, from their saltbox at West Hills the Whitmans could
see to the north the silver streak of the Sound already furrowed
by steamboats,
  and to the south on clear days, scallopings of the surf on
the Atlantic beaches— (p. 5)

partly because New Jersey is a microcosm, a mixture of terrain, but
terrain particularly urban, and fast-paced urban at that. Like Dos
Passos' other fiction, *Century's Ebb* is a kaleidoscope; but unlike
his other montage writing, it is almost entirely visual. Instead of
"Newsreel" or "Sounds from the Air" (the original title for the
"Documentaries" in *Midcentury*), "Turnpike" is the title Dos Passos chose in *Century's Ebb*:

Out of the Jersey truckfarms, the cornfields, the green
slopes golden with Guernseys; cowbarns sporting a silo the

way a church sports a steeple; bright watertanks, one a huge
ball rolling through treetops; the toycolored plants of new
industries . . .

SCENICRUISER FOR ECONOMY
Go Greyhound

. . . the sixlane highway
that arches the reedy rivers and skirts the fields of red clover,

now in whine of windfriction, hiss of tires . . .
plunges under a rampaging bridge,
sixlane under sixlane (p. 15)

Whizzing down an expressway, the average American has only a
fragmented view of his country. Billboards and other commercial
ploys of one kind or another simultaneously distort and obscure
his vision. The turnpike is complete with accidents (carefully impersonal), New York City (all its problems from *Manhattan Transfer* multiplied to the nth power), "exhausts, petroleum essences and,
like death immediate and undetectable, carbon monoxide" (p. 17).

New Jersey is also the point of origin for Jay Pignatelli and Danny
DeLong. Dos Passos' focus in time for their stories is 1937; most
of Pignatelli's story in the first part of the novel is that of the Spanish Civil War, the production of the film, and the execution of José
Robles, with evocative scenes about the conflicts Pignatelli experiences, personally and with his friends.

That Dos Passos, in the book that he considered his last novel,
turned once again to the materials he had already used in *Adventures of a Young Man* shows the real importance of Robles' death
—and people's reactions to it—to Dos Passos. More than a "moment
of truth," the experience seems to have continued to touch his life,
informing it, as he kept learning about human beings through their
reactions to events.

> My observations in Spain brought about my complete dis-
> illusion with Communism and the Soviet Union. The Soviet
> government operated in Spain a series of "extra legal tribunals,"
> more accurately described as murder gangs, who put to death
> without mercy all whom they could reach and who stood in
> the way of Communists. Subsequently they smeared their
> victims' reputations. . . .[20]

In this re-creation of event, as throughout *Century's Ebb*, Dos
Passos has turned from a comparatively objective use of experience

to an apparently candid revelation: history (the Spanish Civil War) has become less important than its characters, than biography (José Robles); similarly, rapportage has changed to more personal narrative, perhaps indicating the accuracy of Ralph Waldo Emerson's observation that

> you can only live for yourself; your action is good only while it is alive–whilst it is in you. The awkward imitation of it by your child or your disciple is not repetition of it, is not the same thing, but another thing. The new individual must work out the whole problem of science, letters and theology for himself; can owe his fathers nothing. There is no history; only biography.[21]

When Delmore Schwartz wrote so perceptively in 1938 that one of Dos Passos' strengths in *U.S.A.* was his persona as "a sensitive, unassuming, anonymous observer who is intent upon seeing all that is to be seen,"[22] he could not foresee that the time would come when that observer would have reported all he could and would have been dissatisfied with the process. The whole modernist ethic of presentation, of noninterference, to which Dos Passos had adhered for thirty years, was failing him; his satisfaction in his writing, his satisfaction with American culture, were ebbing with the century. In his later novels, Dos Passos remained "intent upon seeing all that is to be seen," but he used that material more in the vein Whitman had suggested, with the artist speaking as interpreter rather than observer. And in his creation of a Jay Pignatelli and a Ro Lancaster, in coming as close to an autobiographical protagonist as he had in his early fiction with Fibbie, John Andrews, and Martin Howe, Dos Passos repeats the pattern of other great modern writers who finally chose to emphasize clarity at whatever costs–Faulkner in *The Reivers*, for example; William Carlos Williams in "Asphodel"; Ezra Pound in the last *Cantos*; Charles Olson in the later *Maximus* poems.

Dos Passos' immersion in the Robles affair once again–followed as it is in *Century's Ebb* with a candid account of his deep disappointment in his friends' reactions–is another indication of the mature writer's state of psychological health. The writer who had to keep his parentage an enigma and who had finally written that story –with sympathy, not bitterness–in *Chosen Country*, was now able to express the other major disillusionments of his life–the break with Hemingway and other liberal writers, Katy's death, his diminishing career. In *Century's Ebb*, Jay Pignatelli expresses each disappointment, or a similar kind of disillusion, with candor and poignancy.

Dos Passos' use of the Pignatelli/Dos Passos story is more than confessional, however, for the story serves to show the blight of the American system on a person who has had all the advantages that privilege could provide (unlike Blackie Bowman, Terry Bryant, even Jasper Milliron—all of whom were men at the mercy of the economic system). This is a story Dos Passos knows well; he does not need the McClellan reports to learn the details. This is also a story that parallels the later segments of Whitman's, that of helping others understand their culture, their lives—the loner, the outsider, Vag as artist. As Alfred Kazin had written so accurately,

> Dos Passos has always been so detached from all group
> thinking that is it impossible to understand his development
> as a novelist by identifying him with the radical novelists of
> the Thirties. He began earlier. He has never been a Marxist,
> and in all periods he has followed his own perky, obstinately
> independent course.[23]

The Spanish Civil War experience was crucial to Dos Passos partly because it confirmed this view of himself. Rejected by his former friends, he had to realize that some people are essentially—and in no way romantically—alone; and that, except for Katy, he seemed at this stage of his life to be one of them.

After years spent trying to identify the qualities of the heroic American, through studying and writing about his culture both present and past and implicitly trying to become an American hero (or at least, more modestly, to belong somewhere), Dos Passos learned after 1937 that the only true heroism was individual, to be gained by (given the state of present America) staying outside the very complex he formerly had wanted to experience so fully. In short, Dos Passos' personal direction was reversed, and the year 1937 was pivotal. His use of the biography of George Orwell in this section of *Century's Ebb* is more appropriate than it might at first seem, not only because Orwell was consistently closed out of both literary and social worlds, but also because, in spite of personal tragedies, he wrote what he wanted, was able to convey his angst through satire, and—beyond personal expectations—endured.

In the second part of the novel, "Life's Gymnasium," Dos Passos explores the reasons for the changes between Whitman's affirmation of the future and Orwell's *1984*. The title of the section comes

from Whitman's plea in *Democratic Vistas* that the country counteract what has happened (already, in 1862) to the promise of young
America. For Whitman believed that

> the ulterior object of political and all other government
> [was] . . . to develop, to open up to cultivation, to encour-
> age the possibilities of all beneficent and manly outcroppage.
> . . . Political democracy as it exists and practically works in
> America, with all its threatening evils, supplies a training
> school for making first class men. It is life's gymnasium.
> (p. 104)

The biography of John Dewey, which is titled "American Philosophy, 1859–1952" and thus includes nearly a century itself, summarizes Dos Passos' and Whitman's themes in this longest of the
novel's five parts. The irony about Dewey as "the layman's philosopher" was that "he embodied the American virtues, tolerance,
and altruism, sympathy with the poor and oppressed, impatience
with dogmatism" (p. 113), but somehow his brilliance went awry:
"Pragmatism, experimentalism, instrumentalism dribbled away
into the doctrine that anything goes" (p. 123). What might have
been a paean to Dewey's accepting intellect, set as the description
is in the context of modern American culture, became censure: "In
education John Dewey was the apostle of experiment, learn by doing. His followers made experiment their dogma. When their ex-
periments didn't work, they ignored the results. Failure became
their vested interest" (p. 125).

In his letters from this late period, Dos Passos laments, with more
rancor than impartiality, "The rank criminal idiocy of the younger
generation in this country is more than I can swallow."[24] "I blame
everything on TV. What we are suffering from is the generation
weaned and raised on TV."[25] As he expresses the connection in the
Dewey biography, however, the blame cannot rest entirely on the
young or the media:

> As the twentieth century advanced, the American genius
> rose to paramount heights in the organization of technol-
> ogy, but philosophy in the true sense languished. Nobody
> propounded a scheme for living to replace the disintegrating
> ethos of Protestant Christianity. . . . Young men looked in vain
> for the deeprooted substance of belief they needed to face death
> and disaster. American thought was left, as Whitman put it,
> a hundred years before, "a dangerous sea of seething cur-

rents, cross and counter currents, all so dark and untried;
and whither shall we turn?" (p. 123)

Episodes around the Dewey biography illustrate Dos Passos' concern, but from the end of the second part, *Century's Ebb* is less tightly structured than in its opening 250 pages. There is thematic connection, but many sections seem less complete than they might be—i.e., they seem rhythmically awkward, compared with the total effect of *Midcentury*. Worksheets from that novel and *U.S.A.* show, for example, that in the process of revising, Dos Passos frequently lengthened sections rather than condensing them. Each passage has a kind of rhythmic identity that becomes especially noticeable in the revision process.[26] That Dos Passos may have shortened the second half of *Century's Ebb* rather than complete it as he had planned (or perhaps the book was partially unfinished) seems likely, judging from a 1967 letter to Lovell Thompson, in which Dos Passos describes the plan for the book:

> Well the central story seems to be still "The Later Life
> and Deplorable Opinions of Jay Pignatelli." Interwoven
> with that are several stories; a young Greek business man; a
> character who turns out to be a cross between Eddy Gilbert
> and Bobby Baker who ends up in Brazil; an Iowa seed corn mag-
> nate. The final part will be about the building of one of these
> new from the ground up cities—like Columbia, Md. Of course
> it may develop entirely differently, but that's the way it
> looks now from the notes and scattered semicomplete bits.[27]

Whether or not *Century's Ebb* is as polished as it might have been, what is impressive about the novel is that Dos Passos' narrative control in each segment—the pace with which he tells the stories, the timing in the "Turnpike" collage sections—is undiminished. And the third part illustrates well the kind of cohesion of segments possible when Dos Passos is at his best.

"The Green Revolution," the third part, is a montage of American pastoral. Opening with lines from Whitman's "Song of Myself" ("Over the sharp-peaked farmhouse with its scallop'd scum of slender shoots from the gutters/ . . . walking the path worn in the grass"), this section portrays the American farmer whose independence, in Dos Passos' eyes, allows him to work for the common good instead of only for personal profit. The biographies in this section, of Henry Wallace and Robert Hutchings Goddard, stress a beneficent purpose; the narratives of the Edwardses and Will Henning, whose work in the hybridization of corn combines the practical American grasp of need and a visionary ability to improve the culture, carry a similar emphasis: "Will Henning didn't care too much about money; what he cared for was growth and production and sales and the endless detail of the business that kept him busy from dawn to dark" (p. 320). Dos Passos' move to a rural area of Virginia may have been of more influence than he realized; as he had written a decade before,

> Perhaps it was from living so much abroad as a child that
> I imbibed a stubborn love of my country that no amount
> of disillusion has been able to weaken. . . . In the fifties I find
> myself loving my country and its people more than ever, and
> living in the part of it I first knew as a child deep down among
> the weeds in the Northern neck of Virginia.[28]

As in much of Dos Passos' later work, his heroes are selfless yet aware, willing to work, compassionate; increasingly, they are rural and self-employed.

Set against this positive, fertile center of American promise (even geographically) is the emptiness of America in the fourth part, "The Image." Dos Passos in his continuing campaign against irresponsible use of the media (newspapers, radio, TV, now photography) explores the power of the visual image in American news. His biography in this part is of George Eastman and the Kodak industry, followed by an interesting juxtaposition of the false, yet photographed, views of the modern country and Whitman's even more vivid verbal depictions from *Democratic Vistas*. The deception of the image–people's concern with their "image" as opposed to the reality of their spirit–comes to undermine the characters of both Paul Edwards and Danny DeLong; and the momentum of distorted vision/values carries through the last section, "Of Fortune and Misfortune," in which Dos Passos concludes the narrative lines but also spends much attention on the assassinations of John F. Kennedy and Malcolm X.

"The Coming of the Assassins" is his title for the Lee Harvey Oswald biography, in which the media are once again blamed for many of the unfortunate events of modern life. Dos Passos had written just after the assassination, "What a strange and grewsome [sic] business was the shooting of Kennedy. The response from the mass misinformers has been to me more grewsome than the nasty crime itself."[29] His overstatement suggests the perspective once again of his search for cause. For Dos Passos, mourning an event was never sufficient. As with the Sacco and Vanzetti case and the death of José Robles, the event was only the symptom.

Dos Passos' biography of Lee Harvey Oswald is sympathetic. Oswald's murder of Kennedy, and his attempted murder of General Edwin A. Walker, is a fairly predictable result of his unstable childhood and his susceptibility to the false media. "Having committed the deed which he believed would make him famous in the history books" (p. 440), Oswald goes, satisfied, to his cell, apparently untouched by the enormity of his crime. Years of seeing screen "heroes" commit violent acts on television, years of being told that he was nothing—even by his family, years of finding whatever sense of identity he had in subversion: this accumulation of anger mixed with the firmly entrenched Horatio Alger ideal, that any American could become anything he dared, and Oswald saw no limits to his plan. He would aim high, literally: he would kill not just anyone; he would kill the president. Oswald's "ambition" was the legacy of the new American regime of hate. And in Dos Passos' view, the media had created that regime; it was fitting that the media reap the message of the second murder, that of Oswald himself: "The television networks had the satisfaction of being able to exhibit a film which clearly showed the assassination of the assassin" (p. 442).

Malcolm X's assassination is also an indictment against his culture, regardless of his color. Dos Passos explains well the ironic situation of Malcolm X's being killed by his black friends because he had learned the real meaning of brotherhood:

> Malcolm had two conversions. The first was in Norfolk
> prison, when he decided that the Islam of the Honorable
> Elijah Muhammad was the creed for the Negro and changed
> his name to Malcolm X, and the second was in Jeddah, when he
> discovered that the real Islam meant brotherhood, the brother-
> hood of all believers without regard to race or color. . . . When
> he got home he tried to undo the harm he felt he had done.
>
> That was why they killed him.
>
> His father,
>   a freelance preacher who agitated for Marcus Garvey's Back
> to Africa Movement,
>   went that way before him.

A few years before Earl Little was killed, nightriders
burned his house in Lansing, Michigan. . . . (p. 443)

The right to become an individual, to change according to knowledge, information, should be the basic right of every American; Dos
Passos laments not only the stereotypical patterns established by
modern American culture but also the constant misinformation
(conveyed by the "mass misinformers") available even to those
eager to learn. Only in the twentieth century had the lack of conformity become punishable by death, however; and Dos Passos presents with a kind of controlled horror the accounts of "the coming
of the assassins."

It is a passionate indictment, of the culture perhaps more than
the individual killers, because Dos Passos believes that he has
earned the right to be passionate. The artist must be an involved
participant, rather than an observer–a Walt Whitman, not a Henry
James. "Camerado, this is no book," Whitman writes at the conclusion of "So Long": "Who touches this touches a man. . . . From behind the screen where I hid I advance personally solely to you."[30]
The responsibility of the artist is full participation, full comprehension; otherwise, he cannot write well about his subject, the world
and its people. As Whitman stated so clearly in *Democratic Vistas*,

> when I mix with these interminable swarms of alert, tur-
> bulent, goodnatured, independent citizens, mechanics, clerks,
> young persons–at the idea of this mass of men, so fresh and
> free, so loving and so proud, a singular awe falls over me. I
> feel with dejection and amazement that among our geniuses
> and talented writers or speakers, few or none have yet really
> spoken to this people, created a single imagemaking work for
> them or absorbed the central spirit and the idiosyncrasies
> which are theirs and which thus in highest ranges so far
> remains entirely uncelebrated, unexpressed. (p. 352)

Dos Passos would accept this definition of the American artist and
Whitman's sense of need to have a literature that "absorbed the
central spirit," but after his half century of trying to do just that,
he could speak convincingly of the difficulties involved in the process:

> The chief difficulty you have to meet when you try to
> write about the world today is that the shape of society is
> changing so fast that the ethical and analytical part of the

human mind has not been able to keep up with it. The old standards of good and evil have broken down and no new standards have come into being to take their place. A couple of generations have been brought up on the theory that standards of behavior don't mean anything. The basic old rocky preconceptions—call them prejudices if you want—on which a writer, whether he was for them or against them, used to find a ground to stand on, have been so silted over with the doubletalk of various propagandas that he can't get a foothold on them any more. You are left wallowing in the quicksand of the theory that nothing really matters. Morals? ethics? How shall we behave? Let's just pull it out of the air. An old time Christian named John Bunyan called that quicksand the Slough of Despond.

The generation I got my education from, the generation that cut its eyeteeth on the deceptions and massacres of the First World War still had a fervent sense of right and wrong. We thought civilization was going to hell in a hack. But we did believe too that if people used their brains the modern world could produce a marvelous society. There was a germ of truth in both conceptions.[31]

The position was not new: in his 1932 essay, quoted here in the preface, he had begun his list of the American writer's purposes, "to convince people of something. . . . that's preaching, and is part of the business of everybody who deals with words."

Embarrassed as some critics have been about Dos Passos' late insistence that the moral position become explicit rather than implicit in his writing, their attitudes may be more reactionary than his own philosophical positions. For America's contemporary writers— novelists like Norman Mailer in *Armies of the Night*, for example, and countless poets, from W. S. Merwin and Adrienne Rich to Robert Creeley and Denise Levertov—have turned increasingly to writing that is revolutionary, that does show process rather than mask it.[32] Writers today share with their readers their own experiences, convictions, attitudes, uncertainties; the act of reading Creeley's *A Day Book* is the act of coming to know Creeley. The same kind of statement could easily be made about *Century's Ebb*. One thinks of Whitman's assertion a century ago, "Behold, I do not give lectures or a little charity,/When I give I give myself."[33]

The emphasis on stating a moral position, on sharing sentiment, that had been seen in the 1950s as a weakness in Dos Passos' work may have been evidence of his struggling to become more in tune with contemporary thinking. His "contemporary chronicles" really did stay contemporary, not only in themes but also in method. The present demand for a feeling of intimacy in our relationship with a writer, the urge to understand not only the written book but the person responsible for it: Dos Passos was responding to those needs of readers as he wrote some of the *District of Columbia* material and *Chosen Country, Most Likely to Succeed*, and *The Great Days*. The technical problems with these books were chiefly those of a transitional mode of writing, not unlike Hemingway's problems in writing *To Have and Have Not*.[34] Dos Passos knew he wanted different effects, but his methods in *U.S.A.* and *Manhattan Transfer* had been so conspicuous, so many readers had discussed style in commenting on those books, that he naturally decided that to change effect, he should change method. The most obvious tactic seemed to be simplification, in both plot and texture. But Dos Passos' simplification (for all his variety within it) was disappointing. Just as he could never satisfactorily write short stories,[35] so Dos Passos was not at his best working a single story line handled "straight." As a child of the ironic patterns of modern life, Dos Passos wrote best when he could manipulate those countless, unexpected strands of life into some ironic pattern of his own devising.

And so the excellence of the last two novels, *Midcentury* and *Century's Ebb*. Themes had not changed since the *District of Columbia* trilogy, but Dos Passos' use of a montage of techniques was never surer. As John Brantley concluded,

> John Dos Passos is a better biographer than a poet, a better
> poet than historian, a better historian than a novelist. He chose
> to write novels; therefore his best novels are those which make
> most use of his other talents, which are considerable. It is this
> set of circumstances which makes *Manhattan Transfer, U.S.A.*
> and *Midcentury* his best works.[36]

In addition, in the last novels, through the less disguised use of autobiographical elements, readers feel involved with Dos Passos as person. They are surrounded by the tapestry of the time, a tapestry dominated not only by the larger-than-life saints he had described earlier, but by the equally larger-than-life authorial consciousness. The effect was that writing was taken out of some remote province of "literature" and into the reader's life. Compelling in its intimacy, Dos Passos' late work conveys a sense of the writer that is absent in the early fiction: we are conscious of his intensity, his earnestness, his search—first for America (in the period up to and including *U.S.A.*), then for hero, and ultimately his search for himself.

Dos Passos as person, revealed in these last two novels, is hardly an enigma. As Malcolm Cowley said in his review of *Century's Ebb*,

> Jay is of course the author himself transparently disguised as a lawyer. . . . never the most dependable of prophets or the wisest of political commentators. . . . One could do without many of his opinions, but the character is fascinating: shy, persistent, often disappointed by persons he trusted, and determined to maintain a stubborn integrity. It is the picture of Dos Passos we might have gained from his previous books, but here he reveals himself candidly at moments of personal crisis.[37]

Cowley links Dos Passos' strangely optimistic vision with typically American naivete, and one thinks of Albert Gelpi's description in *The Tenth Muse* of the great American poets (read *writers*), people marked by

> the high hopes and the fear of failure, the arrogance and the defensiveness, the bold front and vulnerable flank, the loud mouth and soft heart, the energy at once searching and unsophisticated, the thrust toward originality against the domination of the past, the sense of limitations and the refusal to rest in them, the lonely isolation and the consequent assertion of individuality, the soaring idealism and the sober realism, the insistence on absolutes and the impatience with imperfections.[38]

For Gelpi, American writers also share "an insistent and subsuming theme . . . the enigma of their identity." Dos Passos surely fits this description of American writer.

There is as well another important quality, which Tony Tanner and Irving Howe have long emphasized—the sense of wonder, of awe, as the American writer, regardless of period and age, keeps discovering his country—and in that discovery, finds a new language. As Howe expressed it, "With America, a new idea comes into the world; with American literature a new voice. . . . Thought and language, idea and image fold into a new being, and we have the flowering of our literature."[39] Whether we speak of naivete or innocence, of Williams or Cummings or Sherwood Anderson or John Dos Passos, the fact remains that part of the American writer's accomplishment depends (and depended) on his optimism, his willingness to try new themes, his curiosity, and a resulting need to go places no one else had ever been.

Because few American writers have remained more consistently optimistic, productive, inventive, and curious than Dos Passos, his closing image in *Century's Ebb* seems more than an accidental choice. For Dos Passos, the landing on the moon was more than a technological feat: it was also some kind of mystical full circle from his earliest romantic dream, Fibbie's beating on the moon in *Seven Times Round the Walls of Jericho*; Tom and Jane's escaping to the moon in *The Garbage Man* (*The Moon Is a Gong*). In 1917, when he had first worked with that image, no one was predicting a moon landing fifty years later; yet somehow, and from America, the space voyage was launched. Dos Passos' openness to the future, to promise, to the life of the imagination remained his hallmark, and one finds even in his comparatively dour late years, a continuous curiosity. "That curiosity," Cowley concludes, "panoramic in scope and combined with old-fashioned patriotism, is the central emotion conveyed by his contemporary chronicles."[40]

In 1920, Dos Passos had also used the image of reaching the moon in a letter to Rumsey Marvin, describing himself and his friend as future writers:

> And Rummy, when are you and I going to walk together
> to the moon and back?
> Haveyouwritten any verse recently?[41]

Rummy and Dos Passos: it is the artist who can walk to the moon; it is all that possibility of reach, of greatness, that always attracted Dos Passos who could reminisce, not quite sadly, some forty years later, "There was, among many of the young people of my generation, a readiness to attempt great things. . . . It was up to us to try to describe in colors that would not fade, our America that we loved and hated. . . ."[42] The essential elements of Dos Passos' art were present early—audacity, subject matter, and an impressionistic craft that defied age. There was also, most importantly, a questioning and rich imagination that understood not only human beings but the patterns of forces with which they had to contend. If some of Dos Passos' last writing is flawed by an overinsistence on opinions readers might not share, we can lament both that overemphasis and those opinions, but, as Joseph Epstein concludes, "It is still possible to recognize a good man behind them."[43] The praise may not, in some final analysis, be so faint as it first seems.

The closing section of *Century's Ebb*, then, is clearly affirmative. Focusing on the journey to the moon is, for Dos Passos, external image, social image, fact-made-personal—a fusion of accessible information and private sensibility, giving any reader insights into the fiction and maintaining as well the continuum of personal meaning that connects all his writing. A half century of work focused on the search for country, hero, and self: *U.S.A.*, John Dos Passos, *Midcentury*, *Century's Ebb*, John Dos Passos, *Manhattan Transfer*, *Streets of Night*, John Dos Passos, *One Man's Initiation: 1917*, John Dos Passos, John Dos Passos, John Dos Passos, John

Dos Passos

He alone of American writers has been able to show to Europeans the America they really find when they come here. Even in translation his vitality, his observation, his broad culture, his honesty and his passion persist. . . .

He has all the honesty that is the lone virtue of our dull writers; . . . and he combines with it the vigor and invention of a true creative writer. . . .

What he writes is damned interesting.[1]
—Ernest Hemingway

Notes

Introduction:
The Americanization of John Dos Passos

1. John Dos Passos, "The New Masses I'd Like," *New Masses*, 1 (June 1926), 20.
2. Ibid.
3. Townsend Ludington, in his commentary to *The Fourteenth Chronicle: Letters and Diaries of John Dos Passos*, p. 207.
4. Ibid., p. 252.
5. Ibid., p. 294.
6. Ibid., p. 346.
7. John Dos Passos, "Against American Literature," *New Republic*, 8 (October 14, 1916), 269–71.
8. Dos Passos had written many essays for *The Harvard Monthly* from 1913 to 1916, but only a few went into detail about literature and its techniques. In his review of *Lord Jim* he comments on Conrad's "remarkable narrative method . . . interwoven, complex, taking sudden leaps forward and back, constantly changing point of view" (July 1915, Vol. 60, 151–54). He praises the Imagist poets for their innovation, their attempts to "add something, to impose a new trend of throught on current literature" (March 1916, Vol. 62, 92–94). In none of his early criticism was Dos Passos concerned with American culture per se.
9. See David Sanders' recent essay, "John Dos Passos as Conservative," in *A Question of Quality: Popularity and Value in Modern Creative Writing*, ed. Louis Filler, pp. 115–23.
10. John Dos Passos, "Business of a Novelist," review of *The Shadow Before*, by William Rollins, Jr., *New Republic*, 78 (April 4, 1934), 220.
11. John Dos Passos, "The Duty of the Writer," in *Writers in Freedom*, ed. Herman Ould, p. 25.
12. Alfred Kazin, "John Dos Passos: Inventor in Isolation," *Saturday Review*, 52 (March 15, 1969), 16.

13. Harry T. Moore, "The Return of John Dos Passos," (review of *Midcentury*), *New York Times Book Review*, February 26, 1961, pp. 1, 51.
14. Joseph Epstein, "The Riddle of Dos Passos," *Commentary*, 61, no. 1 (January 1976), 64.
15. John Dos Passos, *The Best Times: An Informal Memoir*, p. 291; see also p. 169.
16. John Dos Passos, "The Situation in American Writing," *Partisan Review*, 6 (Summer 1939), 27.
17. John Dos Passos, "A Question of Elbow Room," in *Occasions and Protests*; "There Is Only One Freedom," '47, 1, no. 2 (April 1947), 74–80; and see David Sanders, "The Art of Fiction 44, John Dos Passos," *Paris Review*, 46 (1969), 160.
18. John Dos Passos, "What Makes a Novelist," *National Review*, 20 (January 16, 1968), 31.
19. One of Dos Passos' answers to a questionnaire included as an appendix to Thomas Chilton Wheeler's honors essay, "The Political Philosophy of John Dos Passos," Harvard College, History, Government, Economics, 1951, p. 2.
20. Granville Hicks, "The Politics of John Dos Passos," *Antioch Review*, 10, no. 1 (Spring 1950), 85–98. The range of critical judgment about Dos Passos' attitudes is suggested by comparing Maxwell Geismar, "Young Sinclair Lewis and Old Dos Passos," *American Mercury*, 56 (May 1943), 624–28, and "John Dos Passos: Conversion of a Hero," in *Writers in Crisis*, pp. 87–139, and Malcolm Cowley, "John Dos Passos: The Poet and the World," *New Republic*, 70 (April 27, 1932), 303–5, "Dos Passos: The Learned Poggius," in *A Second Flowering*, pp. 74–89, and "*Century's Ebb*," *New York Times Book Review*, November 9, 1975, p. 6. Like many critics, Alfred Thimm in the introduction to the Dos Passos issue of *Idol* (1969), pp. 3–4, finds Dos Passos' views remarkably consistent but not exactly "conservative"–more like Ibsen's or Strindberg's "contempt for the majority." See also David Sanders, "'Lies' and the System: Enduring Themes from Dos Passos' Early Novels," *South Atlantic Quarterly*, 65 (Summer 1966), 215–28.
21. "What Makes a Novelist," p. 31
22. Ibid.
23. Ibid., p. 32.
24. Ibid., p. 31.
25. Ibid.

26. Jean Paul Sartre, "John Dos Passos and *1919*," in *Literary Essays*, pp. 88–96.
27. D. H. Lawrence, *Phoenix, The Posthumous Papers (1936) of D. H. Lawrence*, ed. Edward D. McDonald, p. 363.
28. Epstein, p. 64.
29. Joseph Warren Beach, "Dos Passos: 1947," *Sewanee Review*, 55 (Summer 1947), 410.
30. John Dos Passos, "Faulkner," in *Occasions and Protests*, pp. 275–77.
31. "What Makes a Novelist," p. 30.
32. *Occasions and Protests*, pp. 6–8.

1. Reaching Past Poetry

1. Among the most interesting of Dos Passos' comments as critic in the *Harvard Monthly* are his stress on characterization in his reviews of Louis Couperus' *Small Souls* (February 1915, p. 169) and Joseph Conrad's *Lord Jim* (July 1915, pp. 151–54) and his enthusiastic review of *Des Imagistes* in contrast to *The Catholic Anthology*, the poems of which he found weak because of the poets' "desolating attempts to be new, to be bold, to be smart, to be naughty" (May 1916, pp. 92–94).
2. John Dos Passos, *The Best Times: An Informal Memoir*, p. 23. Charles W. Bernadin gives excellent detail about this period in "Dos Passos' Harvard Years," *New England Quarterly*, 27 (March 1954), 3–26.
3. *Occasions and Protests*, p. 5.
4. Foreword to Blaise Cendrars, *Panama, Or, The Adventures of My Seven Uncles*, p. vii.
5. In the same foreword, Dos Passos termed the years of imagism "a period of virility, intense experimentation and meaning in everyday life." The fullest statements of the imagist credo are found in Ezra Pound and F. S. Flint, "A Few Don'ts by an Imagiste," and "Imagism," both in *Poetry* 1, no. 6 (March 1913), 199–201; Ezra Pound, "Vorticism," *Fortnightly Review*, 96 (September 1, 1914), 469; and Stanley K. Coffman, Jr., *Imagism* (Norman, Okla.: University of Oklahoma Press, 1950).
6. Foreword, John Howard Lawson, *Roger Bloomer*, p. vi.
7. Labeled *A Pushcart at the Curb*, the folder holds most of Dos Passos' poems–those sent in letters to friends but never pub-

lished, some published but not in book form, others never published. Permission to quote from the latter, courtesy of Alderman Library, The University of Virginia, and Mrs. Elizabeth Dos Passos.

8. *A Pushcart at the Curb*, p. 43. Subsequent references in the text are abbreviated as *PAC*.
9. Ludington, *Fourteenth Chronicle*, p. 26.
10. Ibid., p. 42.
11. Ibid., p. 33.
12. Ibid., p. 118.
13. Ibid., p. 33.
14. Ibid., pp. 26–27.
15. Ibid., p. 38.
16. Ibid., p. 52.
17. Ibid., p. 74.
18. This phrase occurs only in the early draft of the poem found in a March 1920 letter to Marvin (ibid., pp. 283–84); it is deleted from the *PAC* version, pp. 151–52.
19. His father, John Roderigo Dos Passos, could not marry his mother, Lucy Addison Sprigg Madison, until his first wife, long an invalid, had died. The son, therefore, carried the name John Roderigo Madison through his years at Choate School, until in 1910, his parents were married and he could later assume the name of John Dos Passos.
20. *The Best Times*, p. 44.
21. Ibid.
22. Ludington, *Fourteenth Chronicle*, p. 129.
23. John Dos Passos, *One Man's Initiation: 1917*, pp. 44–45. A more factual re-creation of a similar scene occurs in *The Best Times*, p. 48.
24. John Dos Passos, *Three Soldiers*, pp. 180–81.
25. Ibid., pp. 188–89.

2. History as Autobiography: Dos Passos' Early Protagonists

1. *Three Soldiers*, p. 458.
2. Critics are fond of saying that Dos Passos kept writing out of his World War I experiences, implying that the physical events of the war framed his subsequent education. What is more likely

is that his involvement in the war crystallized his philosophy and attitudes. It gave him different experiences than had his secluded years at Choate and Harvard, brought him to the literal life-and-death issues that he had longed for, and changed his life—though perhaps less dramatically than it did that of Hemingway or Cummings.

3. Ludington, *Fourteenth Chronicle*, pp. 218–19.
4. Ibid., p. 259.
5. As Dos Passos recounts in the 1951 interview, the novel was partially completed in the summer of 1916, then "redone after *Three Soldiers*" [1921], Wheeler, Appendix, pp. 1–2. See *Fourteenth Chronicle*, pp. 335, 337.
6. John Dos Passos, *Streets of Night*, pp. 68–69.
7. Wheeler, Appendix, p. 2.
8. John Dos Passos, manuscripts for "Seven Times Round the Walls of Jericho," University of Virginia Collection, pp. 5, 7 (much of the manuscript is unpaged). Hereafter cited in text.
9. John Dos Passos, "The Future of Socialism," University of Virginia Collection, pp. 3–4, 8.
10. John Dos Passos, notes to Joseph Waldmeir, Michigan State University, p. 2. Used by permission of Professor Waldmeir.

3. History as Travel: Dos Passos on the Road to America

1. Ludington, *Fourteenth Chronicle*, p. 321.
2. Ibid., p. 328.
3. Edmund Wilson, *The Twenties*, ed. Leon Edel, p. 323.
4. Wheeler, Appendix, p. 2.
5. John Dos Passos, notes to Waldmeir, p. 1.
6. *Fourteenth Chronicle*, p. 328.
7. Ibid., pp. 279–81. The "colossal" opportunity for the *Dial* is expressed with the same exuberance: "You have such a gorgeous chance. . . . you can impress yourself on chaotic unleavened America as no one has ever impressed himself before. The pot is coming to a boil. All depends on the moulds that are made new whether civilization or barbarism rules our continent and the world. . . . The *Dial* is the one hope for all people who, like you and I, want to express themselves freely and still remain Americans."

8. *Streets of Night*, p. 200.
9. John Dos Passos, *Rosinante to the Road Again*, pp. 52–53.
10. *Fourteenth Chronicle*, pp. 276–77; see also p. 265.
11. Ibid., p. 328.
12. Ibid., p. 260.
13. John Howard Lawson, "Debunking the Art Theatre," *New Masses*, 1 (June 1926), 22, describes *Manhattan Transfer* as a picaresque novel.
14. John Dos Passos, review of *Insurgent Mexico*, by Jack Reed, *The Harvard Monthly*, 59 (November 1914), 67–68; he admired its "sympathetic understanding of the Mexicans" and its "impressionistic descriptions of the life and scenery of Mexico." See also his review of *Brittany with Bergère*, by William M. E. Whitelock, *Harvard Monthly*, 59 (March 1915), 200.
15. John Dos Passos, *Journeys Between Wars*, p. 12.
16. John Dos Passos, *Orient Express*, p. 2.
17. Notes to Joseph Waldmeir, p. 3.
18. *Fourteenth Chronicle*, p. 286.
19. Foreword to Blaise Cendrars, *Panama*, p. 8. As Cendrars noted in his *Paris Review* interview, Dos Passos looked, properly, to the French for the "grand reportage"; and thanks to his attention, American writers of that generation "renewed the genre" (George Plimpton, ed., *Writers at Work, The Paris Review Interviews, III*, pp. 48–49).
20. *Fourteenth Chronicle*, p. 171.

4. *Manhattan Transfer*: The Beginning of the Chronicles

1. Sinclair Lewis, *John Dos Passos' Manhattan Transfer*, pp. 3, 4, 6.
2. E. D. Lowry, "The Lively Art of *Manhattan Transfer*," *PMLA*, 84 (1969), 1628–38; David Sanders, "*Manhattan Transfer* and 'The Service of Things,'" in *Themes and Directions in American Literature, Essays in Honor of Leon Howard*, eds. Ray B. Browne and Donald Pizer, pp. 171–85; and Blanche H. Gelfant, *American City Novel*. See also Eugene Arden, "*Manhattan Transfer*: An Experiment in Technique," *University of Kansas City Review*, 22 (1955), 153–58; Robert Gorham Davis, *John Dos Passos*, pp. 18–21; and Georges-Albert Astre, *Thèmes et structures dans l'oeuvre de John Dos Passos*, pp. 156–200.

3. Sinclair Lewis, p. 9, contrasts Dos Passos' methods with those of Dickens and Thackeray: "Their chronicle is a patchwork quilt. . . . In Dos Passos it is a skein of many-colored threads, each thread distinct yet all of them proceeding together."

4. John Dos Passos, "The Beginning of the Contemporary Chronicles," University of Virginia Collection, pp. 2, 4; published as "Contemporary Chronicles," *The Carleton Miscellany*, 2, no. 2 (Spring 1961), 25–29 in a shortened version.

5. It is this sense of impersonality and distance that most impresses Olga Vickery, who sees Dos Passos' New York as an echo of Dante's City of Dis ("The Inferno of the Moderns," in *The Shaken Realist, Essays in Modern Literature in Honor of Frederick J. Hoffman*, ed. Melvin J. Friedman and John B. Vickery, pp. 147–64).

6. John Dos Passos, *The Theme Is Freedom*, p. 43.

7. John Dos Passos, *Manhattan Transfer* (New York: Bantam, 1925), p. 91. Hereafter cited in text.

8. University of Virginia Collection. Of some importance here also is the fact that in *U.S.A.* the play being produced is, first, Hardy's *Return of the Native*; later in *1919*, the stage production is *Tess*.

9. Thomas Hardy, *Tess of the d'Urbervilles, A Pure Woman*, p. 40. Hereafter cited in text.

10. Several critics, thinking of *Manhattan Transfer* as a naturalistic novel, see only evil in all of Ellen's choices. As Charles Child Walcutt describes her, with some inaccuracies from the text, "Ellen has a full-scale Oedipus complex; she drifts from man to man and does not 'love anybody for long unless they're dead.' [Walcutt seems to suggest that this line refers to Ellen's father, but it clearly relates to Stan Emery.] Hovering in the background is her father with whom she had a relation so close as almost to displace the mother whom they both rejected. . . . Ellen for a while is a beautiful and successful actress, married to a homosexual, while Jimmy watches her with doglike devotion from a distance. After a divorce, and a couple of her affairs have dwindled away, she marries Jimmy and has a child; but then Jimmy loses his job, and when Ellen goes back to work she drifts into a new affair with an old friend. Presently she divorces Jimmy to marry this rising politician" (*American Literary Naturalism: A Divided Stream*, p. 182). For further attention to Ellen and Dreiser's *Sister Carrie*, see Renate Schmidt-von Bardeleben, *Das Bild New Yorks im Erzählwerk von Dreiser und Dos Passos*.

11. E. D. Lowry, *"Manhattan Transfer*: Dos Passos' Wasteland,"
    University of Kansas City Review 30 (October 1963), 47–52.
12. Dos Passos makes the remark in "An Interview with John Dos
    Passos" (with Frank Gado), *Idol*, 1969, p. 24 that he included
    news clippings in *Manhattan Transfer* "to show that I knew
    more or less what was going on in the world in which my char-
    acters lived. It was important to know what these people were
    reading, seeing, thinking." For the first attempt to trace the clip-
    pings Dos Passos had in mind in the novel, see Craig Carver,
    "The Newspaper and Other Sources of *Manhattan Transfer*,"
    Studies in American Fiction, 3, no. 2 (Autumn 1975), 167–80.
    See also Vladimir Pozner, "L'Ecrivain devant l'actualité: John
    Dos Passos," *Les Nouvelles Littéraires* (September 8, 1936), 6.
13. University of Virginia Collection.
14. "The New Masses I'd Like," p. 20.
15. Arthur Mizener, "The Gullivers of Dos Passos," in *Dos Passos,
    A Collection of Critical Essays*, ed. Andrew Hook, pp. 164–65.
16. Herbert Marshall McLuhan, "John Dos Passos: Technique vs.
    Sensibility," in *Dos Passos, A Collection of Critical Essays*, p.
    160.
17. *The Theme Is Freedom*, pp. 175–76.
18. Vickery sees this image as a direct parallel to Dante's (see note
    5).
19. John Wrenn, *John Dos Passos*, p. 127, thinks Congo Jake is a
    surrogate father to Jimmy Herf. While it is true that Congo is
    seldom depicted with the bitterness that accompanies some of
    Dos Passos' characters, the absence of the trait is hardly enough
    to convey a paternal resemblance.
20. Quoted by Melvin Landsberg, *Dos Passos' Path to U.S.A., A
    Political Biography, 1912–1936*, p. 98.
21. University of Virginia Collection. See also *The Best Times*, p.
    172. John Howard Lawson, "Debunking the Art Theatre," p. 22,
    seemed to find Herf central, however, because he identified the
    novel as being in the "picaresque mood of *Tom Jones*."
22. University of Virginia Collection.
23. "The Beginning of the Contemporary Chronicles," University of
    Virginia Collection.
24. Michael Gold, "A Barbaric Poem of New York," *New Masses*, 1
    (August 1926), 25–26.
25. John Dos Passos, "What Makes a Novelist," p. 31.
26. John Dos Passos, "Towards a Revolutionary Theatre," *New
    Masses*, 3 (December 1927), 20.

5. "Politics" and the New Drama

1. Gold, "Barbaric Poem," p. 25.
2. Ludington, *Fourteenth Chronicle*, pp. 383–85.
3. John Dos Passos, Preface to *First Encounter* (*One Man's Initiation: 1917*), 1945 ed., p. 38. See also *Occasions and Protests*, pp. 26–27.
4. Preface to *First Encounter*, p. 37. See also *The Theme Is Freedom*, pp. 1–4.
5. John Dos Passos, Preface to *One Man's Initiation: 1917*, 1968 ed., p. 2.
6. See, for example, his 1920 letter to Marvin, Ludington, *Fourteenth Chronicle*, p. 276.
7. Quoted by Dos Passos in "Two Approaches to Individuality," University of Virginia Collection. Phrases from the quotation also appear on a folder of essays, suggesting that Dos Passos might have been planning an essay collection around this concept ("Politics, the great sense, that sublime science. . . .").
8. John Dos Passos, *Facing the Chair, Story of the Americanization of Two Foreignborn Workmen*, p. 124.
9. See Townsend Ludington, "The Neglected Satires of John Dos Passos," *SNL* 7 (1966), 127–36, and Allen Belkind, Introduction to *Dos Passos, the Critics, and the Writer's Intention*, pp. xxxvii–xlvi. Dos Passos' own discussion of satire occurs in his essays on George Grosz, "Satire as a Way of Seeing," *Occasions and Protests*, pp. 20–32, and Luis Quintanilla, Harvard Collection, Houghton Library.
10. *New Masses*, 1 (June 1926), 8.
11. "The New Masses I'd Like," p. 20; "The Pit and the Pendulum," *New Masses* (August 1926), 10–11, 30; "An Open Letter to President Lowell," *Nation*, 125 (August 24, 1927), 176; "'They Are Dead Now–,'" *New Masses*, 3 (October 1927), 7. The same impressionistic techniques are used in his Mexican essays (*New Masses*, 1927), the Harlan, Kentucky, coverage (*New Republic*, 1931), and "Detroit: City of Leisure," *New Republic*, 71 (July 27, 1932), 280–82.
12. *Fourteenth Chronicle*, p. 371.
13. Wilson, *The Twenties*, pp. 388–89.
14. Lawson, "Debunking the Art Theatre," p. 22, and Dos Passos, "Is the 'Realistic' Theatre Obsolete?" *Vanity Fair*, 24 (May 1925), 64.
15. Knox and Stahl, *Dos Passos and "The Revolting Playwrights,"*

p. 17, explain expressionism as the attempt to "'express' some permanent truth or principle, an inner meaning of things as revealed to the interpreting mind of the dramatist." All characters and staging effects are directed toward the expression of that paramount theme. Impressionistic drama is more content to record sensational perception for itself. See also Landsburg, pp. 107–86, and Dos Passos' novel *Most Likely to Succeed*.

16. John Dos Passos, Foreword to Lawson's *Roger Bloomer* and "Introduction: Why Write for the Theatre Anyway," in *Three Plays* (New York: Harcourt, Brace and Co., 1934), xxii; latter essay first published in *New Republic*, 66 (April 1, 1931), 171.

17. Dos Passos, "Towards a Revolutionary Theatre," p. 20.

18. "Revolutionary Theatre," *New Masses*, 3 (1927), 20.

19. *Paris Review* interview, pp. 153–54.

20. Foreword to *Roger Bloomer*, pp. vi–vii.

21. "Is The 'Realistic' Theatre Obsolete?" p. 64.

22. *Three Plays*, p. 75.

23. Knox and Stahl, p. 29.

24. *Fourteenth Chronicle*, p. 368.

25. University of Virginia Collection.

26. Russel B. Nye, *The Unembarrassed Muse*, p. 170.

27. John Dos Passos, "Novelist Hits Review," *The Daily Worker*, January 20, 1928, p. 4.

28. *The Garbage Man*, in *Three Plays*, p. 46.

29. University of Virginia Collection.

30. Edmund Wilson, "Dos Passos and the Social Revolution," in *Shores of Light*, pp. 429–35.

31. *Three Plays*, p. 93.

32. Knox and Stahl, p. 75.

33. University of Virginia Collection.

34. *Three Plays*, p. xxi.

35. Ibid., p. 163.

36. Landsberg, p. 175.

37. John Dos Passos, "Looking Back on *U.S.A.*," *New York Times*, October 25, 1959, sec. 2, p. 5.

6. Dos Passos' Search for U.S.A.

1. The character of Moorehouse is based in part on that of Ivy Lee, public relations expert who was instrumental in creating pro-

American feeling during and after World War I. Lee's smugness seems to have been particularly offensive to Dos Passos. See Dos Passos' essay, "Wanted: An Ivy Lee for Liberals," *New Republic*, 63 (August 13, 1930), 371–72.

2. University of Virginia Collection.
3. Wheeler, Appendix, p. 2.
4. As Daniel Aaron describes Dos Passos' evolution, "The radicalism of Dos Passos simmered in the early twenties, boiled furiously between 1927 and 1932, and began to cool thereafter. At no time did he consider joining the Communist party . . ." (*Writers on the Left*, p. 348).
5. Gado, p. 14.
6. Ibid., p. 13. Dos Passos also speaks admiringly of the panoramic murals of Diego Rivera, Orozco, and Montenegro.
7. John Dos Passos, "Statement of Belief," *Bookman*, 68 (September 1928), 26.
8. Gado, p. 14.
9. John Dos Passos, "The Business of a Novelist," p. 220.
10. *The Theme Is Freedom*, p. 252.
11. Critics that are particularly helpful on the methods of *U.S.A.* are Blanche H. Gelfant, "John Dos Passos: The Synoptic Novel," in *The American City Novel*, pp. 133–51; John Lydenberg, "Dos Passos' *U.S.A.*: The Words of the Hollow Men," in *Essays on Determinism in American Literature*, ed. Sydney J. Krause, pp. 97–107; Melvin Landsberg, *Dos Passos' Path to U.S.A.: A Political Biography 1912–1936*; James N. Westerhoven, "Autobiographical Elements in the Camera Eye," *American Literature*, 48, no. 3 (November 1976), 340–64; Alfred Kazin, "Dos Passos and the 'Lost Generation,'" in *On Native Grounds*; Malcolm Cowley, "John Dos Passos, The Poet and the World," in *Think Back on Us*, pp. 205–18, 298–301; Wrenn, *John Dos Passos*, pp. 154–66.
12. Gado, p. 14.
13. *Paris Review* interview, p. 161.
14. Wheeler, Appendix, p. 2.
15. The best description of Dos Passos' methods of satirizing is Ludington's ("Neglected Satires"). Dos Passos himself explains the healthy purposes of satire in the exhibit catalog for Luis Quintanilla's showing at the Pierce Matisse Gallery, New York: "A satirist is a man who can't see filth, oppression, the complacency of the powerful, the degradation of the weak without

crying out in disgust. A great satirist can turn disgust into violent explosive beauty."

16. University of Virginia Collection.

17. John Dos Passos, *The Big Money* (New York: New American Library Signet, 1969), p. 119. Hereafter cited in text as *BM*; 42 for *The 42nd Parallel* and 1919 (same publication dates).

18. That Dos Passos thought of himself as a Jamesian observer is suggested frequently in his drafts. In one diagram of the plan of the trilogy, he listed the names of five major cities, with his character "Observer" listed in the lower margin. And in *The Best Times* he recalled that his active participation in protests during the late 1920s surprised even him, "true to my conviction that I should stick to the position of observer" (p. 172).

19. John Dos Passos, "On the National Hookup," *In All Countries*, p. 243.

20. *Fourteenth Chronicle*, pp. 403–4.

21. That Dos Passos was none too pleased with his cast of women characters seems evident from his 1932 comment to Hemingway. "Whole trouble with the opus is too many drawing room bitches—never again—it's like fairies getting into a bar—ruin it in no time" (ibid., p. 408). In *The Best Times*, he later recalls the kind of woman who must have served in part as model for the Eveline or Eleanor characters: "Esther had been one of many attractive young women who pour into New York from the Middle West, learn diction at a drama school and yearn for the ill-defined glamor of a stage career. When that didn't work Esther took a job with *Women's Wear Daily*" (p. 135).

22. Two representative paragraphs from the University of Virginia manuscripts of *The 42nd Parallel*. The first would have appeared with p. 128:

> Eleanor used to tell herself a long involved story about how her father was not really her father, but her stepfather, and that her real father was a sad pale tall man with red hair, the last of the Stuarts, dressed in black, living in Florence, Italy in an old Italian garden, waited on by old retainers and sometimes riding out at night, when clouds were scudding across the face of the haggard moon on a mysterious errand, riding a great black horse and with a black cloak thrown across his shoulders slightly stooped by poring [sic] over books, riding out across the Italian hills on a mysterious errand.

(And of Janey Williams:)
and she thought when she unwrapped the tissuepaper to
look at them that must be how Joe felt when he sent her
things from foreign places. She wished she had news of Joe;
she wanted to see him and have a long talk with him. It
would be terrible if he got to be just a common sailor all
his life. She felt now maybe she was in a position to do
something for Joe. (Used by permission of the Alderman
Library, University of Virginia.)

23. Ray Eldon Hiebert, *Courtier to the Crowd* (Ames, Iowa: Iowa
State University Press, 1966), p. 25.
24. *The Theme Is Freedom*, p. 260.
25. Ibid., p. 2.
26. Ibid., p. 253.
27. Wheeler, Appendix, p. 2.
28. John Dos Passos, "Wanted: An Ivy Lee," p. 371.
29. John Dos Passos, "Whither the American Writer," *Modern
Quarterly*, 6 (Summer 1932), 11–12.
30. *Occasions and Protests*, p. 15, p. 11.
31. Samuel Johnson's biography of Savage is a poignant testimony
to his admiration for the talented maverick (*Life of Savage*, ed.
Clarence Tracy, Oxford: Clarendon Press, 1971).
32. University of Virginia Collection.
33. John W. Aldridge, *After the Lost Generation*, p. 73.
34. Alfred Kazin, *On Native Grounds* in Hook, pp. 109–11.
35. University of Virginia Collection.
36. "Whither the American Writer," p. 12.
37. George A. Knox, "Dos Passos and Painting," *Texas Studies in
Literature and Language*, 6 (1964), 22–38.
38. University of Virginia Collection, "Contemporary Chronicles,"
pp. 2, 1.
39. As stated in Gado, p. 18.
40. *Paris Review* interview, p. 171.
41. *42*, pp. 50–52. All citations of manuscript versions refer to
the University of Virginia Collection.
42. University of Virginia Collection.
43. University of Virginia Collection.
44. Kenneth S. Lynn, Introduction to *World in a Glass*, p. xv.

7. *District of Columbia*: Mecca or Dis?

1. *The Theme Is Freedom*, p. 103.
2. Ibid.
3. Ludington, *Fourteenth Chronicle*, p. 459; see also the correspondence from Wilson to Dos Passos in *New York Review of Books*, 24, no. 3 (March 3, 1977), 13–18.
4. *Fourteenth Chronicle*, p. 461; see also his 1937 letter to Lawson, ibid., p. 514.
5. *The Theme Is Freedom*, pp. 128–29. See Ludington's summary of the situation—especially the rift between Dos Passos and Hemingway—in *Fourteenth Chronicle*, pp. 495–96 and Scott Donaldson's account in *By Force of Will, The Life and Art of Ernest Hemingway*, pp. 104–5.
6. *Fourteenth Chronicle*, p. 453.
7. John Dos Passos, "Farewell to Europe," *Common Sense*, 6 (July 1937), 9–11.
8. John Dos Passos, "The Communist Party and the War Spirit," *Common Sense*, 6 (December 1937), 11–14.
9. *Fourteenth Chronicle*, p. 529.
10. Alfred Kazin, "John Dos Passos," p. 17.
11. *Fourteenth Chronicle*, p. 488; see Ludington's confirmation, ibid., p. 424.
12. Ibid., p. 507.
13. Ibid., p. 536.
14. John Dos Passos, *The Ground We Stand On: Some Examples from the History of a Political Creed*, pp. 205, 204. In his 1904 letter to Edmund Wilson, Dos Passos makes this thematic emphasis even more explicit (*Fourteenth Chronicle*, pp. 531–32) and speaks of subtitling the book *The Establishment of an American Bent* rather than the subtitle it finally carried.
15. Ibid., p. 193.
16. John Dos Passos, "Tom Paine," Introduction to *The Living Thoughts of Tom Paine* (London: Cassell and Company, 1940), p. 12.
17. Dos Passos' praise for Fitzgerald's *The Last Tycoon* was based on his having finally attained such a position. "A firmly anchored ethical standard is something that American writing has been struggling toward for half a century" ("A Note on Fitzgerald," in *The Crack-Up*, ed. Edmund Wilson, p. 339).

18. John Dos Passos, *Adventures of a Young Man*, p. 147. Hereafter cited in text.
19. *Occasions and Protests*, p. 36.
20. Wilson, in "Letters to John Dos Passos," *New York Review of Books* (March 3, 1977), 17, criticizes his "generalized commonplaces," mourns his "appalling" comments, and says bluntly, "I never expected to see you develop into such a hot-air artist."
21. *Fourteenth Chronicle*, p. 512.
22. Ibid., p. 469.
23. As quoted by Ludington, *Fourteenth Chronicle*, p. 498, as being part of the draft of the novel.
24. John Dos Passos, *Number One* in *District of Columbia*, p. 242.
25. John Dos Passos, *State of the Nation*, pp. 10, 11.
26. *Fourteenth Chronicle*, p. 552.
27. John Dos Passos, *The Grand Design* in *District of Columbia*, p. 12.
28. David Sanders, Preface to *The Merrill Studies in U.S.A.*
29. *Number One*, p. 243.
30. *State of the Nation*, p.141.

8. The Search for an American Hero

1. Ludington, *Fourteenth Chronicle*, p. 626.
2. Ibid., p. 610.
3. Wrenn, *John Dos Passos*, p. 131.
4. John P. Diggins, "Visions of Chaos and Visions of Order: Dos Passos as Historian," *American Literature*, 46 (November 1974), 343. Subsequent quotations are found on pp. 331, 337, 339, and 344.
5. *Fourteenth Chronicle*, p. 460. John R. Dos Passos, *The Anglo-Saxon Century and The Unification of the English-Speaking People* (New York: G. P. Putnam's Sons, 1903).
6. John Dos Passos, *The Prospect Before Us* (London: John Lehmann, 1951), p. 287.
7. Ibid.
8. John Dos Passos, *The Head and Heart of Thomas Jefferson*, p. 77.
9. John Dos Passos, *The Shackles of Power, Three Jeffersonian Decades*, pp. 298–99, and see p. 312.
10. Diggins describes Jefferson as "a statesman who could be at once

a democrat and an aristocrat, a nationalist and a cosmopolite, a speculative philosopher and a practical politician, a Lockean who denied innate ideas and a humanist who believed in 'self-evident' truths, a theorist of limited government and a practitioner of national sovereignty, a champion of the Bill of Rights and a violator of civil liberties, an advocate of freedom and an apologist for slavery" (Diggins, "Visions of Chaos and Visions of Order," p. 341).

11. John Dos Passos, Foreword to *Prospects of a Golden Age*, p. vii.
12. John Dos Passos, *Chosen Country*, p. 485.
13. John Abbott Clark, "Saving Our Republic Is Individual Job," *Chicago Tribune Books* (December 17, 1950), 8.
14. *Fourteenth Chronicle*, p. 456; see also his disappointment at *Across the River and Into the Trees*, in ibid., p. 591.
15. John Dos Passos, *Most Likely to Succeed*, p. 17.
16. John Dos Passos, *The Great Days* (New York: Sagamore, 1958), pp. 296–97.
17. John Dos Passos' positive picture of Forrestal appears in *The Theme Is Freedom*, pp. 166–67.
18. "What Makes a Novelist," p. 30.
19. Lewis Gannett to Dos Passos, April 27, 1962, Houghton Library Collection, Harvard Library.
20. *42nd Parallel*, p. xx.
21. John Dos Passos, *Easter Island: Island of Enigmas*, p. 122.
22. John Dos Passos, *Century's Ebb: The Thirteenth Chronicle*, p. 323.
23. Ibid., p. 393.
24. *42nd Parallel*, p. 210.
25. Ibid., p. 104.
26. John Dos Passos, *Midcentury*, p. 228.
27. John Dos Passos, *Brazil on the Move*, p. 1.
28. Ibid., p. 125.
29. *Fourteenth Chronicle*, p. 639.
30. *Great Days*, p. 68.

9. The End of the Search

1. Ludington, *Fourteenth Chronicle*, pp. 582, 617.
2. Michael Millgate, "John Dos Passos," in *American Social Fiction: James to Cozzens*, pp. 128–41; this excerpt from pp. 134–35.

3. See the correspondence throughout *Fourteenth Chronicle* and March 1977 *New York Review of Books*. Of special interest is Wilson's letter to Dos Passos in 1932 (February 29) about his being in Kentucky:

> The whole thing was very interesting for us–though I don't know that it did much for the miners. One of the organizers was shot that day–the governor called out troops to keep people from attending his funeral–and another was badly beaten up. I came back convinced that if the literati want to engage in literary activities, they ought to organize or something independently–so that they can back other people besides the comrades and so that the comrades can't play them for suckers.

4. University of Virginia Collection; see also his letter to Edward Grant Taylor, *Fourteenth Chronicle*, pp. 614–15.
5. Wheeler, p. 93.
6. University of Virginia Collection.
7. *Midcentury*, pp. 3, 5.
8. Lynn, Introduction to *World in a Glass*, pp. xi–xii.
9. *Century's Ebb*, p. 467.
10. *Fourteenth Chronicle*, p. 632.
11. Ibid., pp. 628–29.
12. To sample the opinion, the range might run from a survey of Marxist comment like Martin Kallich's "John Dos Passos, Fellow-Traveler: A Dossier with Commentary," *Twentieth-Century Literature* 1 (January 1956), 173–90. Among the most vehement was Maxwell Geismar, "The Failure of Nerve" and "Finale" in *American Moderns: From Rebellion to Conformity*, pp. 76–90. See also Irving Howe, "John Dos Passos: The Loss of Passion," *Tomorrow*, 7 (March 1949), 54–57; Richard Chase, "The Chronicles of Dos Passos," *Commentary*, 31 (May 1916), 395–400; Malcolm Cowley's "Disillusionment," *New Republic* (June 14, 1939), 163, and "Success That Somehow Led to Failure," *New York Times Book Review*, April 13, 1958, 4, 45; and the moderate Daniel Aaron, "The Riddle of Dos Passos," *Harper's*, 224 (March 1962), 55–60.
13. John Dos Passos, Question 5, *Partisan Review*, p. 27.
14. *The Best Times*, p. 134.
15. *Partisan Review*, p. 127.
16. Cesare Pavese, "John Dos Passos and the American Novel," *American Literature, Essays and Opinions*, pp. 91–106.

17. *Partisan Review*, p. 126.
18. *Fourteenth Chronicle*, p. 579.
19. Ibid., p. 516.
20. *Fourteenth Chronicle*, pp. 600–1.
21. Ralph Waldo Emerson, excerpt from *The Journals and Miscellaneous Notebooks of Ralph Waldo Emerson*, eds. William H. Gilman et al. (Cambridge, Mass.: Harvard University Press, 1960–).
22. Delmore Schwartz, "John Dos Passos and the Whole Truth," *Southern Review*, 4 (October 1938), 353.
23. Alfred Kazin, p. 16.
24. *Fourteenth Chronicle*, p. 643.
25. Ibid., p. 638.
26. Materials at the University of Virginia Collection would illustrate this almost at random, particularly the reworkings of the *U.S.A.* Biography sections and the prose-poems.
27. *Fourteenth Chronicle*, p. 629.
28. "Biographical Statement," University of Virginia Collection, pp. 1–2.
29. *Fourteenth Chronicle*, p. 625.
30. Walt Whitman, *Leaves of Grass and Selected Prose*, ed. John Kouwenhoven (New York: Modern Library), p. 391.
31. University of Virginia Collection.
32. For a more complete discussion than space permits here, see my "Modern American Literature: The Poetics of the Individual Voice," *Centennial Review*, 21, no. 4 (Fall 1977), 333–54.
33. *Leaves of Grass*, p. 62.
34. See chapter 4 in my *Hemingway and Faulkner: inventors/masters* (Metuchen, New Jersey: The Scarecrow Press, 1975).
35. Gado, *Idol*, p. 18.
36. John D. Brantley, *The Fiction of John Dos Passos*, p. 127.
37. Malcolm Cowley, "*Century's Ebb*," *New York Times Book Review*, November 9, 1975, p. 6.
38. Albert Gelpi, *The Tenth Muse, The Psyche of the American Poet*, p. 11.
39. Irving Howe, "The American Voice–It Begins on a Note of Wonder," *New York Times Book Review*, July 4, 1976, pp. 1–3; and see Tony Tanner, *The Reign of Wonder: Nativity and Reality in American Literature* (Cambridge: Cambridge University Press, 1965).
40. Cowley, "*Century's Ebb*."

41. *Fourteenth Chronicle*, p. 282.
42. "What Makes a Novelist," p. 30.
43. Joseph Epstein, "Riddle of Dos Passos," p. 66.

Coda

1. Ernest Hemingway, from the Hemingway Collection, Federal Archives Building (temporary J. F. Kennedy Library), Waltham, Massachusetts. Used by permission of the collection and Mrs. Mary Hemingway.

Bibliography

Primary Sources

Books

1920. *One Man's Initiation: 1917*. London: Allen & Unwin; rpt. as *First Encounter*. New York: Philosophical Library, 1945. And as *One Man's Initiation: 1917*. Ithaca, N.Y.: Cornell University Press, 1969.

1921. *Three Soldiers*. New York: George H. Doran Company.

1922. *A Pushcart at the Curb*. New York: George H. Doran Company.

1922. *Rosinante to the Road Again*. New York: George H. Doran Company.

1923. *Streets of Night*. New York: George H. Doran Company.

1925. *Manhattan Transfer*. Boston: Houghton Mifflin Company.

1926. *The Garbage Man: A Parade with Shouting*. New York: Harper and Brothers.

1927. *Facing the Chair: Story of the Americanization of Two Foreignborn Workmen*. Boston: Sacco-Vanzetti Defense Committee; rpt. New York: Da Capo Press, 1970.

1927. *Orient Express*. New York: Harper & Brothers.

1928. *Airways, Inc.* New York: Macaulay Company.

1930. *The 42nd Parallel*. New York: Harper and Brothers.

1932. *1919*. New York: Harcourt, Brace and Company.

1934. *In All Countries*. New York: Harcourt, Brace and Company.

1934. *Three Plays* (includes *Fortune Heights*). New York: Harcourt, Brace and Company.

1936. *The Big Money*. New York: Harcourt, Brace and Company.

1937 *U.S.A.* (*The 42nd Parallel*, *1919*, and *Big Money*). New York:
–38. Harcourt, Brace and Company.

1937. *The Villagers Are the Heart of Spain*. New York: Esquire-Coronet.

1938. *Journeys Between Wars*. New York: Harcourt, Brace and Company.

1939. *Adventures of a Young Man*. Boston: Houghton Mifflin Company.
1940. *The Living Thoughts of Tom Paine*. New York: Longmans, Green.
1941. *The Ground We Stand On: Some Examples from the History of a Political Creed*. New York: Harcourt, Brace and Company.
1943. *Number One*. Boston: Houghton Mifflin Company.
1944. *State of the Nation*. Boston: Houghton Mifflin Company.
1946. *Tour of Duty*. Boston: Houghton Mifflin Company.
1949. *The Grand Design*. Boston: Houghton Mifflin Company.
1950. *The Prospect Before Us*. Boston: Houghton Mifflin Company.
1951. *Chosen Country*. Boston: Houghton Mifflin Company.
1952. *District of Columbia*. Boston: Houghton Mifflin Company.
1954. *The Head and Heart of Thomas Jefferson*. Garden City, N.Y.: Doubleday and Company.
1954. *Most Likely to Succeed*. New York: Prentice-Hall.
1956. *The Theme Is Freedom*. New York: Dodd, Mead and Company.
1957. *The Men Who Made the Nation*. Garden City, N.Y.: Doubleday and Company.
1958. *The Great Days*. New York: Sagamore Press.
1959. *Prospects of a Golden Age*. Englewood Cliffs, N.J.: Prentice-Hall.
1961. *Midcentury*. Boston: Houghton Mifflin Company.
1962. *Mr. Wilson's War*. Garden City, N.Y.: Doubleday and Company.
1963. *Brazil on the Move*. Garden City, N.Y.: Doubleday and Company.
1964. *Occasions and Protests*. Chicago: Henry Regnery Company.
1966. *The Shackles of Power, Three Jeffersonian Decades*. Garden City, N.Y.: Doubleday and Company.
1966. *The Best Times: An Informal Memoir*. New York: New American Library.
1969. *The Portugal Story: Three Centuries of Exploration and Discovery*. Garden City, N.Y.: Doubleday and Company.
1971. *Easter Island, Island of Enigmas*. Garden City, N.Y.: Doubleday and Company.
1975. *Century's Ebb: The Thirteenth Chronicle*. Boston: Gambit.

Selected Essays

1914. Review of *Insurgent Mexico* by Jack Reed. *Harvard Monthly*, 59 (November), 67–68.

1915. Review of *Small Souls* by Louis Couperus. *Harvard Monthly*, 59 (February), 169.

1915. Review of *Brittany with Bergère* by William M. E. Whitelock. *Harvard Monthly*, 59 (March), 200.

1915. "Conrad's 'Lord Jim.'" *Harvard Monthly*, 60 (July), 151–54.

1915. "Summer Military Camps: Two Views, I." *Harvard Monthly*, 60 (July), 156. Unsigned.

1915. "Romantic Education." *Harvard Monthly*, 61 (October), 1–4.

1916. "The World Decision." *Harvard Monthly*, 62 (March), 23–24.

1916. Reviews of the *Catholic Anthology* and *Georgian Poetry, 1913–1915*. *Harvard Monthly*, 62 (May), 92–94.

1916. "A Conference on Foreign Relations." *Harvard Monthly*, 62 (June), 126–27.

1916. "A Humble Protest." *Harvard Monthly*, 62 (June), 115–20.

1916. Review of *The War in Eastern Europe* by John Reed. *Harvard Monthly*, 62 (July), 148–49.

1916. "Against American Literature," *New Republic*, 8 (October 14), 269–71.

1917. "Young Spain." *Seven Arts*, 2 (August), 473–88.

1920. "In Portugal." *Liberator*, 3 (April), 25.

1920. "Farmer Strikers in Spain." *Liberator*, 3 (October), 28–30.

1920. "A Novelist of Disintegration." *Freeman*, 2 (October 20), 132–34.

1920. "America and the Pursuit of Happiness." *Nation*, 111 (December 29), 777–78.

1921. "The Misadventures of 'Deburau.'" *Freeman*, 2 (February 2), 497–98.

1921. "Benavente's Madrid." *Bookman*, 53 (May), 226–30.

1921. "Out of Turkish Coffee Cups." *New York Tribune*, October 2, sec. 5, p. 2.

1921. "In a New Republic." *Freeman*, 4 (October 5), 81–83.

1922. "One Hundred Views of Ararat." *Asia*, 22 (April), 272–76, 326.

1922. "Two University Professors." *Broom*, 2 (April), 59–71.

1922. Review of *The Enormous Room* by E. E. Cummings. *Philadelphia Ledger*, May 27, unpaged in clipping form.

1922. "The Opinions of the 'Sayyid.'" *Asia*, 22 (June), 461–66.

1922. "Off the Shoals." *Dial*, 73 (July), 97–102.

1922. "The Caucasus Under the Soviets." *Liberator*, 5 (August), 5–8.

1923. "Baroja Muzzled." Review of *The Quest* by Pïo Baroja. *Dial*, 74 (February), 199–200.

1923. Foreword to John Howard Lawson, *Roger Bloomer*. New York: Thomas Seltzer, Inc. Pp. v–viii.

1925. "Is the 'Realistic' Theatre Obsolete?" *Vanity Fair*, 24 (May), 64, 114

1926. "The New Masses I'd Like." *New Masses*, 1 (June), 20.

1926. "300 New York Agitators Reach Passaic." *New Masses*, 1 (June), 8.

1926. "Abd el Krim." *New Masses*, 1 (July), 21.

1926. "The Pit and the Pendulum." *New Masses*, 1 (August), 10–11, 30.

1926. "Homer of the Transsiberian." *Saturday Review of Literature*, 3 (October 16), 202, 222.

1926. "Porto Maurizio." *Dial*, 81 (November), 425–26.

1926. "Two Interviews." *Official Bulletin of the Sacco-Vanzetti Defense Committee of Boston, Massachusetts*, 1 (December), 3–4.

1927. "Paint the Revolution!" *New Masses*, 2 (March), 15.

1927. "Relief Map of Mexico." *New Masses*, 2 (April), 24.

1927. "Lèse Majesté." *New Masses*, 3 (July), 3.

1927. "An Open Letter to President Lowell." *Nation*, 125 (August 24), 176.

1927. "Zapata's Ghost Walks." *New Masses*, 3 (September), 11–12.

1927. "'They Are Dead Now–.'" *New Masses*, 3 (October), 7.

1927. Review of *Henry Ward Beecher: An American Portrait* by Paxton Hibben. *New Masses*, 3 (December), 26.

1927. "Towards a Revolutionary Theatre." *New Masses*, 3 (December), 20.

1928. "Novelist Hits Review." *Daily Worker*, January 20, 4.

1928. Letter to the editor. *Daily Worker*, January 28, 6.

1928. "A City That Died by Heartfailure." *Lantern*, 1 (February), 11–12.

1928. Letter on E. E. Cummings' play *Him. New York Times*, April 22, sec. 9, p. 2.

1928. "They Want Ritzy Art." *New Masses*, 4 (June), 8.

1928. "Statement of Belief." *Bookman*, 68 (September), 26.

1929. "Rainy Days in Leningrad." *New Masses*, 4 (February), 3–5.

1929. "Did the New Playwrights Theatre Fail?" *New Masses*, 5 (August), 13.

1929. "Books." Review of Hemingway's *Farewell to Arms*. *New Masses*, 5 (December), 16.

1929. "Edison and Steinmetz: Medicine Men." *New Republic*, 61 (December 18), 103–5.

1930. Report of encounter with Jack Reed. *Monde* (Paris), January 18, p. 3.

1930. "Back to Red Hysteria!" *New Republic*, 63 (July 2), 168–69.

1930. "Whom Can We Appeal To?" In "A Discussion: Intellectuals in America," *New Masses*, 6 (August), 8.

1930. "Wanted: An Ivy Lee for Liberals." *New Republic*, 63 (August 13), 371–72.

1931. Advertisement signed by Dos Passos. *Left*, 1, no. 2, 100.

1931. Foreword to Blaise Cendrars, *Panama, Or, The Adventures of My Seven Uncles*. New York: Harper and Brothers.

1931. "Harlan: Working Under the Gun." *New Republic*, 69 (December 2), 62–67.

1931. "In Defense of Kentucky." *New Republic*, 69 (December 16), 137.

1931. "Red Day on Capitol Hill." *New Republic*, 69 (December 23), 153–55.

1932. "Whither the American Writer." *Modern Quarterly*, 6 (Summer), 11–12.

1932. *Harlan Miners Speak*. National Committee for the Defense of Political Prisoners. New York: Harcourt, Brace and Company. Pp. 91–228 and 277–97 include material written by Dos Passos.

1932. "Washington and Chicago. I: The Veterans Come Home to Roost. II: Spotlights and Microphones." *New Republic*, 71 (June 29), 177–79.

1932. "Out of the Red with Roosevelt." *New Republic*, 71 (July 13), 230–32.

1932. "Detroit: City of Leisure." *New Republic*, 71 (July 27), 280–82.

1932. "Help the Scottsboro Boys." *New Republic*, 72 (August 24), 49.

1932. "The Two Youngest." *Nation*, 135 (August 24), 172.

1932. "An Appeal." *Student Review*, 2 (October), 21.

1932. "Four Nights in a Garden: A Campaign Yarn." *Common Sense*, 1 (December 5), 20–22.

1933. "Hicks and 'Forgotten Frontiers.'" *New Republic*, 74 (March 29), 190.

1933. "Thank You, Mr. Hitler!" *Common Sense*, 1 (April 27), 13.

1933. A Letter. *Common Sense*, 2 (September), 30.

1933. "Fortune Heights." *International Literature* (October), 52–67.

1934. "The Radio Voice." *Common Sense*, 3 (February), 17.

1934. "The Unemployed Report." *New Masses*, 10 (February 13), 11–12.

1934. Letter, quoted in the editorial "Unintelligent Fanaticism." *New Masses*, 10 (March 27), 6, 8.

1934. "Spain Gets Her New Deal." *American Mercury*, 31 (March), 343–56.

1934. "Business of a Novelist." Review of *The Shadow Before* by William Rollins, Jr. *New Republic*, 78 (April 4), 220.

1934. "The World's Iron, Our Blood, and Their Profits." *Student Outlook*, 3 (October), 17–18.

1934. "Etcher and Revolutionist." *New Republic*, 81 (November 28), 73; with Malcolm Cowley.

1935. "Two Views of the Student Strike." *Student Outlook*, 3 (April), 5.

1935. "The Writer as Technician. *American Writers' Congress.* Ed. Henry Hart. New York: International Publishers. Pp. 78–82.

1935. "A Case of Conscience." *Common Sense*, 4 (May), 16–19.

1936. "Poor Whites of Cuba." *Esquire*, 5 (May), 110.

1936. "Grosz Comes to America." *Esquire*, 6 (September), 105, 128, 131.

1936. "Big Parade–1936 Model." *Nation*, 143 (October 3), 392–93.

1936. "Grandfather and Grandson." *New Masses*, 21 (December 15), 19.

1937. "Satire as a Way of Seeing." Introduction to *Interregnum*. Ed. Caresse Crosby. New York. pp. 9–19.

1937. "Farewell to Europe." *Common Sense*, 6 (July), 9–11.

1937. "Tin Can Tourist." *Direction*, 1 (December), 10–12.

1937. "The Communist Party and the War Spirit." *Common Sense*, 6 (December), 11–14.

1938. "Migratory Worker." *Partisan Review*, 4 (January), 16–20.

1939. "The Situation in American Writing." *Partisan Review*, 6 (Summer), 26–27.

1939. "Tom Paine's 'Common Sense.'" *Common Sense*, 8 (September), 3–6.

1939. "Tom Paine's 'Rights of Man.'" *Common Sense*, 8 (October), 12–15.

1942. "Duty of a Writer." *Writers in Freedom*. Ed. Herman Ould. London: Hutchinson and Company. Pp. 24–26.

1945. "A Note on Fitzgerald." *The Crack-Up*. Ed. Edmund Wilson. New York: New Directions. Pp. 338–43.

1947. Reactions to a questionnaire. *Time*, 50 (August 4), 83.

1950. "The General." *The Modern Millwheel* (General Mills, Inc.), 14 (January–July).

1956. "Reminiscences of a Middle-Class Radical." *National Review*, 1 (January 18), 9–11.

1956. "Adlai Stevenson: Patrician with a Mission." *National Review*, 2 (October 27), 11–15.

1958. "Acceptance by John Dos Passos," *Proceedings of the American Academy of Arts and Letters*, 2d ser., no. 8. New York. P. 193.

1958. "What Union Members Have Been Writing Senator McClellan." *Reader's Digest*, 73 (September), 25–32.

1959. "Looking Back on *U.S.A.*," *New York Times*, October 25, sec. 2, p. 5.

1961. "Contemporary Chronicles." *The Carleton Miscellany*, 2, no. 2 (Spring), 25–29.

1966. "The New Left: A Spook Out of the Past." *National Review*, 18 (October), 1037–39.

1968. "What Makes a Novelist." *National Review*, 20 (January 16), 29–32.

1971. "On the Way to the Moon Shot." *National Review*, 23 (February 9), 135–36.

Selected Secondary Sources

Aaron, Daniel. "The Riddle of Dos Passos." *Harper's*, 224 (March 1962), 55–60.

———. *Writers on the Left, Episodes in American Literary Communism*. New York: Harcourt, Brace and Comapny, 1961.

Aldridge, John W. *After the Lost Generation*. New York: McGraw-Hill, 1951.

Anson, Cherrill. "Dos Passos: Changing with the Times." *Baltimore Sunday Sun Magazine*, January 22, 1961, p. 7.

Arden, Eugene. "*Manhattan Transfer*: An Experiment in Technique." *University of Kansas City Review*, 22 (1955), 153–58.

Astre, Georges-Albert. *Thèmes et structures dans l'oeuvre de John Dos Passos*. Paris: Lettres Modernes, 1956.

Beach, Joseph Warren. *American Fiction: 1920–1940*. New York: Macmillan, 1941.

———. "Dos Passos: 1947." *Sewanee Review*, 55 (Summer 1947), 406–18.

———. *The Twentieth-Century Novel: Studies in Technique*. New York: Appleton-Century, 1932.

Becker, George J. *John Dos Passos*. New York: Frederick Ungar, 1974.

Belkind, Allen, ed. *Dos Passos, the Critics, and the Writer's Intention*. Carbondale, Ill.: Southern Illinois University Press, 1971.

Bernardin, Charles W. "Dos Passos' Harvard Years." *New England Quarterly*, 27 (March 1954), 3–26.

Blake, N. M. *Novelists' America: Fiction as History, 1910–1940*. Syracuse, N.Y.: Syracuse University Press, 1969.

Borenstein, Walter. "The Failure of Nerve: The Impact of Pío Baroja's Spain on John Dos Passos." *Nine Essays in Modern Literature*. Ed. Donald E. Stanford. Baton Rouge: Louisiana State University Press, 1965.

Brantley, John D. "Dos Passos' Conversion from Class Struggle to Moral Middle-Class Mobility." *Lost Generation Journal*, 5 (Spring 1977), 20–21.

———. *The Fiction of John Dos Passos*. Studies in American Literature, vol. 16. The Hague: Mouton, 1968.

Carver, Craig. "The Newspaper and Other Sources of *Manhattan Transfer*." *Studies in American Fiction*, 3, no. 2 (Autumn 1975), 167–80.

Chase, Richard. "The Chronicles of Dos Passos." *Commentary*, 31 (May 1961), 395–400.

Clark, John Abbott. "Saving Our Republic Is Individual Job." *Chicago Tribune Books*, December 17, 1950, p. 8.

Cooperman, Stanley. *World War I and the American Novel*. Baltimore: Johns Hopkins University Press, 1967.

Cowley, Malcolm. "Afterthoughts on John Dos Passos." *New Republic*, 88 (September 9, 1936), 134.

———. "*Century's Ebb*." *New York Times Book Review*, November 9, 1975, p. 6.

———. "Disillusionment." *New Republic*, 99 (June 14, 1939), 163.

———. "Dos Passos and His Critics." *New Republic*, 120 (February 28, 1949), 21–23.

———. "The End of a Trilogy." *New Republic*, 88 (August 12, 1936), 23–24.

———. *Exile's Return*. New York: Viking Press, 1951.

———. "John Dos Passos: The Poet and the World." *New Republic*, 70 (April 27, 1932), 303–5.

———. *A Second Flowering*. New York: Viking Press, 1973.

———. "Success That Somehow Led to Failure." *New York Times Book Review*, April 13, 1958, pp. 4, 45.

———. *Think Back on Us*. Carbondale, Ill.: Southern Illinois University Press, 1967.

Davis, Robert Gorham. *John Dos Passos*. Minneapolis: University of Minnesota Press, 1962.

Diggins, John P. *Up from Communism, Conservative Odysseys in American Intellectual History*. New York: Harper and Row, 1975.

———. "Visions of Chaos and Visions of Order: Dos Passos as Historian." *American Literature*, 46 (November 1974), 329–46.

Donaldson, Scott. *By Force of Will, The Life and Art of Ernest Hemingway*. New York: Viking Press, 1977.

Epstein, Joseph. "The Riddle of Dos Passos." *Commentary*, 61, no. 1 (January 1976), 63–66.

Farrell, James T. "Dos Passos and the Critics." *American Mercury*, 47 (August 1939), 489–94.

Foley, Barbara. "From *U.S.A.* to *Ragtime*: Notes on the Forms of Historical Consciousness in Modern Fiction." *American Literature*, 50, no. 1 (March 1978), 85–105.

Freedman, Ralph. *The Lyrical Novel*. Princeton, N.J.: Princeton University Press, 1963.

Frohock, W. M. *The Novel of Violence in America*. Dallas: Southern Methodist University Press, 1957.

Geismar, Maxwell. *American Moderns: From Rebellion to Conformity*. New York: Hill and Wang, 1958.

———. *Writers in Crisis*. Boston: Houghton Mifflin Company, 1942.

———. "Young Sinclair Lewis and Old Dos Passos." *American Mercury* 56 (May 1943), 624–28.

Gelfant, Blanche H. *American City Novel*. Norman, Okla.: University of Oklahoma Press, 1954.

———. "The Search for Identity in the Novels of John Dos Passos." *PMLA* 76 (March 1961), 133–49.

Gelpi, Albert. *The Tenth Muse, The Psyche of the American Poet*. Cambridge, Mass.: Harvard University Press, 1975.

Gold, Michael. "A Barbaric Poem of New York." *New Masses*, 1 (August 1926), 25–26.

Gurko, Leo. "John Dos Passos' 'U.S.A.': A 1930's Spectacular." *Proletarian Writers of the Thirties*. Ed. David Madden. Carbondale, Ill.: Southern Illinois University Press, 1968.

Hardy, Thomas. *Tess of the d'Urbervilles, A Pure Woman*. New York: Macmillan, 1891; rpt. 1974.

Hernadi, Paul. *Beyond Genre: New Directions in Literary Classification*. Ithaca, N.Y.: Cornell University Press, 1972.

Hicks, Granville. *The Great Tradition*. New York: Macmillan, 1935.

———. "The Politics of John Dos Passos." *Antioch Review*, 10, no. 1 (Spring 1950), 85–98.

Hoffman, Frederick J. *The Twenties*. New York: Viking Press, 1955.

Holditch, Kenneth. "*One Man's Initiation*: The Origin of Technique in the Novels of John Dos Passos." *Explorations of Literature*. Ed. Rima D. Reck. Baton Rouge: Louisiana State University Press, 1966. Pp. 115–23.

Hook, Andrew, ed. *Dos Passos, A Collection of Critical Essays*. Englewood Cliffs, N.J.: Prentice-Hall, 1974.

Howe, Irving. "The American Voice–It Begins on a Note of Wonder." *New York Times Book Review*, July 4, 1976, pp. 1–3.

———. "John Dos Passos: The Loss of Passion." *Tomorrow*, 7 (March 1949), 54–57.

Howe, Irving, and Lewis Coser. *The American Communist Party: A Critical History (1919–1957)*. Boston: Beacon Press, 1957.

Kallich, Martin. "John Dos Passos Fellow-Traveler: A Dossier with Commentary." *Twentieth-Century Literature*, 1 (January 1956), 173–90.

———. "John Dos Passos: Liberty and the Father Image." *Antioch Review*, 10 (March 1950), 100–5.

Kazin, Alfred. "John Dos Passos: Inventor in Isolation." *Saturday Review*, 52 (March 15, 1969), 16–19, 44–45.

———. *On Native Grounds*. New York: Harcourt, Brace and Company, 1942.

Knox, George A. "Dos Passos and Painting." *Texas Studies in Literature and Language*, 6 (1964), 22–38.

Knox, George A., and Herbert M. Stahl. *Dos Passos and "The Revolting Playwrights."* Uppsala: Uppsala University Press, 1964.

Landsberg, Melvin. *Dos Passos' Path to U.S.A.: A Political Biography 1912–1936*. Boulder: Colorado Associated University Press, 1972.

Lawrence, D. H. *Phoenix, The Posthumous Papers (1936) of D. H. Lawrence*. Ed. Edward D. McDonald. New York: Viking Press, 1936.

Lawson, John Howard. "Debunking the Art Theatre." *New Masses*, 1 (June 1926), 22.

Lee, Brian. "History and John Dos Passos." *The American Novel and the Nineteen Twenties*. Ed. M. Bradbury and D. Palmer. London: Edwin Arnold, 1971.

Lehan, Richard. "The Trilogies of Jean-Paul Sartre and John Dos Passos." *Iowa English Yearbook*, 9 (1964), 60–64.

Lewis, Sinclair. *John Dos Passos'* Manhattan Transfer. New York: Harper and Brothers, 1926.

Lowry, E. D. "The Lively Art of *Manhattan Transfer*." *PMLA*, 84 (1969), 1628–38.

———. "*Manhattan Transfer*: Dos Passos' Wasteland." *University of Kansas City Review*, 30 (October 1963), 47–52.

Ludington, Townsend, ed. *The Fourteenth Chronicle: Letters and Diaries of John Dos Passos*. Boston: Gambit, 1973.

———. "Life among the American Rover Boys." *Lost Generation Journal*, 5 (Spring 1977), 12–16.

———. "The Neglected Satires of John Dos Passos." *SNL*, 7 (1966), 127–36.

Lydenberg, John. "Dos Passos' *U.S.A.*: The Words of the Hollow Men." *Essays on Determinism in American Literature*. Ed. Sydney J. Krause. Kent, O.: Kent State University Press, 1964. Pp. 97–107.

Lynn, Kenneth S., ed. Introduction to *World in a Glass: A View of Our Century Selected from the Novels of John Dos Passos*. Boston: Houghton Mifflin Company, 1966. Pp. v–xv.

Magny, Claude-Edmonde. *L'âge du roman américain*. Paris: Editions du Seuil, 1948.

Millgate, Michael. "John Dos Passos." *American Social Fiction: James to Cozzens*. New York: Barnes and Noble, 1964.

Miner, Ward L., and Thelma M. Smith. *Transatlantic Migration: The Contemporary American Novel in France*. Durham, N.C.: Duke University Press, 1955.

Mizener, Arthur. "The Big Money." *Twelve Great American Novels*. New York: New American Library, 1967.

———. "The Gullivers of Dos Passos." *Saturday Review* (June 30, 1951), 6–7, 34–35.

Moore, Harry T. "The Return of John Dos Passos." Review of *Mid-century. New York Times Book Review*, February 26, 1961, pp. 1, 51.

Nostrand, Albert Van. *Everyman His Own Poet*. New York: McGraw-Hill, 1968.

Nye, Russel B. *The Unembarrassed Muse*. New York: The Dial Press, 1970.

Pavese, Cesare. "John Dos Passos and the American Novel." *American Literature, Essays and Opinions*. Berkeley: University of California Press, 1970.

Pearse, Andrew. "Dos Passos and the American Theme." *Focus One*. Eds. B. Rajan and Andrew Pearse. London: Dennis Dobson, 1945.

Plimpton, George, ed. *Writers at Work, The Paris Review Interviews, III*. New York: Viking Press, 1967.

Potter, Jack. *A Bibliography of John Dos Passos*. Chicago: Normandie Press, 1950.

Pound, Ezra. "Vorticism." *Fortnightly Review*, 96 (September 1, 1914), 469.

———, and F. S. Flint. "A Few Don'ts by an Imagiste." *Poetry*, 1, no. 6 (March 1913), 199–201.

———, and ———. "Imagism." *Poetry*, 1, no. 6 (March 1913), 199–201.

Pozner, Vladimir. "L'Ecrivain devant l'actualité: John Dos Passos." *Les Nouvelles Littéraires* (September 5, 1936), 6.

Reinhart, Virginia S. "John Dos Passos Bibliography: 1950–1966." *Twentieth-Century Literature*, 13 (1967), 167–78.

Rideout, Walter B. *The Radical Novel in the United States: 1900–1954*. Cambridge, Mass.: Harvard University Press, 1966.

Sanders, David. "The 'Anarchism' of John Dos Passos." *South Atlantic Quarterly*, 60 (Winter 1961), 44–45.

———. "The Art of Fiction 44, John Dos Passos." *Paris Review*, 46 (1969), 160.

———. "'Lies' and the System: Enduring Themes from Dos Passos' Early Novels." *South Atlantic Quarterly*, 65 (Summer 1966), 215–28.

———. "John Dos Passos as Conservative." *A Question of Quality: Popularity and Value in Modern Creative Writing*. Ed. Louis Filler. Bowling Green, O.: Bowling Green Popular Press, 1976. Pp. 115–23.

———. "*Manhattan Transfer* and 'The Service of Things.'" *Themes and Directions in American Literature, Essays in Honor of*

Leon Howard. Eds. Ray B. Browne and Donald Pizer. Lafayette,
Ind.: Purdue University Studies, 1969. Pp. 171–85.
———. *The Merrill Studies in U.S.A.* Columbus, O.: Charles E.
Merrill Publishers, 1972.
Sartre, Jean-Paul. "John Dos Passos and *1919*." *Literary Essays*.
Trans. Annette Michelson. New York: Philosophical Library,
1957. Pp. 88–96.
Schmidt-von Bardeleben, Renate. *Das Bild New Yorks im Erzähl-
werk von Dreiser und Dos Passos*. Munich: Max Hueber, 1967.
Scholl, Peter A. "Dos Passos, Mailer, and Sloan: Young Men's Initi-
ations." *Lost Generations Journal*, 5 (Spring 1977), 2–5, 23.
Schwartz, Delmore. "John Dos Passos and the Whole Truth." *South-
ern Review*, 4 (October 1938), 351–67.
Smith, James S. "The Novelist of Discomfort: A Reconsideration
of John Dos Passos." *College English*, 19 (May 1958), 332–38.
Steiner, George. *Language and Silence*. New York: Atheneum,
1967.
Thimm, Alfred. Introduction to Dos Passos issue of *Idol*. 1969.
Vanderwerken, David. "*Manhattan Transfer*: Dos Passos' Babel
Story." *American Literature*, 49 (May 1977), 253–67.
Vickery, Olga. "The Inferno of the Moderns." *The Shaken Realist,
Essays in Modern Literature in Honor of Frederick J. Hoffman*.
Eds. Melvin J. Friedman and John B. Vickery. Baton Rouge:
Louisiana State University Press, 1970.
Walcutt, Charles Child. *American Literary Naturalism: A Divided
Stream*. Minneapolis: University of Minnesota Press, 1956.
Westerhoven, James N. "Autobiographical Elements in the Camera
Eye." *American Literature*, 48, no. 3 (November 1976), 340–64.
Wheeler, Thomas Chilton. "The Political Philosophy of John Dos
Passos." Unpublished undergraduate honors thesis. Harvard
College, 1951.
Whitman, Walt. *Leaves of Grass and Selected Prose*. Ed. John Kou-
wenhoven. New York: Modern Library.
Wickes, George. *Americans in Paris*. New York: Doubleday, 1969.
Wilson, Edmund. "Letters to John Dos Passos." *New York Review
of Books*, March 3, 1977, pp. 17–18.
———. *Shores of Light*. New York: Farrar and Straus, 1952.
———. *The Twenties*. Ed. Leon Edel. New York: Farrar, Straus, and
Giroux, 1975.
Wrenn, John H. *John Dos Passos*. New York: Twayne Publishers,
1961.

Index